# Planning for Technology

*Dedicated to our wives: Charlotte Whitehead, Sandra Jensen, and Marlys Ann Boschee.*

# Planning for Technology

## A Guide for School Administrators, Technology Coordinators, and Curriculum Leaders

*Second Edition*

**Bruce M. Whitehead**

**Devon F. N. Jensen**

**Floyd Boschee**

**CORWIN**
A SAGE Company

**CORWIN**
A SAGE Company

FOR INFORMATION:

Corwin

A SAGE Company

2455 Teller Road

Thousand Oaks, California 91320

(800) 233-9936

www.corwin.com

SAGE Publications Ltd.

1 Oliver's Yard

55 City Road

London EC1Y 1SP

United Kingdom

SAGE Publications India Pvt. Ltd.

B 1/I 1 Mohan Cooperative Industrial Area

Mathura Road, New Delhi 110 044

India

SAGE Publications Asia-Pacific Pte. Ltd.

3 Church Street

#10-04 Samsung Hub

Singapore 049483

Acquisitions Editor:   Arnis Burvikovs

Associate Editor:   Desirée A. Bartlett

Editorial Assistant:   Ariel Price

Production Editor:   Amy Schroller

Copy Editor:   Lana Todorovic-Arndt

Typesetter:   C&M Digitals (P) Ltd.

Proofreader:   Penelope Sippel

Indexer:   Sheila Bodell

Cover Designer:   Edgar Abarca

Printed in the United States of America

*A catalog record of this book is available from the Library of Congress.*

ISBN 9781452268262

This book is printed on acid-free paper.

SUSTAINABLE FORESTRY INITIATIVE

Certified Chain of Custody
Promoting Sustainable Forestry
www.sfiprogram.org
SFI-01268

SFI label applies to text stock

13 14 15 16 17 10 9 8 7 6 5 4 3 2 1

# Contents

# Foreword

This textbook, *Planning for Technology: A Guide for School Administrators, Technology Coordinators, and Curriculum Leaders* (second edition), provides educators with indispensable tools that engage learners and enhance learning. In the 21st century, the way we engage learners to their learning is often electronic. The transition to an electronic, mobile environment requires educators to create a classroom environment that allows students to become more active participants in their own education. This learning environment is a complex interplay among content, pedagogy, and technology.

At the core of a successful education system is an effective technology plan. The authors masterfully outline the complexity of this plan into a practical reality. The plan focuses on increased student achievement as the overall goal. The authors also help readers reflect on the importance of effective professional development, identification of emerging technologies to promote student engagement, selection and financing of technologies, evaluation of the general educational program, and the development and implementation of a successful public relations program.

Within the book, readers are shown that a modern technology plan respects that students are demanding a rich learning environment that utilizes their knowledge of complex social networks, instant information retrieval, and real-time feedback that provides up-to-the-minute performance evaluations. This changing environment that goes beyond the classroom walls requires educators to satisfy the following concepts of negotiation, relationship, commitment, and engagement as they engage with students and their learning. The technology plan that supports this evolution must be fluid, flexible, and responsive to individual student needs and also place teachers and administrators in their proper roles to coordinate and implement a learning community that promotes digital citizenship through responsible and safe use.

The challenge in all school districts is the identification of technologies and a plan for securing, deploying, and replacing outdated equipment. The authors recognize that most school administrators struggle with shrinking resources and the financial commitment necessary to keep effective tools in the hands of educators and their students. Included in this textbook are activities for securing grants, ideas for reallocation of school resources, and evaluation instruments to assess the effectiveness of their technology infrastructure, applications, and programs.

The authors use the term *future proofing* when talking about their technology infrastructure to assist readers in understanding the impact an effective technology plan has on the quality and sustainability of today's learning environment. In their presentation of school technology, the authors also help readers understand that the development and implementation of a successful public relations plan are instrumental to educating parents, district patrons, and local, state, and federal legislators needed to create policy and financial resources to support equitable access to quality education in the 21st century.

At the core of all successful educational plans is the presence of quality leadership in guiding educational reform. The authors stress the importance of shared leadership in providing a vision for information literacy and global awareness as a major part of our daily lives. This shift requires school administrators, technology coordinators, and curriculum leaders to understand the need for changing learning environments and the implementation of innovation in meeting the increasing challenge of cultural diversity and equitable access for all students.

The authors provide an organized approach for school leaders to move through the book, chapter by chapter, and develop a strategic plan for improving learning in their school district. While the book presents material in a spiraling order, each chapter provides educators with information that can stand alone or build on information from other chapters.

Although each school district has unique needs, the information provided in each chapter is presented in such a manner that it could serve as a template for a successful local technology plan. For example, the charts, cases, applications, study questions, and exercises, and activities included in each chapter provide ready-to-use information for developing technology plans, promotional brochures, and technological resources for administrators, teachers, parents, and community patrons. In addition, the authors provide reflective activities that encourage readers to personalize the information and apply it to their local situations. To accomplish this, each chapter concludes with a series of reflective activities and questions that encourage readers to reflect on and enhance their personal understanding and interpretation of school technology as it relates to the concepts presented in that chapter.

The authors have successfully updated the first edition to reflect the changes in education and the use of technology in schools in the 21st century. The second edition outlines specific changes, and it also recognizes the need for providing increased flexibility for educational systems to adapt in an environment of continual change. Innovation and flexibility are central to our competitive global society, and successful education systems are those that provide learning environments that go beyond the walls of the school building.

Additionally, the authors have placed greater responsibility on educational leaders and educators to develop a shared vision, mission, and goals to promote the use of technology in addressing a more diverse and mobile student population. Professional learning communities and distributive leadership models provide an innovative platform for promoting school reform through technology. This climate of change is exciting for students and offers greater parent participation in sharing the responsibility for safe and effective use of technology during the school day and extending the learning activities outside of the regular school day.

Cloud computing and expanded wireless networks provide a flexible and connected learning environment that requires school leaders to create an infrastructure that is adaptive to the ever-changing reality of technology. The need to create better cybersecurity and develop students' knowledge of digital citizenship through safe, responsible use is central to provide anytime-anywhere 21st century learning.

*Planning for Technology: A Guide for School Administrators, Technology Coordinators, and Curriculum Leaders* (second edition) is a must-have for school leaders and educators interested in designing educational systems and learning environments to prepare students to compete in a global society. The promotion of a shared vision and the practical framework for planning, developing, implementing, and evaluating learning environments supported with the infusion of technology reflects the wisdom of leadership theory and practice.

The formal educational background and practical experience of the authors make this book a real treasure. This one-of-a-kind book serves as a great reference for school districts that choose to develop quality learning environments and embed technology, innovation, equity, and engagement as central to the development of life-long learning.

*Dr. Daniel J. Hoesing, Superintendent*
Schuyler Community Schools
Schuyler, Nebraska

# Preface

**M**ilestones in science and technology have marked the march of human progress. Gutenberg's creation of movable type in the 15th century laid the foundation for universal literacy. Watt's invention of the steam engine in the 18th century launched the Industrial Revolution. The inventiveness of Bell and Marconi in the 19th and 20th centuries—creating the telephone and radio—helped bring a global village into being. However, as Shakespeare wrote, "What's past is prologue." In the 21st century, "we must begin to think far more seriously about what our current education is prologue to—and whether that is enough" (Prensky, 2013, p. 27). The global economy is being reshaped by machines that generate and analyze vast amounts of data; by devices such as smartphones and tablet computers; by smarter, nimbler robots; and by technology services that let businesses rent computer power when they need it. In essence, computers and information technologies are transforming nearly every aspect of American life. America's schools cannot be an exception to this information revolution. Computers and information technologies must be a part of the way most American students learn. As a high school student told Marc Prensky (2013), "you think of technology as a tool, we think of it as a foundation; it underlies everything we do" (p. 23). Prudent integration of our evolving and powerful technology demands that we rethink our curriculum.

## RATIONALE AND PURPOSE

The reason for updating the bestselling first edition of *Planning for Technology: A Guide for School Administrators, Technology Coordinators, and Curriculum Leaders* is to assist school administrators, technology coordinators, and curriculum leaders in their never-ending quest for a shared vision to improve schooling. The role and use of newly emerging technologies has had a massive impact on changing how learning happens. We have shifted to concepts like mobile learning, digital learning, social network learning, and BYOD (Bring Your Own Device). To enhance equity and eliminate pockets of excellence, current and future school leaders need an all-encompassing vision of how technology can help transform teaching and learning at all levels. As part of this shared vision, school administrators also need a toolbox containing tried-and-true examples of what actually works. By collectively brainstorming strategies and reviewing best practices across the globe, the authors have collected a true balance of ideas, models, and strategies that have been proven successful in many schools.

The fundamental purpose of the text is to offer educators practical exercises that will help form a technology vision and plan related to their local context. This unique book provides essential information and activities that will help school administrators, technology coordinators, and curriculum leaders as they seriously consider deepening their understanding of technology and establishing a school plan for effectual integration of emerging technologies in their schools.

This is a must-read textbook for anyone wanting to know what is new and what really works in our technology-rich schools. The three main reasons why this is a must-have book are as follows:

- It strategically and intentionally connects the dots for leadership and instructional change as it relates to 21st century learning.
- It empowers leaders to act boldly and creatively when integrating evolving technology demands and how we need to rethink curriculum.
- It provides an incredibly powerful planning tool to move our nation's classrooms technologically into the future.

## WHAT'S NEW IN THIS BOOK?

The title of Chapter 1 has been changed from "Changing Strategies in Technology" to "Changing Environments in Technology" to shift from discussing specific strategies to exploring technology as a reality that is much deeper than just a set of strategies. Readers are introduced to the concept of 21st century schools in this chapter. The chapter also recognizes the different nature of students and their relationship with technology and how this is impacting the practical use of technology in schools. There is also an important discussion on how technology is integral in school reform. Readers are also introduced to the role that social media can have in 21st century classrooms.

Chapter 2 refocuses the reader's attention to the important role of the school leader in bringing school reform through technology. In this sense, the concept of distributive leadership is discussed as a means for integrating technology. There is also an important discussion on setting up a climate of technology change through leadership that is tied to technology standards for school leaders. Some necessary changes were also made to the Project Outline activity that will help readers through vision, mission, and goal setting.

Substantial changes were made to Chapter 3. A whole new practical activity is provided to help readers link professional development to learning powered by technology for 21st century learning. There is also a new and important discussion on professional learning communities in this second edition. In line with this, readers are given a chance to reflect on how understanding concepts of adult learning theory can be a tool for improving professional development.

Although the title of Chapter 4, "Teaching and Learning With Technology," remains the same, the content and focus is completely new. This chapter brings to the reader's attention the concept of the 21st century classroom and what it looks like. In this dialogue, the chapter explores several new models for conceiving the

21st century educational experience. The models presented are Shifting Minds out of Canada, the Partnership for 21st Century Skills, the Organisation for Economic Co-operation and Development (OECD) Framework for 21st Century Learning, and the National Educational Technology Standards for Teachers (NETS-T) Model for 21st Century Competencies. A new activity in Chapter 4 helps readers to reflect on how they can create a 21st century school environment. There is also a new discussion on linking pedagogy to technology. This component explores how pedagogy is changing as a result of a more integrated relationship between technology and the curriculum. Two examples of practitioners questioning mobile technology and its impact on pedagogy are provided. One of the examples is the concept of technological pedagogical content knowledge. In the end, the completely new chapter encourages readers to consider the new relationship among technology, pedagogy, and content in the 21st century classroom.

As a result of the changing context of technology in schools, the authors felt it necessary to add a chapter to the second edition: Chapter 5, "The Culture of Technology." This chapter challenges readers to move beyond understanding technology integration as just a matter of the devices of technology to actually creating a whole new culture of technology in schools. The authors show how the principal is essential in building this culture of technology. Readers are encouraged to reconsider how they conceptualize the idea of control as it relates to technology in the classroom. The nine themes of digital citizenship are presented in addition to an exploration of the new culture of digital citizens. The chapter ends with how educational leaders need to create a culture of responsibility in their schools. The key idea here is that the concept of control and safety with technology has shifted to one of shared responsibility among educators, students, and families.

Chapter 6 is about public relations and technology. It is still a relevant and important consideration for school administrators, and so appropriate changes have been made to make it current and relevant.

In Chapter 7, important new data on the funding of public education is provided to readers. Included are the possible new funding sources derived from federal budget changes as it relates to technology in schools. Changes have been made to the grant proposal activity to make it more workable for readers.

Another exciting new addition explores the concept of future-proofing schools in Chapter 8. The authors discuss creating an infrastructure that is adaptive to the ever-changing reality of technology. Two examples are provided from schools that have future-proofed their technology infrastructure. Readers can use these examples to help inspire their own technology infrastructure to align with 21st century realities. In the discussion, components such as cyberinfrastructure, cybersecurity, wireless networks, cloud computing, and E-Rates are presented to readers.

The final chapter, Chapter 9, "Technology Plan Evaluation," updates the discussion to ensure that technology plans align with state and national standards. The authors added a new Technology Plan Evaluation activity to aid readers in assessing their level of technology maturity as well as a Technology Planning Analysis Rubric to help administrators assess the soundness of their plan.

Each chapter concludes with a series of reflective activities. The purpose of these activities is to allow readers to apply insightful strategies as they attempt to employ the book's technology framework to their local contexts and realities.

With a dependence on innovative educational ideas and advocacy, as well as new phases of anytime-anywhere learning, this book provides school administrators, technology coordinators, and curriculum leaders with the practical tools needed to create a working, technological framework that is appropriate for their schools and students. It is an exciting educational time when educators, students, and families can really come together to create a growing generation of responsible digital and global citizens. The activities, research, theory, and practice contained in this book will assist with the infusion of technology in our 21st century schools.

# Acknowledgments

Corwin would like to thank the following individuals for taking the time to provide their editorial insight and guidance:

Sally Bennett, Curriculum Coordinator
East Poinsett County School District
Joiner, AR

Harry Dickens, Corwin Author
Director of Technology
Arkansas Public School Resource Center
Little Rock, AR

Jill Gildea, Superintendent
Fremont School District
Mundelein, IL

Charles B. Hodges, Associate Professor of Instructional Technology
Georgia Southern University
College of Education
Statesboro, GA

Frances O'Reilly, Assistant Professor
Department of Educational Leadership
The Phyllis J. Washington College of Education and Human Sciences
University of Montana
Missoula, MT

Bess Scott, Director of Elementary Education
Lincoln Public Schools
Lincoln, NE

Patricia Tucker, Retired Regional Superintendent
District of Columbia Public Schools
Washington, DC

# About the Authors

**Dr. Bruce M. Whitehead** has served for more than 30 years as a principal for School District #4 in Missoula, Montana. He is also an adjunct professor of education at the University of Montana. As a result of his impact on education at state, national, and international levels, he received the National Distinguished Principal Award from the National Association of Elementary School Principals (NAESP), the Milken National Educator Award, the John F. Kennedy Center's Award for Arts in Education, Outstanding Contributions to Saudi Arabian Education, and Japan's International Soroban Institute Award. A former secretary of education called Dr. Whitehead "one of the most innovative educational administrators and visionaries in America." He is the author or coauthor of 10 books as well as numerous journal articles.

**Dr. Devon F. N. Jensen** is an associate professor in the Department of Leadership, Technology, and Human Development at Georgia Southern University. He has a professional background in studying educational leadership issues on a global level having worked in the United States, Canada, and Australia. His research into educational matters has taken him to Taiwan, Hong Kong, India, Nepal, Thailand, Mexico, and Singapore. Dr. Jensen teaches classes relating to higher education leadership and educational administration. He also teaches courses that explore the latest research and theory as it pertains to instructional technology for school leaders. Dr. Jensen has also been on the front lines of distance learning, having taught almost exclusively online since 2002.

**Dr. Floyd Boschee** has an extensive background in teaching and educational administration. He served as a teacher, coach, and school administrator in the public schools and as a professor and chairman of departments of education at the collegiate level. Dr. Boschee is professor emeritus in the Division of Educational Administration, School of Education, at the University of South Dakota and a former school board member of the Vermillion School District, Vermillion, South Dakota. During his tenure as a university professor, he consulted with school districts on reorganization; published numerous articles in major educational journals; and conducted workshops on curriculum development and implementation, the teaching and learning process, and school administrator evaluations. He is the author or coauthor of 12 books in the fields of school administration and curriculum and instruction.

# Changing Environments in Technology 1

The role and importance of technology in the curriculum is a given educational reality. With this reality, the challenge facing educational leaders and technology coordinators is to tune into the future direction of education and better synchronize learning with modern, technological pedagogies and curriculum. One justification for this is that with information literacy and global awareness as part of our daily lives, it is important, if not crucial, for educational reform to become a priority, especially when connecting technology to learning. To meet these demands, administrators and technology coordinators, and curriculum leaders must understand the changing environments in technology and pay keen attention to innovative ways of leading schools. Sharing leadership—as well as sharing a vision of technology—is paramount if we are to meet the ever-increasing local and global demands placed on our schools. Understanding that this new reality is upon us, educators worldwide are coming to realize that learners of the 21st century are different and do require modern learning experiences.

## TECHNOLOGY: A CATALYST FOR CHANGE

With technology emerging as a catalyst for real change, school leaders are becoming more fervent about school reform and how students learn. This fervency includes greater insight into the power of technology and how it allows teachers to present information in ways students will more readily understand (Peterson, 2011). At the same time, students are coming into the educational environment with new ideas and intentions for connecting thought, knowledge, and achievement to technology. These students live in a world where technology is how they communicate, socialize, and create. For them, technology makes academic growth exciting. For some ideas on how technology is changing knowledge, see Box 1.1.

> ## BOX 1.1. TECHNOLOGY IS CHANGING KNOWLEDGE
>
> Knowledge is
>
> - hyperlinked;
> - multidimensional;
> - constructed; and
> - held in graphic, audio, and video formats.
>
> In addition, knowledge
>
> - supports dynamic interactions with the user and
> - incorporates powerful search engines.
>
> ---
>
> *Source:* Dron (2005).

As excitement builds over new ways to use and experience technology in schools, educators at all levels are also directing their attention toward differentiated curriculum and evaluation strategies. This is best represented by the movement toward low-cost, portable devices for student use in all schools that assists teachers and students in redirecting learning on a global scale. Responding to this change, there are numerous examples of classroom teachers who are currently communicating and exchanging information worldwide with students via Web-based programs. In these environments, educators are no longer bound by classroom walls and are allowing students to work in multiple settings. As shown in Box 1.2, these virtual communities and learning spaces are exciting ways for students, teachers, and schools to collaborate on a variety of educational projects and relationships. From a school leader's perspective, technology, with its overflowing waves of information and media, appears to be making a difference on *how* teachers teach and *how* students learn. Examples include technology applications promoting investigative skills, making learning more exciting, providing opportunities to apply knowledge, as well as preparing students for an increasingly diverse world. In addition, digital formats and applications are revolutionizing student assessment by allowing teachers and students to instantaneously enter and access pre- and postassessment data. Information from these digital measures can be quickly graded and uploaded to various files for real-time analysis by both teachers and administrators. By and large, all of these changes and applications are providing a starting place for educators who want to channel energies toward technology-related schools and data-driven instruction.

> ## BOX 1.2. TECHNOLOGY IS CHANGING SCHOOL COMMUNITIES
>
> In using technology to go beyond classroom walls and build global communities, technology should satisfy the following concepts:
>
> - *Negotiation:* School participants must agree on protocols for how the interactions will occur.

- *Relationships:* School participants need to establish the degree to which personal information will be shared. Some communities are about seeing how people in other parts of the world live, and so the relationship is closer. Some communities are purely about accessing the knowledge of another community, and so the relationship is more distant.
- *Commitment:* Detailed commitment to the work creates stronger communities.
- *Engagement:* Learners must have opportunities to interact with each other in meaningful ways and be committed to the process. This will encourage engagement in the community.

*Source:* "Characteristics of Virtual Learning Communities" (n.d.).

Technology is also a catalyst for change in that it can provide administrators with access to digitized up-to-the-minute performance information challenging leaders to reconceptualize the meaning of data and how it impacts instruction (Nidus & Saddler, 2011). It is through the use of data-driven instruction that school leaders can now readily analyze, chart, and graph every student, class, and school within a district—or multiple districts as needed. This is very helpful from an assessment, evaluation, and accountability perspective. In the confines of their offices, administrators can now instantly diagnose academic weaknesses and strengths in any school environment—as well as display, annotate, organize, import, capture, record, or share whatever information is provided with anyone across the world—in real time. Naturally, all of this uploaded information is encrypted allowing for data transactions that are private, secure, and safe. More importantly, with up-to-date instantaneous data results that are easy to read and understand, teachers have the resources they need to make data-driven changes. In particular, instructional action will hopefully lead to improved student achievement and create positive change.

## EDUCATIONAL TECHNOLOGY AND INNOVATIONS IN LEARNING

The role of digital learning in schools is tremendously exciting and is sparking creative innovations with instructional methodologies. For example, teachers are now using forms of *flipped instruction* in their classrooms (Saltman, 2012). Flipped instruction is not a new concept and is occasionally referred to as *backwards classroom, reverse instruction,* or *reverse teaching.* Unlike a traditional classroom—where knowledge is conventionally delivered by a teacher—a teacher using a flipped instructional strategy might *first have students studying a topic on their own,* utilizing a variety of technological mediums. Using this approach, the teacher becomes more of a tutor, resource, or facilitator, thus "flipping" the instructional process. In addition to techniques such as flipped instruction, schools are focusing on different ways to use mobile devices and are implementing BYOD or BYOT (Bring Your Own Device/Technology) policies. In fact, mobile devices were recommended for use in schools by the U.S. Department of Education in the National Education Technology

Plan (NETP) as early as 2010 (Scholastic Administrator, 2012). Nonetheless, some educators remain justifiably wary of BYOD/BYOT because of the potential for misuse of mobile devices that can create a host of security concerns, including data protection and compliance with the Children's Internet Protection Act (CIPA).

With new innovations and better security, online educational communities are springing up across the country (Dobler, 2012). According to Banchero and Simon (2011), the state of Virginia authorized 13 online schools, with more to come. Not to be undone, Florida is requiring all public high school students to take at least one class online, partly to prepare them for college cybercourses. Idaho soon will require two. In Georgia, a new app lets high school students take full course loads on their mobile devices. Thirty states now let students take all of their courses online. According to the International Association for K–12 Online Learning, a trade group, an estimated 250,000 students nationwide are enrolled in full-time virtual educational experiences. A general search indicated that there are 18 virtual high schools in Canada and 247 virtual high schools throughout the United States. Whether there is a virtual or hybrid educational experience, technology is changing learning and the ways in which students learn. With all these changes occurring, future educators will need to consider questions such as, Are virtual schools and online learning making a difference, positively or negatively, in educating the youth that will lead in the future?

Along with new developments in technology, systemic planning is melding with up-to-date technological advancements to create digital-aided schools of the future. Moreover, systemic designs are redirecting educational technology away from its use as a mere tool toward its role in addressing the academic needs for a different generation of learners. The concentration of this approach makes implementation and regular use of technology even more student centered while providing a shared vision as well as awareness on how technology can advance learning. In this regard, Salpeter (2012) listed a variety of elements as to how schools can best prepare students to succeed in the first decades of the 21st century.

## Elements of School Improvement

The following are the elements of school improvement:

- Schools need to expand their focus beyond "basic competency."
- Students need to know how to use their knowledge and skills by thinking critically, applying knowledge to new situations, analyzing information, comprehending new ideas, communicating, collaborating, solving problems, and making decisions.
- Technology will continue to be the driving force in workplaces.
- Student experiences need to connect with authentic projects beyond the classroom.
- Content must prepare students to live and work in a 21st century world.
- Assessment includes moving beyond standardized testing as the sole measure of student learning.

This cocreative relationship between technology and innovations in learning is also reaching down to the basic concepts of the essential dispositions we desire all of our learners in the K–12 system to attain. One expression of this comes from the National Common Core State Standards that are a state-led effort coordinated by the National Governors Association for Best Practices (NGA Center) and the Council of Chief State School Officers (CCSSO). The standards were developed in collaboration with teachers, school administrators, and experts to provide a clear and consistent framework that would prepare our children for college and the workforce. Of the standards currently developed, the English Language Arts and Literacy in History/Social Studies, Science, and Technical Subjects have the following as some of its core standards:

- Students employ technology thoughtfully to enhance their reading, writing, speaking, listening, and language use. They tailor their searches online to acquire useful information efficiently, and they integrate what they learn using technology with what they learn offline. They are also familiar with the strengths and limitation of various technological tools and mediums and can select and use those best suited to their communication goals.
- Students can integrate and evaluate content presented in diverse media and formats, including visually and quantitatively, as well as in words. Specifically in Grade 5, with some guidance and support from adults, students use technology, including the Internet, to produce and publish writing as well as to interact and collaborate with others and demonstrate sufficient command of keyboarding skills to type a minimum of two pages in a single sitting.
- New technologies have broadened and expanded the role that speaking and listening play in acquiring and sharing knowledge and have tightened their link to other forms of communication. The Internet has accelerated the speed at which connections between speaking, listening, reading, and writing can be made, requiring that students be ready to use these modalities nearly simultaneously. Technology itself is changing quickly, creating a new urgency for students to be adaptable in response to change.

## Technologies and the Classroom

Every day across America, students are exploring and using a variety of technologies. Currently, K–12 students are accessing and sharing information via Web-based learning, smart boards, and mobile devices. Both mercurial and date sensitive, classroom technology continues to morph and change with the times. One day, classroom students are accessing the *cloud* as well as *skyping*, and the next day they are *moodling*. Moodling refers to a Course Management System (CMS), also known as a Learning Management System, used by educators to create effective online learning sites. Skyping is a Microsoft proprietary Voice over Internet Protocol (VOIP) and software application allowing educators and students to communicate with peers by voice, video, and instant messaging. Finally, cloud computing provides individuals with an efficient way to get applications up and running faster on the Internet, as well as improving manageability and allowing for less maintenance. This type of computing basically entrusts services with a user's data and software over a network. By collaborating in the cloud, students have access to their work anywhere there is an interest. Thus, they do not have to work solely at school and can work wherever they have Internet access. The result is a major step toward individualizing instruction at all levels. With these types of technology applications in schools, many students are developing traits of high-tech experts simply by the way they approach their learning and the digital world around them (Cushman, 2012).

To be sure, mobile devices are fast becoming a way for teachers to deliver instruction. This is specifically true of iPads. Whether they are developing math skills, comprehension, or fluency, iPads are impacting the way teachers teach and the way students learn (Mulholland, 2011). If readers were to spend some time in a classroom using iPads, they would witness students accessing the cloud, being totally immersed in what they are doing, as well as being highly motivated to do more. Fingers fly with images scrolling across an electronic screen as students navigate a variety of apps and sources. Wrapped in interfaces, technology-loving kids are speaking into microphones, recording themselves, playing back voices and/or bringing up interesting photos. This technology-driven classroom is considered to be *mobile learning* and is occasionally referenced as *m-learning.* Certainly, this type of technology advancement has the capability of significantly reshaping the classroom learning experience (Caudill, 2007). Although time will tell, educators are using mobile learning or m-learning as an untethered and more informal approach to instruction. Some teachers even refer to m-learning as "just-in-time" technology because of its acquisition speed for students and because it is more "discovery" in nature. Covering the gamut of on-the-spot informational retrieval, m-learning, as well as the more common fixed-based electronic learning (*e-learning*), continue to revolutionize classrooms in schools today. What is especially exciting for educators is the speed and instant access to data. Just as importantly, high-speed handheld devices are designed to deliver extra feedback via apps and programs—and not extra work for teachers. By providing untapped opportunities for teachers, student performance can be uploaded, graphed, and screened as an assessment tool. Likewise, teachers and administrators can show parents how students are performing individually and are able to chart what is happening at the school or district level. Overall, a survey (Masie & Chan, 2011) conducted by the MASIE Center (described as "an international think tank dedicated to exploring the intersection of learning and technology") found the following as the most used technologies in the classroom:

| Technologies in Classrooms ||
| --- | --- |
| **Technology** | **Percentage** |
| Projector/Display | 85% |
| Blackboard/Whiteboard | 80% |
| Flipchart | 78% |
| Movable furniture | 68% |
| Speakerphone | 59% |
| Microphone/Speakers | 52% |
| Wireless | 49% |

| Technologies in Classrooms | |
|---|---|
| **Technology** | **Percentage** |
| Video conferencing via webinar | 47% |
| Flat screen | 28% |
| High-def projector | 28% |
| Video conferencing via IP/ISDN | 25% |
| Fixed furniture | 25% |
| Camera/Microphone to record class | 23% |
| Dividable spaces | 22% |
| Interactive whiteboard | 22% |
| Video conferencing via desktop | 20% |
| Document camera | 19% |
| Multiple displays | 19% |
| Audience response systems | 13% |
| Tablet control for instructor | 11% |
| Slide projector | 10% |
| Tablet for every learner | 6% |
| Gaming technology | 4% |

Another plus of mobile technology, especially for administrators and supervisors, is the ease in collecting data for program and staff evaluations. While walking from classroom to classroom, building-level supervisors can document, record, and upload data as needed. Thus, with handheld technology, school leaders are better able to capitalize on the interest, energy, and learning needed to better differentiate teaching and learning in individual classrooms. Not only is this useful in the classroom, but these technology advances are also allowing local classrooms to connect with a larger community. As a result, current advances in mobile technology are now providing educators and students everywhere, with a long-awaited window to school reform.

Caution is also essential when integrating technology into the classroom because some community members are expressing concerns over security. Fortunately, the issue of security is being addressed through a series of programs and applications. Systems such as Gaggle (www.gaggle.net) are becoming instrumental in allowing instructors to monitor students by making sure they do not wander on the Internet. Gaggle's control and filtering system gives administrators and teachers a way to protect students from sending and receiving inappropriate e-mail. Instructors can even place restrictions on student accounts controlling with whom they communicate. All student mail that is flagged by the filters is redirected to a Gaggle App account that will determine if it is allowed to go through or should be blocked. Along with improved security, it is crucial for school leaders to develop an acceptable-use policy that addresses mobile electronic devices.

When adapting an acceptable-use policy, school administrators need to make sure the policy addresses such areas as purpose, responsibility, theft or damage, inappropriate use as well as sanctions if policy is violated. Regardless of what type of policy is approved, mobile technology appears to be leaving a legacy of individualized learning, especially as it relates to working with both at-risk students as well as gifted and talented students. What really matters then is that handheld devices are a highly motivational learning tool for potentially increasing the "cool factor" for students. The old adage of "If you can't reach them, you can't teach them" seems to readily apply to today's technology.

## Key Elements Impacting School Change

With a variety of new innovations in technology appearing in classrooms, perhaps it is important to focus on some of the *key elements* impacting teaching and learning (Whitehead, Boschee, & Decker, 2013).

*Time.* Teachers and students in our schools today perceive *working, learning,* and *activities* as being interconnected. As a result, 21st century schools must implement curricula where working, learning, and activities converge allowing learning to occur at any time and any place.

*Relationships.* Students of this century are beginning to reestablish strong interconnections to community and linkages with other cultures via handheld mobile technology. This creates a somewhat fluid society vastly different from that of their parents. Today's Tech-Age students are now learning and growing in communities that are becoming highly diverse in age, religion, culture, language, and location. Within these newly emerging digital communities, collaboration is surfacing as a primary expression of experience, and the working realities of life are becoming focused on being connected.

*Technology.* Students in schools today are living in a reality of reform and changing technologies. Moreover, these students are preparing and constantly waiting for the next level of advancement that will provide them with new ways of learning.

*Learning Style.* Digitally savvy students are now effectively using state-of-the-art technology. This does not mean individual students are spending time working alone, but are reinforcing learning through memberships in a network of socials group—even if those groups are thousands of miles away. As such, students want to solve real problems with hopes they can make a contribution to their school, city, and community. With information and knowledge acquisition expanding and changing, students also desire to formulate analytical skills that will help them succeed in our digitally transforming world.

*Flexibility.* Students participating in the global shift to mobile technology can no longer depend on the stable and unchanging reality of school buildings and classrooms; therefore, they desire a curriculum open to a diverse range of options and educational choices. This is especially true with learning opportunities and knowledge acquisition expanding so rapidly. A result of these transformative changes—school leaders, curriculum designers, and technology coordinators are taking note. Not surprisingly, these educators are now looking for flexibility in allowing students to learn in multiple settings—public and private schools, home schooling, travel, community groups, as well as cloud computing groups.

On a daily basis, educators across the country are seeing an increase in innovative instructional strategies and curriculum changes. Progressive teachers now desire to step into learning environments that were unimaginable only a decade or two ago. With more changes on the horizon, administrators, teachers, and technology coordinators are readying for systemwide school reform. In support of this finding, more evidence is demonstrating that up-to-date technology, if used wisely, can have the following positive effects on students:

- Interesting and engaging websites provide students opportunities to explore the world and access unlimited informational resources.
- Communicating through the Internet enables students to keep in touch with friends and family and to form online communities with others who share their interests.
- New innovations and applications are enhancing instructional assessment practices and student academic performance.
- Advances in media literacy and digital fluency are allowing students to create, design, and invent in much more affordable ways.

Integration of up-to-date transformative technology will be critical for future school success. In addition, it will be crucial for schools to engage students in addressing real-world problems, issues, and questions that matter (Devine, 2012). When focusing on school reform, the reality is that developments in educational technology are changing societal and career needs as well as challenging the very nature of schools.

## Technology and Pedagogy

What is extraordinary is the capability of technology in augmenting educational reform in terms of pedagogies. To prove this point, a model emerging from research in the areas of leadership and technology shows that technology is becoming a force for student growth and achievement (Lytle, 2012). Subsequently, this alters the philosophies that many teachers hold about the nature of instruction. One of the realities found in the literature—from a philosophical level—is how many educators continue to depend on the foundational pedagogies of Piaget, Bruner, and Vygotsky, for example. The struggle is that some pedagogies are based on a nontechnological educational space. This creates a unique philosophical conflict between how learning is conceived and how learning happens when technology is added to the equation. What is required, perhaps, are modern technological pedagogies that are consistent with the technological educational space we now inhabit. A key for transformation is to research and discover how future educators will be able to learn to adapt to tomorrow's pedagogical challenges and opportunities.

## School Technology Realities

A careful look around the country, as well as around the globe, reveals that communities are embracing educational change mostly due to the characteristics (see Box 1.3) of the change agents—school administrators. Just as important, schools are making strides in solidifying research-based reforms. In keeping with this trend, visionary school leaders are now refocusing district and state efforts on how technology can best enhance students' academic and social needs, especially through cloud computing (Damani, 2011/2012). What is even more interesting is that with all these changes, students are matriculating into upper grades with more technical skills as well as a greater desire to learn.

---

### BOX 1.3. TOP CHARACTERISTICS OF CHANGE AGENTS

- Trustworthy
- Resilient
- Manages conflict
- Coaches
- Facilitator
- Excellent communicator
- Emotionally intelligent
- Tolerant
- Service minded
- Active learner

---

Furthermore, these reforms are generating greater interest on the part of parents, teachers, and students as to the real-world relevancy of educational technology.

All of these changes are causing school administrators and technology coordinators to rethink how schools approach teaching and learning. Given the circumstances, perhaps we have reached a tipping point in how schools address reform, especially on how school administrators, technology coordinators, curriculum leaders, board members, trustees, and teachers are reassessing the ways technology can impact instructional delivery. In keeping with this perspective, educational leaders are now compelled to ask some penetrating questions:

- How can technology best be integrated into educational programs?
- Will educationally related technological approaches have the impact we expect?
- Is redirecting our technological program worth the effort?
- Are there technological advances on the horizon that will render our current use obsolete in the not-too-distant future?
- Where can we go to get the best advice about meeting our technological needs?

## Student Achievement and Technology

Using technology to improve student achievement is becoming a major part of school success, but this has not always been the case. An emphasis on higher levels of student achievement has largely been associated with federal and state legislation, regulations, and recommended standards such as the Elementary and Secondary Education Act (ESEA), No Child Left Behind Act (NCLB), Race to the Top, Response to Intervention (RTI), and Common Core State Standards. Results have not necessarily met expectations. In attempting to better understand the connection of technology with student achievement, the Milken Exchange on Education Technology (an independent economic think tank whose mission is to improve the lives and economic conditions of people in the United States and around the world) conducted a meta-analysis of 700 empirical research studies. This research showed that students who had access to

- computer-assisted instruction, or
- integrated learning systems technology, or
- software that teaches higher-order thinking, or
- collaborative networked technologies, or
- design and programming technologies

showed positive gains in achievement on researcher-constructed tests, standardized tests, and national tests. In contrast, Toch (2012) reviewed the outcome of NCLB and found that NCLB's effect on student achievement was mixed, at best. The National Assessment of Educational Progress (NAEP), a rigorous snapshot of student performance nationally, reported that the number of fourth graders scoring proficient or advanced in math increased 11% during the NCLB era (from 2003 to 2011), which is good news. At the same time, this compares to an increase of 23% in the pre-NCLB era (1990 to 2003). The same is true for eighth graders in math—"those scoring proficient or above increased 9% in the NCLB era compared to 17% in the pre-NCLB period" (p. 67).

Regardless of state or federal outcomes, there is a renewed vision of education across the country. Researchers are finding pockets of increased student achievement, even in frontier states such as Montana. One such school is the Hellgate Elementary School District in Missoula, Montana. Hellgate is uniquely named after an adjacent historical canyon and located on the outskirts of Missoula. It is made up of primary Grades P–2, intermediate Grades 3–5, and middle school Grades 6–8. In total, there are over 1,200 students in the district. Student population is 87% Caucasian, 5% Native American, 4% Asian American, 2% Hispanic, 1% African American, and 1% Native Hawaiian. Over 40% of students qualify for free or reduced-price lunch.

According to Superintendent Douglas Reisig, Hellgate Elementary School District failed to meet Adequate Yearly Progress (AYP) mandated by NCLB. Administrators, concerned for the progress and success of students, knew that it was time for a change. After extensive research, the school district selected McGraw-Hill's Direct Instruction reading and math programs, which are fully aligned with RTI, for the entire district's strategic and intensive intervention students. To assist with program implementation, the district engaged with Educational Resources, Inc., a professional staff development company, to aid in the implementation of curriculum and instructional revision.

Along with curriculum changes, classroom teachers integrated technology such as Web-based instruction, Classroom Performance Systems (clickers), and iPads to enhance instruction. With the implementation of direct instruction and improvement of classroom technology, Hellgate has seen improvement in reading and math scores on the annual Criterion Reference Test (CRT). For example, CRT scores for third-grade students at primary levels increased over 10% from 2007 to 2009. In 2010, the district achieved a significant milestone, meeting AYP for the first time in two years. Moreover, the implementation of direct instruction along with technology applications has had a direct impact on economically disadvantaged students, which make up nearly half of the district's student population. Before implementing direct instruction, only 61% of economically disadvantaged students were meeting the standard in math. For the 2010/2011 school year, 84% of these students met projected goals to meet the standard. This marks a vast 23% improvement in math scores in just four years (Kelly, 2011).

Hellgate Elementary School Grade 3 Criterion Reference Test Math Proficiency

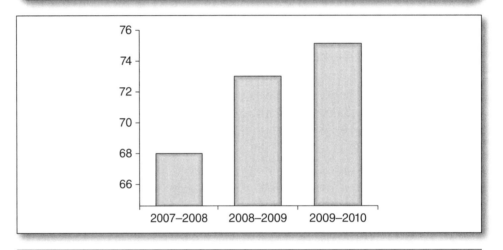

*Source:* Kelly (2011).

Much of Hellgate Elementary School's success is attributed to quality teachers, program changes, as well as changes in the implementation of educational technology. Students have reacted to the program with enthusiasm, noting it is predictable and fun to use. Teachers are pleased and have described the new curriculum and technology as rewarding, especially when they hear previously reluctant students exclaiming, "I love math." To be sure, the success of this Montana school in the area of curriculum revision and technology integration is being replicated across the country, revealing that individual school districts can, and are, moving into the future.

## Impact of Technology on Schools

Along with focusing on student achievement, educational leaders must realize the overall impact of technology on schools. This is especially the case due to educators having a sense of greater ownership as well as having their work on permanent display for the world to see. Naturally, these changes continue to be vastly significant. Keeping with this perspective of a culture of change, educators worldwide are finding that advancements in technology can potentially impact schools in at least 10 major areas (Whitehead, Boschee, & Decker, 2013). Impact areas include the following:

1. **Increased student writing.** Simply measuring the amount that students are using technology applications to write reveals one positive impact of technology. Students are writing more compositions and doing so more often. Many teachers now find that students are producing three times the amount of written documents than they did before word processors were made available to them. Teachers who carefully watch students find that it often appears to be easier for their pupils to use a keyboard and screen than a pen or pencil to write. The direct result is that students are writing more often and with seemingly greater ease. This trend is likely to become even more pronounced with quality voice recognition programs and other technological applications.

2. **Higher quality student writing.** Analysis of student writing by numerous researchers has shown that word processing related program helps students become more effective writers. This is not surprising to anyone who uses digital media to any degree.

3. **Enhanced cooperative learning.** Teachers using mobile technology are finding that this format greatly enhances and supports cooperative learning strategies. When collaborative learning is linked with technology, it is known to have a strong positive influence on student achievement.

4. **Enhanced integration of curriculum.** Instructors having access to cloud computing as well as mobile devices are finding technological applications are making it easier to integrate social studies, literature, math, and science into a more coordinated series of learning experiences for students. A practical example of this is when students use applications to create content-integrated presentations using material from several disciplines. In addition, maps, graphs, tables, and illustrations from a variety of subject areas can be easily shared or incorporated into student projects and visual presentations.

5. **Greater range of learning applications.** Teachers are finding the use of technology helps accommodate different ways students learn. This is best evidenced by research noting certain cognitive skills are strengthened, sometimes substantially, by the use of computers and the Net (Carr, 2011).

6. **Increased applications of cross-age tutoring.** Students using mobile technology now have easy access to information across grade levels. As a result, teachers are finding that older students can work with younger students on cooperative or tutorial projects anytime, anywhere.

7. **Increased teacher communication.** Instructors using mobile technology are finding it easy to communicate with colleagues. Today's technological advances create greater possibility for exchanging information and sharing on local, state, national, as well as global levels.

8. **Greater parent communication.** New technology innovations are proving to be a promising link between home and school. Parents anywhere and at any time can readily receive updated reports on student performance, homework assignments, as well as school activities.

9. **Enhanced community relations.** Bringing the school and community together provides another compelling reason for implementing technology into schools. In many school districts, community residents and local business members often participate in campus training and professional development programs using school technology. As a result, adult education classes are on the rise. In addition, students and teachers across the country are helping civic groups as well as small businesses become more attuned to the latest up-to-date technological advances.

10. **Enhanced global learners.** Never before have educators and students been able to develop a better understanding of other cultures and people than is possible today. Many schools are now using technology applications to access information from all parts of the globe. As one considers this phenomenon, it becomes increasingly evident that technology in schools is paving the way for students, teachers, and citizens to enter into a community of global learners.

## FOCUSING ON SOCIAL MEDIA AND ETHICAL ISSUES

Social media and e-mentoring help to define various generations such as Generation Y, Millennials, Net Generation, and iGeneration. For example, Rosen (2011) referred to the iGeneration as the group who heavily used digital technologies (iPhone, iPod, iPad, Wii, and iTunes). Interestingly enough, regardless of the label, social networking technology uniquely offers new generations an opportunity to interact with an expansive universe of team members, family, and friends (Richardson, 2011).

### Drawbacks

There are, however, some drawbacks to using social networking websites according to Gross and Acquisti (2005). The four areas where social networking can cause individuals personal and professional drawbacks are the following:

1. It must be understood that when making postings on these types of websites, individuals are making public statements and not *private* postings.

2. When posting a statement or story, it is important to note the posting is (and remains) a digital footprint and that it is accessible to the rest of the world. To remove a statement or story, one needs to go through the website policy process for removing information.

3. The Internet is an open unlimited international community in which millions of people have access. Thus, personal responsibility is a critical aspect of being safe on the Internet.

4. There is another point of view to consider: the privacy of others. Privacy is a complicated matter in American law. It evokes everything from the right to family planning through Fourth Amendment search and seizure, to torts, or civil rights (Hodge, 2006). School leaders and staff need to be aware that if they post an alleged fact about someone that proves incorrect, the message writer may be liable for damages under either the defamation or libel. Moreover, if they post photographs or information about someone that can be construed to be an "invasion of their privacy" or "false light," or "misappropriation of likeness," they may also be liable for a tort under the broad rubric of "privacy."

As noted in *The Principal: Leadership for a Global Society* by Whitehead, Boschee, and Decker (2013), social networks are a great innovation allowing users to express their humanity and an opportunity to create new communities. The freedom of the Internet, however, does not suggest individuals can act with impunity. Since we live in a society in which expression is judged in legal policy and even personal ways, it is important to remember the consequences of that expression no matter how ephemeral or fun in the moment it might seem to be. What matters most for educators, however, is to be fully aware and realize that anything posted about them or anyone else, given caching technologies, might prove to be a liability to an ongoing sense of identity over the longer course of history. Behind every device, behind every new program, and behind every technology is a law, a social norm, or a business practice that warrants thoughtful consideration.

## Social Ramifications of Cyberbullying

In our newly developing digital world, the age-old problem of bullying is taking on a whole new agenda that is hidden behind digital screens and cell phones. The term *cyberbullying* is harassment over the Internet or via other technologies. Teasing, name calling, and threats thrive on social media networks as well as text messaging on cell phones and in e-mails. According to Lenhart, Madden, Purcell, and Zickuhr (2011), a research study sponsored by the Pew Research Center titled *Teens, Kindness and Cruelty on Social Network Sites* reported that 9 out of 10 teens say they have witnessed cruelty by their peers on social networks. The survey of 800 children between the ages of 12 to 17 found cyberbullying cuts across all ages and backgrounds. Some 15% of teen social media users who were participants in the Pew Research Center sponsored research indicated that they have experienced such harassment themselves (Guess, 2011).

As part of creating a sense of responsibility, schools are paying closer attention to the cyberbullying experiences that students are having (Guess, 2011). With this in mind, it is important for educational leaders worldwide to not only address the cyberbully issue but to also have counselors available to assist targeted students. Having a plan as well as an authentic problem-based solving approach to help and assist victims of cyberbullying can be just as important as catching the culprit. Students engaged in authentic problem-based learning are encouraged to apply their knowledge to questions they have about why things happen in their world, and thus, are better able to discuss social ramifications often associated with specific issues—such as cyberbullying. Pew Research has identified some areas of interest for school leaders that involve negative impacts of cyberbullying. A substantial number of teens report specific negative outcomes from experiences on social network sites. For example, 41% of teenagers who use social media say they have experienced at least one of the following negative outcomes:

- 25% of social media teenagers have had an experience on a social network site that resulted in a face-to-face argument or confrontation with someone.
- 22% have had an experience that ended their friendship with someone.
- 13% have had an experience that caused a problem with their parents.
- 13% have felt nervous about going to school the next day.
- 8% have gotten into a physical fight with someone else because of something that happened on a social network site.
- 6% have gotten into trouble at school because of an experience on a social network site.

Understanding that technology is constantly evolving, lawmakers are racing to keep up with policies and punishments for cyberbullying. As schools and administrators struggle to keep up with the changes, they must stay on top of this issue for the safety of students who are trying to become young adults in an environment that is constantly changing (Whitehead, Boschee, & Decker, 2013).

## SCHOOL TECHNOLOGY GOALS

Fundamental to the process of planning educational technology is how schools/districts assess needs, develop goals and strategies, and pursue implementation to improve student learning. As discussed in Chapter 2, a key standard for school jurisdictions to consider is the provision of four clear and practical technological goals that will expand the boundaries of traditional schooling and help children reach new levels of learning development. The goals are the following:

- School administrators should coordinate school-based services and resources in order to heighten access to interactive technology for students in their schools.
- Guidelines to enhance communication and technological awareness within communities need to be developed. Improved public awareness of what technology is available often leads to a greater understanding of how technology can benefit students and citizens. Community appreciation also leads to the creation of shared vision and mission statements, joint technology committees, appropriate financing programs, infrastructure development, professional development, maintenance and service arrangements, favorable program evaluation and, finally, successful public relations programs. Education leaders must expand traditional school boundaries to involve the community in planning, financing, implementing, and evaluating technology.
- School leaders would be wise to share school success stories with their communities. Data obtained from student assessments can add substantial

credibility to the positive things happening in schools when effectively presented to the public. This information can be easily retrieved and presented in our digital world.

- Data from student assessments can provide school administrators and teachers with a valuable mechanism to ensure that student performance meets or exceeds Common Core State Standards. In addition, statewide data retrieval systems for student performance are helpful to school leaders in determining aggregate achievement levels for all schools. Likewise, an accompanying item analysis of standardized test questions can provide administrators and teachers with a means of making a sound appraisal of strengths and weaknesses in the school or district curriculum.

As can be seen, it is with the development of clear public information programs that state legislators and citizens will best understand how technology is impacting student achievement. As community support increases, school leaders are better able to provide the administrative support necessary to accommodate the needs of teachers and students. As a result, high-impact school leaders are critical to turnaround success, and pockets of success can be found around the country (Stein, 2012). Community support also helps break down classroom walls by making positive activities in schools more visible and educators more accessible to parents via technology. In retrospect then, there appears to be little doubt about leading-edge technology holding the promise for many positive changes occurring in American education. A few of these positive outcomes will be focusing on exploratory learning, the empowering of teachers, and equipping school leaders with advanced technological resources needed to manage schools. In reality, the task of illuminating the role of technology in our nation's classrooms is complex, but a very important one.

## STRATEGIES FOR SUCCESS

To be successful in our increasingly technological world, it is evident that all educators and learners must be skilled in the use of technology. This is especially important because research on raising student achievement consistently revealed that an effective teacher is the most vital factor in a student's success (Routman, 2012). As a result, to bring about change and establish equity in our schools, factors such as proper professional development programs, technical support, and time for learning must be provided simultaneously as well as the strategies displayed in Box 1.4.

### BOX 1.4. SUCCESSFUL SCHOOL TECHNOLOGY STRATEGIES

- Community involvement in planning and implementing the use of technology in schools should be a high priority for school leaders.
- Developing quality technological leadership and planning for effective technology use within the jurisdiction must receive considerable attention.

*(Continued)*

(Continued)

- Finances for technology and other forms of school technology should become a line item in the general budget of all school districts.
- Emphasis should be placed on incorporating handheld mobile technology into all classrooms.
- Professional development involving technology should be made highly practical by encouraging teachers to teach other teachers.
- Planning and implementation phases for new technology should include assessment and evaluation standards.
- A well-planned public relations program should be a priority of every school district.

By incorporating diverse ideas and strategies into a collective vision, school leaders and technology coordinators can—and will—improve the overall nature of education. Furthermore, there is no question that in our rapidly changing world, the economic vitality of our communities will depend more on students being able to turn information into usable knowledge (Goudvis & Harvey, 2012). Just as important, individual students will be better able to build knowledge, solve problems, and share successes with the larger community.

## State and National Levels of Awareness

State and national organizations are moving forward in their continued support of school technology. Furthermore, it is crucial that educational leaders and organizations at all levels develop a coordinated plan directed at helping schools best use new advances in technology.

---

**TECHNOLOGY THOUGHT**

Review your district's technology plan to ensure that it is developing well-rounded, adept, intuitive, and culturally aware students.

---

In an effort to improve the situation, school administrators are spearheading movements to develop community frameworks to include influential noneducators into the brainstorming and implementation process before bringing technologies into their districts. As will be described in Chapter 3, these efforts have been especially beneficial in formulating professional learning communities (PLCs) as a way to address a multitude of issues including reading and writing academic problems.

Along with PLCs, an ever-expanding state and national focus includes the formation of National Common Core State Standards. These standards are dramatically helping to redefine a basic education as per readiness for college and careers (Rothman, 2012). Moreover, Common Core Standards are addressing as well as clarifying the complexity of today's hi-tech educational landscape. In addition to Common Core State Standards, the Council for the Accreditation of Educator Preparation (CAEP) continues to be highly involved as well. For example, CAEP requires schools of education to meet verifiable technology standards for program accreditation. This accreditation body recognizes the importance of advanced technology in schools and supports this stance by stating that technology needs to move from the periphery to the center of teacher education. In addition, organizations such as the National Association of Elementary School Principals (NAESP), National Association of Secondary School Principals (NASSP), and American Association of School Administrators (AASA) are collaborating to review and endorse highly successful educational technology practices. To make this happen, these organizations are now assisting school technology coordinators with ideas and strategies to help address the issue of equity and cultural diversity on a global level. This is extremely important.

## Fostering a Global Link

As society grows both culturally and globally, educators remain concerned as to how the United States is measuring up academically. Tony Wagner (2008), in *The Global Achievement Gap*, relates how transformations in leadership represent enormous challenges for future educational leaders. He lists a primary challenge as being the ability of educators to prepare students for both analytic and creative thinking. For this reason, Wagner focuses on the development of a global achievement gap. Basically, this gap reflects the distance between what our best public schools are teaching and testing as opposed to what all students need to know in the world today. With an alarming fear of other countries having more success academically, the achievement gap has profound implications not just for work, but also for citizenship and lifelong learning.

To meet these challenges and address any gaps in achievement, schools are using advances in technology to become globally interconnected. This means school leaders are becoming global leaders as well. A global leader is an individual who is aware of universal challenges, world cultures, and the connection between them and the rest of the world. It is crucial for our school leaders to understand how other countries develop curriculum, conduct professional development, and handle school-related issues. It is equally imperative for schools to develop a global perspective through integrated online communities, mobile technology, and other communication sources to gather information about other countries and cultures. Therefore, by rearranging priorities and developing an effective use of technology, every new 21st century learner will have an opportunity to learn from a global audience (Blair, 2012). By and large, an increasing number of school leaders are realizing the potential of technology as a powerful resource for enhancing learning on a global scale. Through advanced technology, it is now possible to share information and classroom projects with educators and schools all over the world. As part of that culture of conversation, school leaders will be better able to formulate a broader perspective of world challenges. Moreover, in the process of encouraging staff and students to become global citizens, teachers can become more interested in using advances in technology to explore civic responsibilities and equity issues, cultural awareness, and the environment. The need for vibrant educational leadership on a global level is here and apparent. Knowing what problems might arise from a worldly perspective and how to deal with complex issues is the reward. Likewise, knowing that this generation of students is more cognizant of world affairs than previous generations will help lead us to an age of global transparency.

## FUTURE CHALLENGES

As educators give further thought to the impact of technology in our present world, it becomes readily apparent that we must carefully merge new technology advances and applications into our educational institutions. The potential for creating schools and school districts of high quality is only possible through the timely application of existing knowledge. In order to benefit from conceptually new ways of learning, it is important that a comprehensive blueprint be adopted and followed. It is recommended that school administrators, technology coordinators, and community leaders carefully consider and adhere to suggestions from the chapters that follow as they explore ways to integrate technology into our schools. What is at stake is *how* students learn, and this may have the greatest impact on our future as a global society.

## REFLECTIVE ACTIVITIES

1. List and analyze the outcomes expected from innovative applications of educational technology.

2. Explain how your school district technology purchases are meeting students' needs. If they are not meeting students' needs, list the shortcomings (e.g., equipment inadequacies, lack of qualified personnel, or infrastructural limitations).

3. Identify other forms of technology available that could improve learning opportunities for students in your school district.

4. Reflect on the type of students you see in your school district today. Compare and contrast their relationship with learning and technology.

5. Consider how instructional strategies in your school have changed as a result of technology being implemented into your curriculum.

6. Analyze the positive and negative aspects of technology use in your school district.

7. Decide how much access community members should have to your school's technologies.

8. Provide a rationale for why school-community communication via e-mail, text messaging, Facebook, Twitter, and other applications should or should not be promoted.

9. Identify what organizations exist in your school district and state for the coordinated implementation of educational technology.

10. If applicable, describe how your school is using technology to align with the Common Core State Standards.

# Leadership and Planning 2

## EDUCATIONAL LEADERSHIP IN THE 21ST CENTURY

School leaders are experiencing a very challenging and exciting time. Clearly, the ever-present dramatic political, social, environmental, and economic changes occurring globally are requiring educational leaders at all levels to become conscious of guiding and directing institutional and academic change relevant to the needs of this modern reality (Goslin, 2012). This change can be both academically threatening and liberating for school administrators, technology coordinators, and curriculum leaders as they consider new approaches and avenues for delivering education to the young people of this country. At this critical juncture, the quality of educational leadership is becoming one of the essential elements required for the organization and realization of successful technology initiatives in schools. Conversely, average leadership will merely maintain the status quo. At its worst, mediocre direction from school leaders and coordinators will likely nullify the positive contributions that technology can make to education, frustrate teachers and their students, and cost taxpayers a good deal in ill-directed expenditures.

### Defining Leadership Values

School leaders are helping to define the future of schools. More to the point, they are making a significant contribution to the teaching and learning process. According to Lytle (2012), successful leaders define their values and vision to raise expectations if they are to set direction and build trust; reshape the conditions for teachers and learning; restructure parts of the organization and redesign leadership roles and responsibilities; enrich the curriculum; enhance teacher quality; enhance the quality of teaching and learning; build collaboration internally; and build strong relationships outside the school community. This lengthy list reveals that school leadership is both dynamic and complex, and as a result, is constantly evolving. With the advent of new educational technologies, coupled with innovative teaching practices, perceptive school leaders are becoming more adept at guiding schools through this dynamic learning environment. Individual school administrators who have the foresight required to create and sustain leading-edge technology programs are certainly worthy of the encouragement and recognition extended by their communities and peers. Through time, energy, and commitment, these visionary leaders are investing in a renewed vision of schooling that can have broader implications for the larger educational community. These are the school leaders who are developing and maintaining technology programs and plans of exceptional quality. At the beginning point in developing exceptional technology programs, school leaders and technology coordinators should attempt to answer four basic questions:

1. What equipment or applications are required to make the improvements we wish to see in the student-centered learning environments of our schools?

2. Why do we want to commit a great deal of time and money to this initiative for specific technological changes, and are our motives focused on improving student learning?

3. Who is the best person to lead the technological initiative we are considering?

4. Who will be best suited to assess and maintain the quality of technology programs after the initial stages of implementation are completed?

Without a doubt, quality leadership involves a unique human ability. This means a successful leader must be able to anticipate change and adapt administrative roles and responsibilities to meet the needs of teachers and students. As part of this process, school leaders must be able to work within a structured organizational framework. This also means knowing how to effectively integrate innovative educational technologies. With this being said, today's management and instructional skills currently require individuals who are flexible and can handle a good deal of change. This flexibility and this adaptability are extremely useful because they allow school leaders to shift from a purely managerial focus to an instructional teacher-learner leadership approach. Additionally, a ranking of the top characteristics of ethical educational leaders are shown in Box 2.1.

---

**BOX 2.1. TOP CHARACTERISTICS OF ETHICAL EDUCATIONAL LEADERS IN ORDER OF IMPORTANCE**

1. Honest
2. Positive
3. Caring/Considerate
4. Fair
5. Professional/Knowledgeable

6. Trustworthy/Reliable

7. Consistent

8. Respectful

9. Open-minded

10. Kind/Friendly

11. Listener

12. High expectations/Standards

13. Accessible/Available

*Source:* National Council of Professors of Educational Administration (n.d.).

## Leadership and Integrity

Perhaps the most critical aspect of quality leadership involves integrity and ethics. Today's school leaders and technology coordinators must act with integrity, fairness, and ethics. When we lose our integrity, we lose our effectiveness. As an administrator, one needs to act consistently and treat all people equitably. Thus, leaders need to show stakeholders in a school and community that they genuinely respect and care about them. Stakeholders need to know that a leader exhibits outstanding character, values honor, and is driven by an unending passion to reach a vision of excellence. Covey (2006), in his book *The Speed of Trust,* ties this concept to the roots of a tree. He stated that even though the roots of a tree are underground and not visible most of the time, they are vital to the nourishment, strength, stability, and growth of the entire tree. Likewise, educational leaders, who do not have strong roots, and thus are withering on the inside, will soon be exposed on the outside. Covey continued defining integrity by saying that, for most people, integrity means honesty. Though some do not consciously realize it, honesty includes not only telling the truth, but also leaving the right impression. It is possible to tell the truth, but leave the wrong impression.

Most school administrators and technology coordinators would describe themselves as being honest. However, many staff members do not believe their administrators and directors are honest or communicate honestly. So, how does one go about increasing his or her integrity? The answer may be in school leaders and technology coordinators taking time to reflect on what degree of integrity they presently possess (see Exhibit 2.1). This is the first step of being truthful. Inherently, most of us know the difference between right and wrong, and we need to evaluate our inner thoughts on *how honest are we with our fellow man.*

Results from the Research from the Schools of Integrity project by Mirk (2009) identified openness, honesty, relationship building, and constant rigorous reflection as key elements in schools that successfully balance academic rigor with ethical development. The Institute for Global Ethics (2006) translated those findings and interviewed six secondary school leaders who were

**Exhibit 2.1** Self-Reflective Integrity Assessment

| Self-reflective integrity assessment. Place a check (✓) mark by those items that you always do, do most of the time, or just sometimes. | Always | Most of the time | Sometimes |
|---|---|---|---|
| • I indisputably try to be honest in all my interactions with others. | | | |
| • I typically "walk my talk." | | | |
| • I am clear on my values. | | | |
| • I feel comfortable in standing up for my values. | | | |
| • I am open to the possibility of learning new truths that may cause me to rethink issues or even redefine my values. | | | |

*Source:* Covey (2006).

recommended on their solid reputations of integrity to learn how ethics and values contribute to leadership effectiveness. Those leaders offered five key recommendations listed below:

- *Lead from your core values.* Deeply held values become an operating platform that works in two directions: compelling constant internal alignment and driving outward actions. In an age of increasing transparency, both functions are essential.
- *Have the courage to connect.* As a leader of a school community, it can take a measure of courage to stick to ideals and share vulnerabilities. A commitment to fairness directs a leader to suspend preconceived ideas or assumptions as they go into potentially tough meetings. By overriding preconceptions about a given situation, an ethical leader can develop the courage and humility to share and connect with others. Effective leaders resist the temptation to impose their beliefs. Instead they opt for a slower and perhaps less convenient route that seeks common ground and mutual respect and, ultimately, leads to meaningful connections. The focus on positive, authentic relationships sets the tone for what the leader wants their school culture to become.
- *Do your homework.* In developing relationships, the ethical leader needs to understand how others think and understand the background of where others are coming from. Thus, the leader has an understanding and respect for the person as well as the issue at hand. Remembering details and giving specific feedback helps others know

they are being respected. The point of not talking jargon but being able to communicate in ways that anyone can understand with clarity is a huge leadership responsibility.

- *Model your outcomes.* School leaders can establish trust through their willingness to be open and transparent with faculty and staff. Being open and forthright is a key ingredient in modeling what you expect your faculty to do with students. As a school leader, exemplifying experimentation and then acting upon feedback is a risk but a huge modeling technique. It will open channels for discussion and reflection and create a culture of improvement.

- *Lean on others for support.* Bringing faculty and staff into conversations about their school shows that you respect them as professionals and you recognize the institution as a community of practice. This leadership approach helps to build values-driven relationships within a school community. When appropriate, asking the question, "What would you do?" opens the door to talk about different points of view regarding decisions that need to be made at the school.

## Distributive Leadership

Sharing leadership is a major part of technology planning and implementation. Keeping with this perspective, a fundamental aspect of distributive leadership is involving teacher leaders. According to Kennedy, Deuel, Nelson, and Slavit (2011), the three major attributes of distributed leadership that support teacher collaboration and professional learning communities are

1. leader's recognition and use of internal intellectual and experiential resources,

2. differentiated top-down and lateral decision-making processes, and

3. culture building through dialogue and collaborative inquiry.

Each of the attributes listed promotes the concept of school administrators sharing expertise and creating a collective responsibility for integrating technology. These efforts are directed toward enhancing student learning as well as teaching leaders the value of inviting teachers into leadership. Such discussions can also build a platform for shared decision making if opportunities are appropriate when considering new technology initiatives. Likewise, significant problems are more likely to be solved when people come together and collaborate (Hoerr, 2012). Readers can refer to the distributive leadership conceptual model presented in Figure 2.1. This model is a visual representation of the core elements that stakeholders and school administrators should consider in creating a culture of shared leadership.

Involving other teacher leaders has real benefits—and in the end, when trying to change school culture, it certainly does make sense to broaden leadership responsibilities and deepen understanding. Whenever the job is too large to be effectively done by one person, there are individuals who can

**Figure 2.1** Distributive Leadership Model

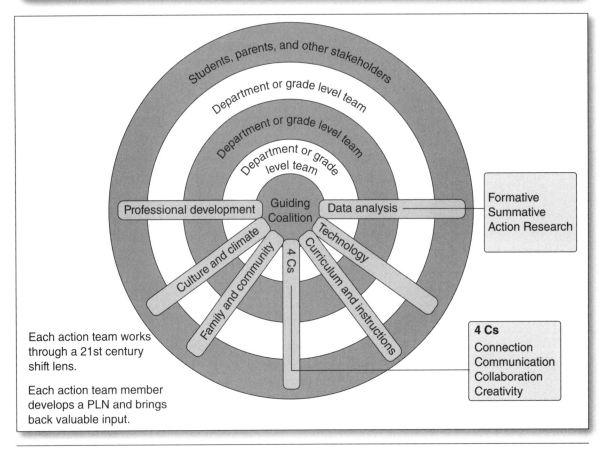

Students, parents, and other stakeholders

Department or grade level team

Department or grade level team

Department or grade level team

Guiding Coalition

Professional development

Data analysis

Formative
Summative
Action Research

Culture and climate

Family and community

4 Cs

Technology

Curriculum and instructions

Each action team works through a 21st century shift lens.

Each action team member develops a PLN and brings back valuable input.

**4 Cs**
Connection
Communication
Collaboration
Creativity

*Source:* "Thinking Hard While Running on Empty" (n.d.).

support in the process of change. Instead of one individual trying to provide adequate leadership, using a team approach to technology planning can be the answer. The corollary to this line of thinking is that if we trust teachers to work with students and make decisions about their academic welfare, school leaders need to be willing to involve teachers in discussions that are technology and leadership related.

## Engaging Stakeholders in Technology Planning

Involving stakeholders in school reform and technology planning has far-reaching implications. Moreover, with technology planning being a multifaceted enterprise, it takes the involvement of various stakeholders to make it all work. For school leaders, this means a school technology advisory committee should include interested teachers, a financial expert, a person knowledgeable about project implementation, another individual with knowledge of professional development strategies, a technology specialist, as well as a person who is proficient in public relations.

Fortunately, there are many schools that have discerning and mindful leaders who instinctively invite these community members into the process. That said, one of the most important steps toward improving public education is deepening an understanding of a school's most important stakeholders, their teachers, parents, and students (Hemmen, 2012). They are the stakeholders at the heart of the institution and it is vital their viewpoints are heard and included.

## School and Community Leadership

Successful educational leaders who make initial changes in planning and technology implementation are usually those same individuals who realize the importance of community involvement. As noted in Chapter 5, public engagement is no longer a theoretical phrase to be used exclusively in discussions between academics. The development of technology initiatives that are broad based and supportive requires foresight on the part of school and teacher leaders. A good deal of this foresight involves the willingness and moxie to cultivate and capitalize on the potential knowledge, energy, and support of parents and community members.

Public disengagement from schools has been a problem in the past, but this can change with sound research practices, information sharing about technology, and quality leadership. If we are to succeed as a global society, educational leaders must involve parents and community members in the development of school technology plans. Understanding how to support educational change via technology advancements, evaluating instructional strategies, and initiating new programs is perhaps one of the critical steps in the leadership process. Likewise, it is important for school leaders to translate their knowledge and abilities into community support for school reform. When considering the great extent to which properly functioning schools can positively influence student lives, there should be little doubt that communities should be major supporters and encouragers of their children's schooling. With a focus on quality leadership and a focus on increasing student achievement, public schools can effectively accommodate the demands for curricular and technological change that are unmistakably evident on the educational horizon.

## Navigating Future Change

The 21st century challenge in education will be to assess curricular and technology credibility in a systematic and sustained way (Abilock, 2012). Subsequently, the art of planning and building successful technology programs will continue to involve a number of important factors. The following important target areas provide a brief overview of individual elements needed for a successful technology outline. In most cases, these target areas provide concise categories as a guideline for school leaders and technology coordinators. For more detailed information, readers are referred to specific chapters.

### Support Student Needs

In any technology initiative, the needs of students must be placed above any other factor being considered. The present interest in mobile technology and mobile learning, or *m-learning*, often derives support from viewpoints that take into account the importance of student needs. Unfortunately, many well-meaning school leaders, coordinators, and committee members make decisions about technology applications that really do not acknowledge the needs of the students who will use it. Educationally questionable reasons for making major decisions about technology include international competitiveness, skilled-labor force, and getting good jobs. As important as these reasons are, no other motivation can be allowed to supplant students' needs as the central focus for schools and their technology programs. For more in-depth information on students' needs, see Chapter 4.

### Combine Teaching and Learning

Teaching and learning are two distinctly complex and yet complementary entities. Therefore, they must be considered simultaneously when deciding how the technology will be brought into the classroom or the school. For a more complete discussion of teaching and learning with technology, see Chapter 4. To begin with, educational administrators can consider the following list as it relates to the effects technology has on teaching and learning:

- Consider carefully how new technology applications will affect teaching and learning. Make sure to have a purpose that reflects teaching and learning when bringing technologies into the school and into classrooms.
- Determine how new technology will coexist with other technologies used throughout the school district.
- Explore and manage bandwidth issues.
- Evaluate applications and purchases as well as coordinate them to student needs.
- Consider features like durability, maintenance, access, and speed.
- Evaluate projected purchases to determine which programs and applications will best complement, support, and expand classroom teaching and learning.
- Evaluate planned purchases for user friendliness. Use is important because ease of use reduces the learning curve and helps ensure that the program will be used.
- Determine the simplest approach that will effectively integrate technology into the teaching and learning environment. Making technology transparent allows stakeholders to support the process more readily.
- Establish dialogues with teachers to evaluate classroom space as it relates to new technology.
- Determine the amount of use teachers will make of the new technology.

### Provide Leadership With Planning

Quality leadership must be evident at all stages of development. Planning can help participants understand the structure of the project and what is required of each committee and person. Planning can also help address the *who, what, when, where, why,* and *how* aspects of the project. The suggestions listed below provide a brief overview of several important factors to consider when a technology project is being planned:

- Keep students' and teachers' needs as the vanguard during the various stages of the technology planning process.
- Consider how students and staff members will be affected by the technology changes and develop appropriate support structures like professional development, changes in classroom layout, and inclusion into curricula.
- Invest in technology for the long haul and not just for a quick fix.
- Review school programs to determine how course subjects may be adjusted to make use of technologies in the classroom.
- Locate research that both supports and counters the major assumptions on which the technology project is based. Make sure everyone knows both sides of the issue.
- Consider the possibility of having to modify school practices or upgrade regulations.
- Look at the likelihood of having to adjust the school's philosophy and mission statements to align with the technology initiative you are creating.
- If necessary, create or borrow surveys to probe stakeholder viewpoints.
- Envision what the completed project will look like and what it will do for teaching and learning. This mental picture can help provide focus for the entire enterprise.

### Provide Professional Development

One of the most important aspects of any technology initiative is professional development. It is critical that consideration be given to teacher learning well in advance. For a detailed description of professional development and its importance to technology implementation, see Chapter 3. Suggestions include the following:

- Formulate detailed plans for professional development and implementation. Plans for training and inservice should be developed well in advance of the actual implementation of technology.
- Decide who will lead professional development programs and evaluate each stage of implementation.
- Determine appropriate professional development activities for special services and support staff.
- Identify who will lead and evaluate professional development for auxiliary staff members.
- Identify in-house technical consultants who will help teachers deal quickly with problems that might arise.
- If possible, seek out a product/technology representative who has already done what you are trying to do.
- Develop a working schedule for the professional development program.

## Understand Financial Management

Most determinations about finance are generally dealt with at middle- and upper-management positions. While many of these deliberations are held in small groups, their impact will be critical to the success of committees that will guide the technology project. For more information about financial management, see Chapter 7. Several points are listed below to provide a general overview of the financial-management process:

- Determine what financial resources are available for in-house projects and equipment.
- Itemize equipment resources owned by the school or district. The goal is to look to reduce unnecessary duplication in new purchases.
- Determine financial resources available 3 to 5 years in advance.
- Consider canvassing civic organizations for financial, material, or equipment support.
- Determine if the proposed equipment or applications will be purchased locally, statewide, or nationally. Decide who will be responsible for handling recommended purchases.
- Review all costs to make sure the technology project is affordable at all phases.

## Analyze the Infrastructure

This should be one of first steps in planning and implementation of technology. When discussing infrastructure, one is generally referring to basic facilities as well as technological capabilities needed in a school. These facilities and installations can impact proposed technology implementations. For a more complete review of infrastructure, see Chapter 8. The following points provide a brief outline of things to consider when reviewing infrastructure:

- Decide how existing infrastructure and capabilities can be integrated into the project.
- Visit other schools to evaluate successful programs for structural adaptations that could be simulated and, in particular, look for unique ideas to solve local problems.
- Ensure infrastructure will accommodate any instructional configuration required by teachers or staff.
- Analyze what space, remodeling, and/or expertise is required for implementation.
- Arrange for professionals to handle infrastructural changes or needs.

## Garner Community Support

In current educational contexts, when planning technology, community support is paramount to success. This is because parents and community members want to be informed especially when costly reforms are undertaken. To find out more about community awareness, planning, and support, see Chapter 6. Several factors are listed below to provide general information to guide your deliberations:

- Evaluate community willingness to fund technology initiatives.
- Determine the level of congruence between the school's technology initiatives and commitment on the part of board members and/or trustees.

- Consider how you will be able to show community members how teachers will integrate technology into their curriculum.
- Address parents' and community members' concerns as to how technology will enhance student learning and achievement.
- Show parents and members of the community the benefits of new technology applications.
- Develop guidelines for presenting information to the public. Be sure all news releases are verified with the superintendent as well as public relations director (if applicable) before they go public.

## Complete an Evaluation

A crucial component of any technology implementation is program evaluation. To learn more about this process, see Chapter 9. The list that follows contains a selection of ideas that are pertinent to evaluation of the technology initiative:

- Decide who will evaluate the overall project and how the evaluations will be done.
- Set a specific timeline for the completion of key events within the evaluation process.
- Outline how changes or revisions will be handled.
- Review various evaluation methods and choose the most appropriate methods available for sharing information with the community.

After reviewing the above factors and tailoring feedback to reflect school or district realities, school leaders will be prepared to develop more specific plans for the initiative or project renewal.

## TECHNOLOGY FOR SCHOOL LEADERS

To specifically define project parameters, school leaders need to follow International Society for Technology in Education standards (ISTE, 2011) as well as Technology Standards for School Administrators (TSSA, 2001). The driving force behind these standards is the assumption that technology reform requires large-scale systemic change. Moreover, these standards can assist school leaders in identifying and specifying future school technology projects. Refer to the following TSSA standards to conceptualize the leadership role in the technology plan.

## Standards

I. **Leadership and Vision.** Educational leaders inspire a shared vision for comprehensive integration of technology and foster an environment and culture conducive to the realization of that vision.

*Educational Leaders:*

A. Facilitate the shared development by all stakeholders of a vision for technology use and widely communicate that vision.

B. Maintain an inclusive and cohesive process to develop, implement, and monitor a dynamic, long-range, and systemic technology plan to achieve the vision.

C. Foster and nurture a culture of responsible risk taking and advocate policies promoting continuous innovation with technology.

D. Use data in making leadership decisions.

E. Advocate for research-based effective practices in use of technology.

F. Advocate on the state and national levels for policies, programs, and funding opportunities that support implementation of the district technology plan.

II. **Teaching and Learning.** Educational leaders ensure that curricular design, instructional strategies, and learning environments integrate appropriate technologies to maximize teaching and learning.

*Educational Leaders:*

A. Identify, use, evaluate, and promote appropriate technologies to enhance and support instruction and standards-based curriculum leading to high levels of student achievement.

B. Facilitate and support collaborative technology-enriched learning environments conducive to innovation for improved learning.

C. Provide for learner-centered environments that use technology to meet the individual and diverse needs of learners.

D. Facilitate the use of technologies to support and enhance instructional methods that develop higher-level thinking, decision-making, and problem-solving skills.

E. Provide for and ensure that faculty and staff take advantage of quality professional learning opportunities for improved learning and teaching with technology.

III. **Productivity and Professional Practice.** Educational leaders apply technology to enhance their professional practice and to increase their own productivity and that of others.

*Educational Leaders:*

A. Model the routine, intentional, and effective use of technology.

B. Employ technology for communication and collaboration among colleagues, staff, parents, students, and the larger community.

C. Create and participate in learning communities that stimulate, nurture, and support faculty and staff in using technology for improved productivity.

D. Engage in sustained, job-related professional learning using technology resources.

E. Maintain awareness of emerging technologies and their potential uses in education.

F. Use technology to advance organizational improvement.

IV. **Support, Management, and Operations.** Educational leaders ensure the integration of technology to support productive systems for learning and administration.

*Educational Leaders:*

A. Develop, implement, and monitor policies and guidelines to ensure compatibility of technologies.

B. Implement and use integrated technology-based management and operations systems.

C. Allocate financial and human resources to ensure complete and sustained implementation of the technology plan.

D. Integrate strategic plans, technology plans, and other improvement plans and policies to align efforts and leverage resources.

E. Implement procedures to drive continuous improvement of technology systems and to support technology replacement cycles.

V. **Evaluation.** Educational leaders use technology to plan and implement comprehensive systems of effective evaluation.

*Educational Leaders:*

A. Use multiple methods to evaluate appropriate uses of technology resources for learning, communication, and productivity.

B. Use technology to collect and analyze data, interpret results, and communicate findings to improve instructional practice and student learning.

C. Assess staff knowledge, skills, and performance in using technology and use results to facilitate quality professional development and to inform personnel decisions.

D. Use technology to evaluate and manage administrative and operational systems.

VI. **Social, Legal, and Ethical Issues.** Educational leaders understand the social, legal, and ethical issues related to technology and model responsible decision making related to these issues.

*Educational Leaders:*

A. Ensure equity of access to technology resources that enable and empower all learners and educators.

B. Identify, communicate, model, and enforce social, legal, and ethical practices to promote responsible use of technology.

C. Promote and enforce privacy, security, and online safety related to the use of technology.

D. Promote and enforce environmentally safe and healthy practices in the use of technology.

E. Participate in the development of policies that clearly enforce copyright law and assign ownership of intellectual property developed with district resources.

# TECHNOLOGY LEADERSHIP ROLES

To formulate a technology mission statement, school administrators should keep the following specific technology leadership tasks in mind. The school superintendent, principal, and district technology coordinator will take on technology leadership roles that provide ways and objectives to solidify overriding goals of technology for a school district.

## Superintendent

Superintendents who effectively lead integration of technology typically perform the following tasks:

### Leadership and Vision

1. Ensure that the vision for use of technology is congruent with the overall district vision.

2. Engage representatives from all stakeholder groups in the development, implementation, and ongoing assessment of a district technology plan consistent with the district improvement plan.

3. Advocate to the school community, the media, and the community at large for effective technology use in schools for improved student learning and efficiency of operations.

### Teaching and Learning

4. Provide equitable access for students and staff to technologies that facilitate productivity and enhance learning.

5. Communicate expectations consistently for the use of technology to increase student achievement.

6. Ensure that budget priorities reflect a focus on technology and its relationships to enhanced learning and teaching.

7. Establish a culture that encourages responsible risk taking with technology while requiring accountability for results.

8. Maintain an emphasis on technology fluency among staff across the district and provide staff development opportunities to support high expectations.

9. Use current information tools and systems for communication, management of schedules and resources, performance assessment, and professional learning.

## Support, Management, and Operations

10. Provide adequate staffing and other resources to support technology infrastructure and integration across the district.

11. Ensure, through collaboration with district and campus leadership, alignment of technology efforts with the overall district improvement efforts in instructional management and district operations.

## Evaluation

12. Engage administrators in using districtwide and disaggregated data to identify improvement targets at the campus and program levels.

13. Establish evaluation procedures for administrators that assess demonstrated growth toward achieving technology standards for school administrators.

## Social, Legal, and Ethical Issues

14. Ensure that every student in the district engages in technology-rich learning experiences.

15. Recommend policies and procedures that protect the security and integrity of the district infrastructure and the data resident on it.

16. Develop policies and procedures that protect the rights and confidentiality of students and staff.

# Principal

Principals who effectively lead integration of technology typically perform the following tasks:

## Leadership and Vision

1. Participate in an inclusive district process through which stakeholders formulate a shared vision that clearly defines expectations for technology use.

2. Develop a collaborative, technology-rich school improvement plan, grounded in research and aligned with the district strategic plan.

3. Promote highly effective practices in technology integration among faculty and other staff members.

## Teaching and Learning

4. Assist teachers in using technology to access, analyze, and interpret student performance data, and in using results to appropriately design, assess, and modify student instruction.

5. Collaboratively design, implement, support, and participate in professional development for all instructional staff that institutionalizes effective integration of technology for improved student learning.

## *Productivity and Professional Practice*

6. Use current technology-based management systems to access and maintain personnel and student records.

7. Use a variety of media and formats, including telecommunications and the school website, to communicate, interact, and collaborate with peers, experts, and other education stakeholders.

## *Support, Management, and Operations*

8. Provide campuswide staff development for sharing work and resources across commonly used formats and platforms.

9. Allocate campus discretionary funds and other resources to advance implementation of the technology plan.

10. Advocate for adequate, timely, and high-quality technology support services.

## *Evaluation*

11. Promote and model the use of technology to access, analyze, and interpret campus data to focus efforts for improving student learning and productivity.

12. Implement evaluation procedures for teachers that assess individual growth toward established technology standards and guide professional development planning.

13. Include effectiveness of technology use in the teaching and learning process as one criterion in assessing performance of instructional staff.

## *Social, Legal, and Ethical Issues*

14. Secure and allocate technology resources to enable teachers to better meet the needs of all learners on campus.

15. Adhere to and enforce among staff and students the district's acceptable-use policy and other policies and procedures related to security, copyright, and technology use.

16. Participate in the development of facility plans that support and focus on health and environmentally safe practices related to the use of technology.

## District Technology Coordinator

District technology coordinators who effectively lead integration of technology typically perform the following tasks:

## *Leadership and Vision*

1. Ensure that program technology initiatives are aligned with the district technology vision.

2. Represent program interests in the development and systematic review of a comprehensive district technology plan.

3. Advocate for program use of promising practices with technology to achieve program goals.

## Teaching and Learning

4. Participate in developing and providing electronic resources that support improved learning for program participants.

5. Provide rich and effective staff development opportunities and ongoing support that promote use of technology to enhance program initiatives and activities.

6. Ensure that program curricula and services embrace changes brought about by the proliferation of technology within society.

## Productivity and Professional Practice

7. Use technology and connectivity to share promising strategies, interesting case studies, and student and faculty learning opportunities that support program improvement.

8. Model, for program staff, effective uses of technology for professional productivity, such as in presentations, record keeping, data analysis, research, and communications.

9. Use online collaboration to build and participate in collaborative learning communities with directors of similar programs in other districts.

## Support, Management, and Operations

10. Implement technology initiatives that provide instructional and technical support as defined in the district technology plan.

11. Determine financial needs of the program, develop budgets, and set timelines to realize program technology targets.

## Evaluation

12. Continuously monitor and analyze performance data to guide the design and improvement of program initiatives and activities.

13. Employ multiple measures and flexible assessment strategies to determine staff technology proficiency within the program and to guide staff development efforts.

## Social, Legal, and Ethical Issues

14. Involve program participants, clients, and staff members in dealing with issues related to equity of access and equity of technology-rich opportunities.

15. Educate program personnel about technology-related health, safety, legal, and ethical issues, and hold them accountable for decisions and behaviors.

16. Inform district and campus leadership of program-specific issues related to privacy, confidentiality, and reporting of information that might impact technology system and policy requirements.

## Formulating Goal and Mission Statements

A project goal and mission statement can be very helpful as a guide to participants in any major project. The key is to note that a goal is an overarching theme. It is crucial that the goal and mission of any individual school remain consistent and in line with the overall goal of the district. Thus, a goal and mission statement (see Box 2.2) including students, learning, and teaching is one that is most likely to direct the project toward successful implementation for students, teachers, and schools. For example, technology-oriented goal and/or mission statements should include

- Statements about student learning
- School and district priorities
- General objective and expectations associated with the shift in technological focus

---

### BOX 2.2. KALAMAZOO PUBLIC SCHOOLS TECHNOLOGY PLAN, MICHIGAN

*Technology Mission Statement*

The technology mission of Kalamazoo Public Schools is to ensure that all students access, process, create and communicate using diverse technology as an integral part of learning.

*Technology Vision*

The technology vision of the Kalamazoo Public Schools is to ensure that all students, supported by staff and community, will demonstrate a high degree of technological literacy in pursuit of life-long learning.

*Technology Belief Statements*

1. All students must have the knowledge and competencies necessary to function in an increasingly technological age.

2. Educational technology, when used appropriately, improves performance, increases achievement and expands the knowledge of both the student and the teacher.

3. The financial commitment of the school district to technology must be continual and ongoing.

4. Technology should be equally accessible for all members of the school community.

5. All students must be provided the opportunities to access, process, create and communicate using various technologies.

6. Technology used in the learning process is project based.

7. Technology instruction must include an understanding of the responsible use of all forms of technology including the social, ethical and legal aspects.

8. Technology integration is an essential component in the school improvement process.

9. The District Technology Benchmarks must be aligned with the State Educational Technology Standards and Expectations and integrated into the district curriculum.

*Source:* Kalamazoo Public Schools (2012).

## ESTABLISHING AND MAINTAINING COMMITMENT

Resilience and support is often what school leaders need the most (Allison, 2012). Obtaining and maintaining commitment from administrators, teachers, parents, and school board members is paramount to the success of each phase of the process. Establishing strong support from each of these groups requires the development of several strategies. Following are a number of approaches for building and maintaining commitment from various groups.

### School Administrators

- Encourage school administrators to attend state and national technology conferences or workshops. Conferences and workshops can bring administrators up-to-date on technological developments and provide useful information to meet district and school needs.
- Allow school administrators to visit schools that have successfully integrated technology into their classrooms. A picture is worth 1,000 words, so get out there and see what is being done.
- Require school administrators to develop management plans for the technology in district schools. School administrators must know that their job is not over when the technology is in place. Their influence and insights will be needed in other areas.

### School Board Members

School board members have the ultimate responsibility and authority for almost all decisions and activities that take place in the school district. Therefore, support from trustees or school board members is critical for the successful implementation of any technology initiative. Some ways to obtain (or maintain) board support and keep board members abreast of new developments in technology are in the following list:

- Encourage board members to attend technology presentations at state and national conferences and workshops.
- Continually upgrade board members' knowledge by making the latest research available to them.
- Keep the school board informed about district technology needs and initiatives.
- Keep board members up to date on the status of technology problems.
- Remember that school board support is important during the entire project but particularly during the planning stages.

The guidelines mentioned above are important because *to compete, public and private school board members across the country need to spend more time and energy focusing on an array of critical issues in their districts.*

## Teachers

Teaching is a complex profession. Initiating advances in educational technology into school learning environments can add to the complexities that teachers must already deal with on a daily basis. Inherent in properly functioning classrooms is an energy that is fully understood only through experience. It is within the hustle and bustle of classroom activities that technology initiatives will ultimately succeed or fail. Successful coordinators will understand this reality and provide a good deal of attention to teachers. The following ideas can help teachers adapt to technological changes:

- Encourage interschool visits for teachers to see what classroom technology use looks like and how it is integrated into the curriculum and regular classroom work.
- Distribute up-to-date literature and research findings about technology use in schools. This will build confidence in the staff when they know that their administrator is informed regarding the research base on this issue.
- Provide in-house workshops for classroom educators. Let teachers know where the expertise is and, more importantly, that it will be shared.
- Consider contacting teachers at specific grade levels to implement pilot projects with the new technological approach. Allow teachers to share with others the advantages they are experiencing and to discuss difficulties encountered.
- Build a user-friendly environment for teachers. Provide prompt access to expert guidance when they have questions or problems. Remember, if teachers become stuck, they rarely have time or energy to deal with technical shortcomings because students come first!
- As part of the budgeting agenda, administrators should set aside funding to send teachers to technology workshops or conferences. This is where

they can learn from those who are already using learning technologies in their classrooms.

- Remember that teacher input and support for the technology projects are critical for real success.

## Parents

Parents comprise a primary group of educational stakeholders whose voice needs to be heard. When working with parents, readers can consider the following approaches:

- Involve parents in the planning process because it can be very beneficial to a project. Make sure they know what is expected of them from the start.
- Arrange for formal and informal meetings between school personnel and parents. These meetings can be used to set positive expectations for the intended technology project.
- Provide the latest information to parents and be willing to discuss information with them.
- When practical, invite parents to attend professional development opportunities.
- Develop working relationships between home and school to provide an avenue for parental viewpoints and contributions. Parent support can help a project immensely.

## Project Calendar

School leaders, technology coordinators, curriculum leaders, and committee members must work closely together to construct a practical calendar for the project. The calendar of events in the Project Outline marks important reference points for the technology advisory committee to reach in order to keep the project on schedule. Realistic target dates are a key ingredient, and committee members should be included as this is the only way to really ensure a workable schedule of events. In this respect, it is important to remember that committee members are usually chosen because they know how to get tasks done, and they are also the ones who usually have the best idea of how long it will take to get these tasks done.

## Developing a Schedule

A technology implementation schedule differs from the calendar in that it is more specific in nature. The calendar sets general benchmarks to notify participants where they are in the process. The schedule, on the other hand, identifies specific tasks assigned to committee members needed to meet the benchmarks outlined in the calendar. Before scheduling begins, all participants must understand their roles in the project. Administrators and coordinators should hold meetings to discuss project guidelines and group responsibilities with the technology advisory committee members. Once a schedule is developed, a second meeting should be convened to discuss the project in more detail. Representation at this meeting should include

- Teacher leaders
- Local technology specialists and company representatives
- Community leaders
- District maintenance advisor
- Members of groups interested in or affected by the project

Keep minutes of meetings to direct the efforts of committee members. During preliminary meetings, list the names of individuals or organizations willing to assist with any aspect of the project. Create an implementation document outlining the duty of each group or individual on the technology advisory committee. This document is important because it ties everyone together and ensures successful scheduling of the project. Building enthusiasm for any technology initiative is crucial. Without this implementation document, the best designed plans have the potential to fail (Overbay, Mollette, & Vasu, 2011). Moreover, precious time, significant sums of district money, and needless duplication of labor can be saved because channels of communication will remain open and responsibilities clearly outlined.

## Project Outline

The Project Outline noted below provides structure and direction for the leadership and committee activities required to make a technology project successful. When using the Project Outline, it is important to note that a needs assessment, professional development, and technology evaluation will continue well beyond the initial 2-year period. Assessing and updating current infrastructure is therefore imperative at this juncture of the planning process. Likewise, lengthening the time span for professional development should be consistent with research showing teachers often require up to 5 years to become proficient in planning and implementing educational technology.

# PROJECT OUTLINE

*Phase One: Initial Planning and Commitment*

Note: This phase deals with organizing people and creating the plans necessary in moving the technology initiative forward.

## Step One: Gaining Support for the Project

| Administrative | Faculty and Staff | School Board |
|---|---|---|
| Commitment | Commitment | Commitment |
| Yes ❑ No ❑ | Yes ❑ No ❑ | Yes ❑ No ❑ |

If "No," indicate reasons.

Parental Commitment          Community Member(s)

Yes ❑ No ❑                         Yes ❑ No ❑

If "No," indicate reasons.

Additional insights and concerns regarding support:

## Step Two: Formulating Core Committees

Note: The number of members on any of the suggested committees will depend on the amount of human resources available.

### Technology Advisory Committee

**Chairperson:**

Administrative Members          Faculty Members
Parent Members                        Community Members

### Steering Committee

**Chairperson:**

Note: These members will come from the technology advisory committee.

**Members:**

**Subcommittees:**

Note: The following list suggests subcommittees that could be established to help with this technology initiative. Some of these can be separate committees, or they can be combined as needed.

### Curriculum Committee

**Chairperson:**

Note: These members will be responsible for developing a working base of information that will assist teachers in implementing the technology in the curriculum.

**Members:**

## Professional Development Committee

**Chairperson:**

Note: This committee will be responsible for ensuring that all staff members receive appropriate professional training regarding the technology initiative.

**Members:**

## Budgeting Committee

**Chairperson:**

Note: This committee will be responsible for dealing with all financial issues associated with the technology project, from garnering financial support to pricing out needed equipment.

**Members:**

## Infrastructure Support Committee

**Chairperson:**

Note: This committee will be responsible for deciding how the technology can best be integrated into the existing school facility. Of primary importance here is assessing as well as updating current infrastructure.

**Members:**

## Evaluation and Assessment Committee

**Chairperson:**

Note: This committee will decide on and formulate the approaches needed in evaluating and assessing all stages of the project.

**Members:**

## Public Relations Committee

**Chairperson:**

Note: This committee will guide and direct how information will be released to the external community.

**Members:**

## Step Three: Determining Leadership Roles

Note: In this area of the project outline, you want to determine the degree of leadership, input, and involvement you want core members to play.

**Superintendent**

| | | | |
|---|---|---|---|
| Leadership: | High ❑ | Medium ❑ | Low ❑ |
| Input: | High ❑ | Medium ❑ | Low ❑ |
| Involvement: | High ❑ | Medium ❑ | Low ❑ |

**Local School Administrators**

| | | | |
|---|---|---|---|
| Leadership: | High ❑ | Medium ❑ | Low ❑ |
| Input: | High ❑ | Medium ❑ | Low ❑ |
| Involvement: | High ❑ | Medium ❑ | Low ❑ |

**Tehnology Instructors**

| | | | |
|---|---|---|---|
| Leadership: | High ❑ | Medium ❑ | Low ❑ |
| Input: | High ❑ | Medium ❑ | Low ❑ |
| Involvement: | High ❑ | Medium ❑ | Low ❑ |

**Teacher Leaders**

| | | | |
|---|---|---|---|
| Leadership: | High ❑ | Medium ❑ | Low ❑ |
| Input: | High ❑ | Medium ❑ | Low ❑ |
| Involvement: | High ❑ | Medium ❑ | Low ❑ |

**Parents**

| | | | |
|---|---|---|---|
| Leadership: | High ❑ | Medium ❑ | Low ❑ |
| Input: | High ❑ | Medium ❑ | Low ❑ |
| Involvement: | High ❑ | Medium ❑ | Low ❑ |

**Community Members**

| | | | |
|---|---|---|---|
| Leadership: | High ❑ | Medium ❑ | Low ❑ |
| Input: | High ❑ | Medium ❑ | Low ❑ |
| Involvement: | High ❑ | Medium ❑ | Low ❑ |

## Step Four: Setting

Whenever addressing these components of your technology project, it is essential to have a clear understanding of your current technology plan. It is suggested that before you begin to work on the following components in the Project Outline, you review Chapter 8 for help in determining the maturity level of your technology plan.

1. Write several possible vision statements: This is to provide general direction for the committees and to align the project with district philosophy statements. Remember that vision statements should align with the school's purpose of educating students and improving learning and be

consistent with the school improvement process. Make sure you are thinking about the future you want, not your current situation. Note: After you have come up with a potential list, rank them from most favored to least favored and defend this ranking. Next, rank from most difficult to least difficult to implement and defend this ranking. Are the two rankings the same or different?

Concepts to consider in your vision statement:

    a.  What do you want your learners to look and be like in the years to come?

    b.  How will curriculum and technology synchronize to impact student learning?

    c.  What is your future concept of instructional delivery?

    d.  What will your classrooms under the new vision look like?

    e.  What impact do you see technology having on your school in the coming years?

    f.  How will the local and larger community be involved in your technology vision?

2.  Write several possible mission statements. Remember that the mission statement is an expression of how the vision will be fulfilled. You can go through the same ranking process you did for your vision statement. Concepts to consider in your mission statement are the following:

    a.  What is your definition of learning?

    b.  How is learning different when technology is added?

    c.  How can you make your vision come to reality?

    d.  What is required to make technology have positive impacts on instruction?

    e.  How do you see technology impacting student achievement outcomes?

    f.  What is unique about the learners and their needs at your school?

**State specific goals:**

Now that you have potential vision and mission statements, you will want to support this with relevant goals. In this sense, you want your goals to be specific statements about how you are going to connect technology to learning. Goals are the technology and learning points you are trying to reach. You want your goals to be realistic, achievable, and adaptable.

Goals List:

1.

2.

3.

4.

5.

6.

7. Other:

**State specific objectives:**

You now need to write some specific objectives for each goal. Objectives are ways that you can measure the accomplishments of your intended goals. You want your objectives to be clear, concise, measurable, adaptable, and observable.

Objectives List

Goal 1

Objectives:

1.

2.

3.

4. Other:

Goal 2

Objectives:

1.

2.

3.

4. Other:

Goal 3

Objectives:

1.

2.

3.

4. Other:

Goal 4: Other . . .

3. Committee recommendations:

This will provide direction for the committees as they work toward a solid technology plan.

Recommendations List:

## Step Five: Establish Communication Networks

Note: Make sure that you provide a list of all committees and their members to everyone involved in the project. In doing so, stress the importance of using proper channels when discussing project issues or concerns. As part of this, project-related communications should go through committee chairs to disseminate to committee members.

## Step Six: Needs Assessment

Note: In this particular category, you want to ask yourself if you have general needs in each of these three areas. The key is that you want to start to consider what already exists in the school and what can be used and what is needed to begin to align your existing technology program with the new technology initiative outlined in this book.

### General Assessment

A. Hardware Needs     B. Software Needs     C. Financial Assessment

Yes ❑ No ❑          Yes ❑ No ❑          Yes ❑ No ❑

| A. Hardware Inventory | | |
|---|---|---|
| **Equipment** | **Current Amount** | **Needed Amount** |
| Faculty desktops | | |
| Faculty mobile devices | | |
| Student desktops | | |
| Student portable devices | | |
| Smart boards | | |
| Available printers | | |
| Wireless routers/Networking system | | |
| Other | | |

### Current Technology Hardware Specifications

❑ **PC**   ❑ **APPLE**   ❑ **Mobile Device**

Processor type: _____

Memory: _____

USB/HDMI ports: _____

Bluetooth: _____

Wireless capability: _____

Operating system: _____

Warranty: _____

Other relevant data:

### B. Current In-School Software and Application Programs

1.

2.

3.

4.

5. Other:

### C. Technology Financial Assessment

| Sources of Funding | Current Amount | Potential Amount |
|---|---|---|
| In-school funding | $ | $ |
| District funding | $ | $ |
| Contributions | $ | $ |
| Grants | $ | $ |
| Donations | $ | $ |
| State initiatives | $ | $ |
| Federal initiatives | $ | $ |
| Fundraising | $ | $ |
| Totals | $ | $ |

## Step Seven: Course of Action

1. List specific purposes for the technology change.

2. Project evaluation: Determine how technology will be evaluated for use.

3. Preliminary supplier evaluation

Company: _____

| | | | |
|---|---|---|---|
| Expertise: | Excellent ❑ | Good ❑ | Poor ❑ |
| Price: | Excellent ❑ | Good ❑ | Poor ❑ |
| Service quality: | Excellent ❑ | Good ❑ | Poor ❑ |

After-sale service: Excellent ❑ Good ❑ Poor ❑

Warranty: Excellent ❑ Good ❑ Poor ❑

- Repeat this process until an appropriate company can be found.
- Preview software and application support services.

Findings:

| 4. Assess general costs for predicted hardware needs. | PC | Apple | Cost per Unit |
|---|---|---|---|
| Faculty desktop | | | $ |
| Faculty mobile device | | | $ |
| Student desktop | | | $ |
| Student mobile device | | | $ |
| Smart board | | | $ |
| Wireless routers/Networking system | | | $ |
| Other | | | $ |

| 5. Estimated Hardware Costs | | | | |
|---|---|---|---|---|
| Users | Total Cost Per Unit | × | Amount Needed | = Total Predicted Cost |
| Faculty desktop | | | | |
| Faculty mobile device | | | | |
| Student desktop | | | | |
| Student mobile device | | | | |
| Smart board | | | | |
| Wireless routers/ Networking system | | | | |
| Other | | | | |
| | | | Total Cost | |

Note: You may not have to purchase all new equipment or devices for a project. Make sure everything is compatible.

**Option:**

Some schools and school districts are opting to lease equipment and systems instead of purchasing them outright. Leasing agreements allow schools to acquire equipment without using capital funds, establish flexible financing, and keep systems current. Most leasing agreements are based on 48-month terms. It is something that could be discussed and considered based on district needs, finances, and resources.

6. Evaluate existing network capabilities. Unless you have a qualified technical expert, it would be best if this was evaluated through school district personnel or contracted privately.

List specific needs:

7. Establish professional development program and prepare budget. Include such factors as

| | |
|---|---|
| *Professional development:* | $ |
| *Conferences:* | $ |
| *Research resources:* | $ |
| *Leave time:* | $ |
| *Travel allowances:* | $ |
| *Other:* | $ |
| *Projected totals:* | $ |

*General comments:*

8. Review all proposed maintenance agreements, contracts, costs, warrantees, legal documents, and so on. Make sure to get the various committees and school officials to double-check and list any concerns.

Notes:

# PROJECT OUTLINE

## *Phase Two: Action Planning and Implementation*

### Step One: Committee Action

Assign specific tasks to committees. Consider factors such as

- Committee description
- Who will participate
- Timelines for work projects

Committees should now be actively working on their areas of focus and should be providing clear direction to how the equipment and devices will be brought into the classrooms.

### Step Two: Financial Review

1. Verify funding sources accessed by appropriate committees. You should now be starting to work with actual figures and not projected numbers.

2. Confirm hardware, software, and application costs.

3. Confirm infrastructure and networking costs.

4. Confirm staff development costs.

5. Finalize financial plans with appropriate district and school authorities.

### Step Three: Public Relations Program

1. Committee chairperson or administrator should now be able to inform the larger community and public of the technology project.

2. Assign school and technology spokesperson.

3. Ensure that parents and the public are appropriately informed of the stages and progress of the technology initiative. This can occur through school website, online and phone message systems, newsletters, articles in the local paper, radio, and television.

### Step Four: Calendar of Events

1. Finalize dates for completion of purchases.

2. Set dates for introduction of new devices into classrooms.

3. Set tentative dates for professional development.

4. Set program evaluation dates.

5. Set dates for public relations information and events.

**Calendar of Events Checklist**

| | | |
|---|---|---|
| District approval | Date: | Done ❑ |
| School board approval | Date: | Done ❑ |
| Financial agreements and contracts signed | Date: | Done ❑ |
| Equipment purchase | Date: | Done ❑ |
| Support materials purchase | Date: | Done ❑ |
| Infrastructure and networking project | Date: | Done ❑ |
| Professional development meetings | Date: | Done ❑ |
| | Date: | Done ❑ |
| | Date: | Done ❑ |
| | Date: | Done ❑ |
| | Date: | Done ❑ |
| Evaluation program schedule | Date: | Done ❑ |
| | Date: | Done ❑ |
| | Date: | Done ❑ |
| | Date: | Done ❑ |
| Public relations announcements and events | Date: | Done ❑ |
| | Date: | Done ❑ |

---

## Step Five: Hardware, Software and Application Implementation Checklist

---

1. Sign contracts to purchase hardware, software, applications, and network accessories.    Done ❑

2. Sign contracts to purchase support materials such as tables, chairs, headsets, extension cords, power strips, etc.    Done ❑

3. Prepare schools and appropriate personnel to facilitate delivery and setup.    Done ❑

4. Check all products for damage.    Done ❑

5. Return damaged materials for replacement.    Done ❑

6. Place equipment in classrooms according to agreed-on plans.    Done ❑

7. Consult teachers to see if changes are needed regarding placement of equipment and devices in their rooms.     Done ❑

8. Load all software and check for problems.     Done ❑

9. Run all factory-installed programs and check for problems.     Done ❑

10. Check network to make sure that connections work as needed.     Done ❑

11. Make sure support materials are available and equitably distributed (manuals, tutorial programs, textbooks, etc.).     Done ❑

12. Run final integrity checks on networks, equipment, software, and applications before clearing the system for classroom use.     Done ❑

13. Sign contract for service and maintenance of system.     Done ❑

14. Develop schedule for regular cleaning and preventive maintenance.     Done ❑

# PROJECT OUTLINE

## *Phase Three: Professional Development and Assessment*

Note: Professional development is critical for the overall success of this technology initiative. It requires foresight and patience by administrators and teachers, because introducing new equipment, mobile devices, and applications into classrooms can require a good deal of time for everyone to adjust. As such, all staff members will need differing levels of technical support, encouragement, and space so that they can find the best ways to link technology with curriculum as well as to their personal teaching style. It is important that professional development programs are developed according to teacher needs. Often, a home-grown program will work best. Also be aware that phase three will begin as phase two is being finalized.

## Instructions for the Professional Development Committee

1. Establish a professional development program that is common sense in focus and will provide essential help to all staff members.

2. Consider various forms of professional development activities: online on-demand programs, conferences, inservice days, staff meetings, individual tutoring, and so on.

3. Identify and hire experts to run key professional development exercises, if needed.

4. Purchase needed materials for professional development meetings and activities.

5. Prepare a budget of expected professional development costs.

6. Set dates for professional development activities and meetings.

7. Set guidelines for evaluation and assessment of professional development activities.

8. Establish a communication network and links so that information and concerns can be shared. This information can be used for future professional development activities.

## Instructions for the Evaluation and Assessment Committee

1. Develop and implement an assessment or evaluation format—online and/or hardcopy.

2. Review summative and formative evaluation information and data to determine strengths and weaknesses and areas requiring alterations.

3. Make necessary alterations and continue evaluating the project.

Keep in perspective that precious time, significant sums of district money, and needless duplication of labor can be saved when channels of communication are open and responsibilities clearly outlined.

The project model will help school leaders develop the core elements necessary to implement this technology initiative. It is intended to help individuals focus on the specific needs of their school and to provide the framework necessary to construct a technology plan based on local contexts. Administrators can use the outline as a model, keeping the plans that are relevant and making changes to suit local needs and conditions when prudent to do so.

## YEARLY PLANS

When the overall three-phased process is finalized in a more specific form and placed on a timeline, it will help school administrators address the technology needs for a school or district.

---

## Calendar Outline

---

### YEARLY PLANS

When this overall, three-phased process is put in more specific form and placed on a timeline, it might look something like the following model:

**YEAR ONE: Phase One—Planning Phase**

| | |
|---|---|
| September | • Determine initial commitment to project. |
| | • Form technology advisory committee. |
| | • Form project steering committee. |
| October | • Develop project philosophy and mission statement. |
| | • Create calendars for specific committee work. |
| | • Develop project benchmarks and indicators. |
| November | • Finalize goals and targets for project. |
| | • Carry out needs assessment. |
| December | • Review relevant literature. |

| | |
|---|---|
| January | • Analyze needs assessment data. |
| | • Disseminate information from literature review. |
| | • Consider possible options available to coordinators. (Look at such elements as hardware, software, application programs, implementation strategies, financing, professional development strategies, and student needs.) |
| February | • Determine course of action based on available options and needs assessment data. |
| | • List needed materials and resources. |
| | • Confirm and formalize school board commitment. |

## YEAR ONE CONTINUED: Phase Two—Implementation and Professional Development

| | |
|---|---|
| | • Establish leadership roles for implementation phase. |
| | • Fix calendar for implementation phase. |
| | • Plan public relations program. |
| March | • Meet with committees to discuss implementation strategies. |
| | • Purchase hardware, software, applications, and other materials. |
| April | • Initiate professional development programs. |
| | • Continue public relations program. |
| May | • Network and/or wireless installation finalized. |
| June–August | • Complete installation and troubleshooting of system. |
| | • Finalize teacher inservice before classes begin. |
| September | • Continue with professional development activities. |
| | • Integrate new technology in instructional program. |
| | • Administrative monitoring of equipment and programs begins. |
| October and | • Public relations program continues. |
| November | • Ongoing help to teachers provided in various forms. |
| December | • Continue administrative monitoring of equipment and programs. |

### YEAR TWO: Phase Three—Evaluation

| | |
|---|---|
| January | • Begin formal project evaluation, which should include |
| | • Reports from administrative monitoring from September to December |
| | • Continuing administrative monitoring |
| | • Feedback from teachers |
| | • Feedback from students |
| | • Feedback from in-house technology experts |
| February | • Continue monitoring and gathering information. |
| March–May | • Complete formal evaluations. |
| | • Make revisions according to information gathered during evaluation phase. |

Note: Planning, implementation, and evaluation schedules are based on a 2-year calendar. Requirements for each month are noted above to simplify and structure the project. As illustrated above, planning and implementation should be completed in year one, with program implementation and evaluation continuing throughout the 2nd year. The professional development phase begins after the planning stage is completed and continues indefinitely.

This project outline will help school leaders develop the core elements necessary to implement a technology initiative. It is intended to assist individuals focus on the specific needs of a school or district as well as to provide the framework necessary to construct this technology plan based on local contexts. School leaders and coordinators can use the outline as a model, keeping the plans that are relevant and making changes to suit local needs and conditions when prudent to do so.

## FUTURE CHALLENGES

If schools are to thrive in the future, technology initiatives and implementation plans must be familiar to everyone—and adaptable enough to reflect situational change. With strong leadership and a vision of what is needed, as well as a solid technology plan in place, school leaders will be better able to build relevancy and create the connections needed to secure student learning. Moreover, if leaders learn to expect the unexpected, lead with wisdom, and stay current with the latest advances in educational technology—our schools will succeed long into the future.

## REFLECTIVE ACTIVITIES

1. Describe your personal philosophy regarding leadership in technology.

2. Indicate why technology planning is important to your school as well as your school district.

3. Analyze the relationship your school has with the community.

4. Identify a school and a school district's technology goal and mission statement as well as objectives. Explain how they meet student needs.

5. List which elements of steps one through seven in the Project Outline are in place at your school or school district.

6. In relation to step three in the Project Outline involving leadership roles, identify and list teacher perceptions regarding technology use in your school. Identify levels of technological expertise.

# 3 Technology and Professional Development

School leaders at all levels recognize the critical importance of professional development. Like their students, teachers must be in a consistent state of learning about their profession, and it is the responsibility of the school to provide the infrastructures to aid in teacher growth. Principals, curriculum leaders, and technology coordinators need to work in unison so that they can respond to and set the direction for 21st century learning in their schools. Concepts such as m-learning, e-learning, and professional learning communities don't just happen. It takes planning, strategy, and collegial reform to make such concepts work. This is largely due to educators being pivotal in determining or altering a student's educational path (Espinoza, 2012). By building awareness and strategic alliances, teachers can, and often do, make a significant difference in the lives of their students. It is for this reason that instituting high-quality professional development, as well as the application of up-to-date educational technology, is so vital to school reform and change.

## PROFESSIONAL DEVELOPMENT BASED ON STRATEGY

The reality of technology reform in schools is that leaders should not be working on ad hoc practices of professional development. When it comes to planning for technology, one benefit is that there is a large base of information available to school leaders in local schools to assist in the process of technology change. There are many groups, societies, and organizations that have thought intently about this issue and have provided public school leaders with the means to help them make informed decisions about technology and professional development in their schools. Utilizing these public sources of data can help local leaders bring strategy to their school technology reform.

For instance, the Office of Educational Technology within the U.S. Federal Department of Education has produced a national education technology plan called Transforming American Education: Learning Powered by Technology 2010. The overall plan sets a vision of a model of learning powered by technology with goals and recommendations in five essential areas:

- *Learning Goal:* All learners will have engaging and empowering learning experiences both in and out of school that prepare them to be active, creative, knowledgeable, and ethical participants in our globally networked society.
- *Assessment Goal:* Our education system at all levels will leverage the power of technology to measure what matters and use assessment data for continuous improvement.
- *Teaching Goal:* Professional educators will be supported individually and in teams by technology that connects them to data, content, resources, expertise, and learning experiences that enable and inspire more effective teaching for all learners.
- *Infrastructure Goal:* All students and educators will have access to a comprehensive infrastructure for learning when and where they need it.
- *Productivity Goal:* Our education system at all levels will redesign processes and structures to take advantage of the power of technology to improve learning outcomes while making more efficient use of time, money, and staff.

In relation to this technology plan and setting a strategic direction for your school's technology reform, educational leaders and technology coordinators can work through the worksheet shown in Exhibit 3.1 to help bring a strategic focus to professional development.

Once this list is completed, principals can have a faculty meeting where these elements are discussed and used as a means to begin to develop professional

---

**Exhibit 3.1** Strategic Professional Development

Teaching and Learning Powered by Technology for the 21st Century

| Educational Need | Are your teachers/ administrators skilled in this? | | Is it relevant to your school? | | Suggested ideas/ opportunities for professional development (if needed) |
|---|---|---|---|---|---|
| | Yes | No | Yes | No | |
| Students need to learn using multimedia content. | | | | | |
| Students need skills in participating and collaborating in online social networks. | | | | | |
| Students need technology to help with personalized learning experiences. | | | | | |

*(Continued)*

**Exhibit 3.1** (Continued)

| Educational Need | Are your teachers/ administrators skilled in this? | | Is it relevant to your school? | | Suggested ideas/ opportunities for professional development (if needed) |
|---|---|---|---|---|---|
| | Yes | No | Yes | No | |
| Students need to be engaged in learning through small and large groups within a local and global community. | | | | | |
| Students need access to a global set of educators such as parents, experts, mentors, and teachers. | | | | | |
| Students need resources that aid in 24/7 and lifelong learning. | | | | | |
| Students need 21st century skills of<br><br>• Critical thinking<br>• Problem solving<br>• Collaboration<br>• Multimedia communication | | | | | |
| Students need exposure to technology that professionals use to help solve real-world problems. | | | | | |
| Teachers need technology-based assessments to both diagnose and modify<br><br>• Conditions of learning<br>• Instructional practices<br>• Level of knowledge<br>• Problem-solving abilities | | | | | |
| Teachers need technology-based assessments to determine what students have learned. | | | | | |
| Teachers need relevant student data at the right time and in the right form. | | | | | |
| Teachers need training to help them manage assessment data. | | | | | |
| Teachers need training to help them analyze relevant data. | | | | | |

| Educational Need | Are your teachers/ administrators skilled in this? | | Is it relevant to your school? | | Suggested ideas/ opportunities for professional development (if needed) |
|---|---|---|---|---|---|
| | Yes | No | Yes | No | |
| Teachers need training to help them act upon results of assessment data. | | | | | |
| Teachers need technology to help them transition into connected teaching. | | | | | |
| Teachers need to be fully connected to school learning data. | | | | | |
| Teachers need technology to help them<br><br>• Create<br>• Manage<br>• Engage<br>• Support students in their learning both inside school and out of school | | | | | |
| Teachers need access to resources that improve their own instructional practices. | | | | | |
| Teachers need to see education as a team activity where they are connected with online learning communities including<br><br>• Students<br>• Fellow educators<br>• Professional experts<br>• Members of relevant learning communities parents | | | | | |
| Teachers need professional development that is<br><br>• Collaborative<br>• Coherent<br>• Continuous<br>• Convenient | | | | | |
| Enabled by online resources and opportunities | | | | | |
| Teachers need professional development that exposes them to | | | | | |

*(Continued)*

**Exhibit 3.1** (Continued)

| Educational Need | Are your teachers/ administrators skilled in this? | | Is it relevant to your school? | | Suggested ideas/ opportunities for professional development (if needed) |
|---|---|---|---|---|---|
| | Yes | No | Yes | No | |
| • Exceptional technology educators<br>• Technology learning systems<br>• Self-directed learning programs | | | | | |
| Schools need technology infrastructure that is<br><br>• Always on<br>• Available to students<br>• Available to educators<br>• Available to administrators regardless of location or time of day | | | | | |
| Schools need technology infrastructures that allow for capturing and sharing knowledge in<br><br>• Multimedia formats<br>• Still and moving images<br>• Audio<br>• Text | | | | | |
| Schools need technology that enables an integration of in- and out-of-school learning. | | | | | |
| Schools need technology infrastructures that ensure the security and privacy of educational data. | | | | | |
| Schools need an interdisciplinary team of professionals to oversee learning that is powered by technology. | | | | | |

development initiatives for the school year. For example, principals can use a nominal group technique to determine where the faculty rate their professional development needs. For this process, you first generate a list of the professional development needs that are "relevant to your school." This can be done on a white board or on several large pieces of paper. From here, each faculty member is given 10 smaller circle stickers and then asked to place them next to the items he or she feels are most relevant to his or her professional development needs. There are no rules regarding how the stickers can be placed. For example, one faculty member could put all ten of their stickers next to one item, or five next to one item and five stickers next to another item, or any other combination. Then, you tally up the stickers next to each item on the list. This will give you a list of the areas that faculty deem their most pressing professional development needs related to technology. You can then begin to fill out the last column of the chart related to "suggested ideas for professional development" on the items that were ranked the highest. This can then be used to define the strategy for professional development in your school for that given academic year.

Applying strategy and focus to any form of professional development in your school is essential to having meaning and purpose behind your efforts. You want to have a vision about how your teachers will be connected with technology and how they can use that to empower learning in the 21st century. The conceptual model from the Transforming Education Through Technology Plan presented in Figure 3.1 is a good image of how these various components can be used to direct professional development in your school.

**Figure 3.1** A Model of Learning, Powered by Technology

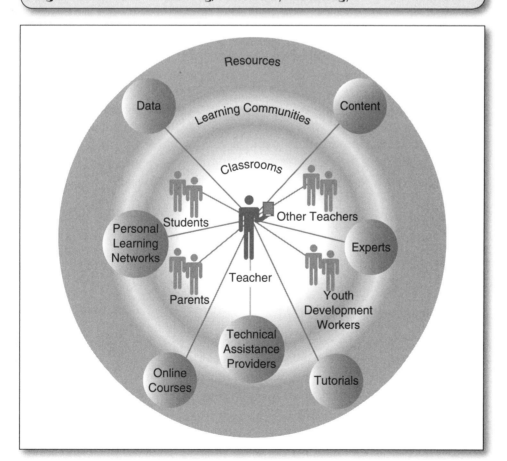

*Source:* U.S. Department of Education, Office of Educational Technology, *Transforming American Education: Learning Powered by Technology,* Washington, DC, 2010.

## Setting Priorities

One of the most important keys to school reform is making professional development a priority. Unfortunately, many teachers do not receive the training and support they need. As a result, large numbers of educators across the nation remain inadequately prepared to best use technology resources such as mobile devices and m-learning applications. This gap between those who are knowledgeable about technology in schools and those who are not continues to be an educational challenge. The crux here is that in an age of global interconnectedness, we cannot afford to work at less than stellar levels when it comes to providing high-quality professional development. According to Sterling and Frazier (2011), leaving teachers on their own to determine how to teach is not an effective way to support staff and is unfair to students. The key then is helping teachers fully understand and appreciate the powerful role technology plays in unlocking student potential.

Within the priorities of 21st century learning then, the focus of technology-based professional development is to assist as many teachers as possible to become digitally literate. In her work on professional development that is connected to technology, Pianfetti (2001) suggests that digital literacy

- produces the ability for lifelong learning;
- often occurs in pursuit of other goals;
- occurs in social context;
- requires strategic competencies; and
- requires critical knowledge of assembly and production.

By incorporating these components into their educational life, teachers are able to process information from a variety of sources and formats so that they can draw upon their own conclusions and create a personal knowledge path about the relationship between technology and learning. In doing so, teachers will be able to empower their students with the skills, knowledge, and dispositions necessary to be successful in a global reality dominated by technology (see Box 3.1).

---

### BOX 3.1. CORE COMPETENCIES FOR DIGITALLY LITERATE TEACHERS

1. *Facilitate and Inspire Student Learning and Creativity:* Teachers use their knowledge of subject matter, teaching, learning, and technology to facilitate experiences that advance student learning, creativity, and innovation in both face-to-face and virtual environments.

2. *Design and Develop Digital Age Learning Experiences and Assessments:* Teachers design, develop, and evaluate authentic learning experiences and assessment incorporating contemporary tools and resources to maximize content learning in context and to develop the relevant knowledge, skills, and attitudes related to content area.

3. *Model Digital Age Work and Learning:* Teachers exhibit knowledge, skills, and work processes representative of an innovative professional in a global and digital society.

4. *Promote and Model Digital Citizenship and Responsibility:* Teachers understand local and global societal issues and responsibilities in an evolving digital culture and exhibit legal and ethical behavior in their professional practices.

5. *Engage in Professional Growth and Leadership:* Teachers continually improve their professional practice, model lifelong learning, and exhibit leadership in their school and professional community by promoting and demonstrating the effective use of digital tools and resources.

*Source:* International Society for Technology in Education (2011b).

Another high priority is funding. The concern here is that schools and state educational agencies are often lacking resources and funding needed to support quality professional development opportunities and school technology. In this regard, both state and national organizations need to step up and explore new ways to enhance training and awareness. In addition, college and university systems need to work collaboratively with school districts, charter schools, and private businesses to develop a cadre of educational leaders versed in state-of-the-art educational technology. Furthermore, and along with this new leadership, a different mindset for teaching through technology must emerge—a mindset that depends on a shift in teacher/student roles (Blair, 2012).

## Dynamic Changes for Professional Development

Exemplary professional development programs involve everyday interactions. Simply put, strong involvement grows from dynamic, collaborative, and intentional plans of school improvement coupled with the latest technology advances. At their core, quality professional development programs commonly reflect a shared vision, mission, and goals, ethics and integrity, as well as collaboration with families and stakeholders. These elements are the essence of every successful professional development program—thus making understanding, building awareness, and healthy relationships major focal points in driving school reform. With this in mind, school leaders can use the following list of creative professional development ideas in building awareness collaboration and understanding:

- Providing teachers and staff with online resources, books, and materials
- Discussing research and applying new ideas and strategies in local settings
- Involving teachers as leaders in special projects and discussions
- Creating release time for faculty to observe other colleagues using technology effectively in classrooms
- Incorporating and appropriately funding teacher mentoring programs
- Encouraging faculty and staff to attend professional inservice opportunities

To go one step further, another untapped opportunity is for school leaders to rethink the structure of a typical school day. In this sense, school district leaders need to provide more flexibility in structuring the school day in a manner to establish time for ongoing, educational professional development programs. In addition, states can require school districts to plan a minimum of one pupil instructional related (PIR) day of technology inservice and training each academic year. A potential up side of this is that states can revise their renewal certification process to reflect educational technology professional development.

Each of the above ideas can truly make a difference in the outcome of any professional development program. But, to really accomplish measurable change and reform, school administrators, technology coordinators, and curriculum leaders must think not only out of the box but also think way beyond the box. This is where guiding preservice teachers and data-driven programs can play a huge role.

## Guiding Preservice Teacher Development

A general consensus among school leaders is that preservice teachers, graduating from teacher education programs at both university and college levels, need to receive more guidance in using classroom technology. For example, there needs to be more awareness on the part of new teachers as to how to best integrate technology into various subject areas and across the curriculum. Likewise, preservice teachers must know how to acquire and best utilize the latest technological information, especially technology applications involving assessment. With this being said, each state needs to appropriately fund universities and colleges in a manner that will allow them to explore the dynamics and benefits of educational technology. To meet these challenges, many states are revising their teacher education program standards to require a course in technology applications as well as instruction in how to integrate and effectively use technology in an instructional setting. (For more information on preparation needs of preservice teachers and technology in education, see Box 3.2.)

---

### BOX 3.2. PRESERVICE TEACHING AND TECHNOLOGY

Preparation needs of preservice teachers and technology in education:

1. Preservice teachers need to see how technology theory aligns with practice. Education students need to know the theory presented during class lectures and need to see how this can be applied through real-world class examples.

2. Preservice teachers need teacher educators as role models. Education students need to observe teachers and professors using technology in their instruction so they can imagine ways to use technology in their own teaching.

3. Preservice teachers need opportunities to reflect on their attitudes about the role of technology in education. Education students need opportunities to dialogue with peers, professors, and teacher mentors about technology in the classroom so they can develop their own technological attitudes.

4. Preservice teachers need specific direction on how to incorporate technology into their regular instructional design. Education students need opportunities to go through the planning and preparation process so they can see how to implement lessons incorporating technology.

5. Preservice teachers need time to collaborate with peers. Education students need opportunities to work in groups when learning about technology use in the classroom so they can discuss and share concerns.

6. Preservice teachers need to be able to scaffold their technology learning experiences. Education students need opportunities to try out their ideas for incorporating technology into their lesson plans with appropriate supports to provide feedback and direction for improvement.

7. Preservice teachers need access to appropriate technology resources. Education students need to see and have hands-on experience with resources essential to technology integration in the curriculum.

*Source:* Tondeur et al. (2012).

What matters most, however, is that there be a commitment and consistent delivery of professional development throughout the entire system. Especially needed is a model that coordinates professional development with a variety of educational related organizations. With proper training and inservice as a unifying theme, school leaders and organizational leaders can hopefully form a partnership in addressing true school reform. The goal then is to change the culture of schooling through strong leadership, collaboration, data-driven programs, and most importantly, quality professional development. And, in doing so, school leaders will discover and realize the importance of valuing and involving teachers.

## Data-Driven Programs

Numerous schools are using comprehensive data and other management tools to help facilitate professional development. What's important is having teachers using information databases to find accurate and appropriate knowledge quickly when solving problems (Chesley & Jordan, 2012). Good and reliable data can lead to amazing results, especially if channeled through well-led teachers. For example, databases in the area of curriculum can

1. Determine professional development interests and needs

2. Develop a background of skills and usage

3. Identify individuals willing to share ideas and techniques as well as to inventory the type and level of materials and resources used in the classroom

Utilizing high-quality and effective data-driven applications should be a part of every school's planning and professional development program.

With ever-present new advances in data-driven instruction and the advent of Common Core State Standards, teachers are now better able to transition schools into digital places of learning. In addition to the Common Core State Standards, the National Educational Technology Standards (NETS) developed by the International Society for Technology in Education (ISTE) set a standard of excellence and best practices in learning, teaching, and leading with technology in education (ISTE, 2011a). The benefits of using the NETS include the following:

- Improving higher-order thinking skills, such as problem solving, critical thinking, and creativity
- Preparing students for their future in a competitive global job market
- Designing student-centered, project-based, and online learning environments
- Guiding systemic change in our schools to create digital places of learning
- Inspiring digital-age professional development models for working, collaborating, and decision making

Clearly, advances in data-driven instruction and professional development are continuing to change the way teachers teach as well as the way students learn. As rapid new innovations in technology place demands on educators and students, the level and quality of professional development become more crucial.

## Digital-Age Leadership

Regarding digital-age leadership, professional development and data informational systems are becoming crucial elements in school reform and change. School leaders are thus playing a critical role in determining how well technology is used in their schools. Today's school leaders are certainly becoming more aware of the importance of a global curriculum fueled by new economic, social, political, and technological changes. The hope is to inspire and motivate school leaders to rise to the challenge of our increasingly changing world. According to Yong Zhao, university professor and founding director of the Center for Teaching and Technology, College of Education, Michigan State University, "If we are to be competitive in a world market, we need to foster a broader perspective of education" (Richardson, 2010, p. 15). In addition, he added, "The United States should deepen what it does best, rather than trying to catch up to developing nations" (p. 15). Thus, the role of school leadership is fundamental to enhancing Americans' global perspective of education. As such, school leaders, and the roles they play in guiding teachers and preparing students, can and will do much to foster a milieu of creativity, networking, and adaptability.

**TECHNOLOGY THOUGHT**

Experience has found the most efficient way for educational leaders to evoke change is through providing relevant support and direction for faculty and staff to be their best rather than exerting power and authority over them.

With our ever-present educational web of knowing, school leaders worldwide are now working together in greater numbers to identify the forces and trends affecting education today. With constant vigilance, these same leaders are projecting how trends in professional development and professional learning communities may conceivably play out in the future. Consequently, it is important to note that as demands on education continue to expand, it is becoming even more apparent for school leaders to lead from community-based strengths. It is through this process of focusing on collective community-based strengths that may prove to be a turning point in bringing about major educational changes and reforms in our digital world.

## Online and Web-Based Programs

Online and On-Demand programs such as PD 360 are becoming more prevalent in schools (School Improvement Network, 2012). These programs are easy to access and provide for a systematic approach to professional development. What is especially important is that each plan is personalized for each teacher and is in sync with district goals. By compiling essential learning elements and the availability of thousands of videos of best practices by master teachers, staff members can create, differentiate, and personalize their own portfolio as well as professional development plan. Moreover, all plans are developed with administrative approval and can be tracked online.

# PROFESSIONAL DEVELOPMENT MODELS

Although many variations exist in the specifics of professional development, there are three models that school leaders have used successfully. As noted in Whitehead, Boschee, and Decker (2013), these professional development models include the following:

## Model 1: Prior to Major Program Change

Professional development sessions are held prior to any major change in program. The intent of this model, then, is to update teachers' knowledge about new developments in the field, as well as to provide skills they need for specific curriculum and instructional materials. In addition, this model also provides opportunities for teachers to exchange and try out new ideas.

## Model 2: Subsequent to Program Change

Professional development sessions are held subsequent to program change. New learnings become the basis for a series of professional inservice and mentoring plans offered immediately prior to the introduction of any program. This essentially is the model used in most hands-on implementation projects. The chief advantage of this model is the close fit between program change and professional development.

## Model 3: Professional Learning Community (PLC) Based

A more contemporary approach for professional development is the *community-based learning model.* An example would be the Teacher Leaders Network (TLN). TLN is a professional community of accomplished educators dedicated to sharing ideas and expanding the influence of teachers (Education Week, 2012). These online networks are designed to allow educators in any state, region, or nation to bond together as influential professional learning communities.

Each of the three models, as shown in Box 3.3, represents a creative and innovative use of professional development practices. In addition, each model can make a difference as to whether school change will be both successful and lasting.

---

### BOX 3.3. SUCCESSFUL TECHNOLOGY PROFESSIONAL DEVELOPMENT CONCEPTS

1. Learn from case studies.

2. Work with your strongest people and develop them into mentors.

3. Build online communities where dialogue and information sharing about technology can happen.

4. Technology professional development needs to be ongoing in response to the rapidly changing context of technology.

5. Get faculty to collaborate.

---

According to Routman (2012), ongoing PLCs are considered the bedrock of current professional development practices. This is largely due to PLCs being literacy based and dedicated to improving lifelong skills, which in turn allows educators to translate changing beliefs and practices into more effective teaching. A direct benefit of PLCs is a dramatic increase in public awareness. Likewise, community members have a tendency to become more positive about their local schools. As an example, business leaders often begin to recognize the connection between students' technological skills and their ability to be successful in the world of work. This increased awareness leads to more collaborative efforts between schools and businesses and thus translates into even more support for local schools down the line.

The key is for schools to make professional learning communities a living reality. More importantly, educational leaders need to use professional learning communities and quality professional development models to guide the process of school reform—especially if we are to make schools better for everyone. The core concept here is that integrating technology is essential to school reform leading to 21st century schools. Huffman and Hipp (2003) indicated that PLC is a setting where "a school's professional staff members continuously seek to find answers through inquiry and act on their learning to improve student learning" (p. 4). They further stated that PLC is "the most powerful professional development and change strategy available" (p. 4). In setting up a solid PLC, school districts should create the following educational and professional context:

> *Shared Beliefs, Values, and Vision.* All members of the school must be focused on continuous learning with a clear direction toward improving student learning. Everyone in the school must have a common educational purpose.

> *Shared and Supportive Leadership.* Mutual respect is an essential component of making PLCs work. In this sense, influence, authority, and decision making are shared and promoted throughout the school. Here, the principal must nurture this culture throughout the school.

> *Collective Learning and Its Application.* All the staff and faculty in the school must work together to apply what is learned. It is not enough to learn how to be a good school but you must make it happen.

> *Supportive Conditions.* Leaders in the school must show that they value PLC and provide appropriate time to meet, dialogue, and plan. Leaders must provide faculty with avenues to relate, form social networks, and create a caring culture.

> *Shared Personal Practice.* Teachers need opportunities to examine and learn from each other's practice, assessment, and management behaviors (Ruebel, 2011).

So in reflecting on this, school leaders should understand these ideas as the primary tenets of PLCs. The key reality behind PLCs is the concept of shared leadership and bringing people together. Educational leaders can refer to Box 3.4 for ways that technology can bring a variety of educational stakeholders together around a common purpose.

---

### BOX 3.4. COMMUNITY SUPPORT FOR TECHNOLOGY

- Mobile devices and cloud computing foster community awareness of student exploration.
- Mobile technology provides a powerful tool that accents constructivist teaching methods.
- Technological awareness gives teachers an added sense of professionalism.
- Online and On Demand communications reduce isolation and lead to the development of professional communities.
- Specialized technology advancements allow educators to mark and measure academic progress as well as to assess individual student performance.
- Data-driven technology is streamlining information collection and is enhancing school reform and change at community levels.

## STRATEGIES FOR SUCCESS

A creative and innovative use of resources for professional development is often a turning point for school success. Keeping with this perspective, it is the establishment of a vision, creation of a sound plan, and actual implementation that determines the outcome of any program. Below, the authors have listed a series of tried-and-true professional development ideas and strategies for school leaders and technology coordinators.

## Management Planning Matrix

The Northwest Regional Educational Laboratory's (1990) Management Planning Matrix continues to be one of the most successful tools in designing effective professional development programs. This user-friendly matrix assists school leaders and technology coordinators in the actual process of planning, implementing, and evaluating technology programs. Basically, it directs coordinators to formulate professional development goals as well as lay the groundwork to create measurable indicators of success. As school leaders navigate future-oriented change, the matrix assists them in detailing activities, setting leadership roles, and establishing implementation and evaluation dates. See Exhibit 3.2 for the Management Planning Matrix.

**Exhibit 3.2** Management and Monitoring Matrix

Target Area _____   Product _____
1. GOAL _____   End Point _____

| 6. STATUS TODAY<br><br>What is the situation today? | 5. ACTIVITIES<br><br>What must be done to get from 4 to 3? | 4. LEADERSHIP<br><br>Who is responsible to initiate and follow through with activities? | 3. SCHEDULE<br><br>What is the time frame for accomplishing each activity being monitored? | 2. INDICATORS<br><br>If the goal were attained, what would really be happening? What would the target area look or be like? List 8 to 10 indicators. |
|---|---|---|---|---|
| A. | | | | A. |
| | | | | |
| | | | | |
| | | | | |
| B. | | | | B. |
| | | | | |
| | | | | |
| | | | | |

| 6. STATUS TODAY<br><br>What is the situation today? | 5. ACTIVITIES<br><br>What must be done to get from 4 to 3? | 4. LEADERSHIP<br><br>Who is responsible to initiate and follow through with activities? | 3.SCHEDULE<br><br>What is the time frame for accomplishing each activity being monitored? | 2. INDICATORS<br><br>If the goal were attained, what would really be happening? What would the target area look or be like? List 8 to 10 indicators. |
|---|---|---|---|---|
| C. | | | | C. |
| | | | | |
| | | | | |
| | | | | |
| D. | | | | D. |
| | | | | |
| | | | | |
| | | | | |

*Source:* Northwest Regional Educational Laboratory. (1990). Modified and adapted from Whitehead, B. M., Jensen, D. F. N., & Boschee, F. (2003). *Planning for technology: A guide for school administrators, technology coordinators, and curriculum leaders,* p. 73. Thousand Oaks, CA: Corwin.

## Project-Based Approach

A team of five to six individuals is selected from building or district staff periodically to meet with the school leaders and technology coordinators in a project-based setting. An administrator then sets a specific amount of funding and asks the group to come up with a project that best uses technology to increase student achievement. Most importantly, allotted money is primarily set for professional development associated with the project. With dollars up front, the team cannot use funding as an excuse in not taking a risk and/or trying something unique and innovative. The only requirement is that the group sets (in writing) predetermined measurable assessment indicators.

## Flexible Scheduling

The rule of flexible scheduling is to align or arrange preparation periods to best assist teachers needing assistance when implementing a new program or application. Preparation periods (art, music, library, physical education, and music) can then be scheduled in a manner that matches an experienced teacher with a colleague needing assistance. This provides quality time for both mentor and mentee to get together and share ideas. This newfound relationship helps alleviate any misunderstandings as well as opens the door to future professional development opportunities.

### Rule of Traveling Pairs

This strategy recommends having a minimum of two teachers traveling together when attending workshops, seminars, and conferences. By strengthening partnerships, teachers feel more comfortable, safe, and supported. Having at least *two* faculty members (preferably from the same grade level or department) on the team is a tremendous way to increase success. Many programs have failed because a single teacher receiving training feels isolated or does not have the time or energy to carry a program through all stages of implementation.

### "Early-Out Time" for Students

Numerous schools are adjusting schedules to provide a minimum of 1 hour (or more) of planning and professional development time per week for teachers. The key here is to maintain and honor contractual agreements, as well as state requirements for student contact time. In some schools, teachers have agreed to start earlier as well as extend the length of each day thus creating extra blocks of time for professional development. School leaders can also rearrange recess and lunch schedules (depending on contractual agreements). The goal here is to free up a specific block of time allowing schools to schedule professional development opportunities. A tip for school leaders is to schedule at least one block of time, solely devoted to technology, per month.

### Presenter Stipends

Paying a nominal fee to building-level teachers to direct professional development sessions is proving to be beneficial. These sessions can be held after school, on weekends, or during summer months. Again, this is a small nominal fee for planning and teaching a professional development session. The purpose is not to extend salary commitments, but to reward building-level teachers. With this in mind, emphasis should be placed on having a classroom teacher who has credibility with the staff and/or school system to be the presenter.

### Substitute Rotation

Innovative school districts are currently developing blocks of time by having a set of substitutes rotate through a schedule. For example, a set of five substitutes can release five teachers in the morning—then, the same five substitutes can be used to release another set of teachers in the afternoon. However, this procedure should be used sparingly in that regular teacher and student contact time can be diminished. Nonetheless, this process does work, especially when scheduling a consultant for a specific period of time.

### Free Consulting Services

National consultants can be used to provide curriculum ideas and strategies. For example, some companies are willing to provide free consultants to a district—generally in hopes of their series, programs, or materials being selected. Naturally, some publishers do provide such services while others do not. It is up to creative school leaders and technology coordinators to contact companies for possible free-consulting services. A key here is to work with company representatives and, if possible, collaborate with several adjoining school districts to justify costs and be successful.

## Regional Resource Centers

An important step in planning and implementation of any quality preservice and professional development programs is the formulation of regional as well as statewide resource centers. Resource centers can provide the background and awareness needed to forge a more vibrant system of professional development. The key, however, is to appropriately fund and place technology resource centers strategically throughout all states.

## Technology for Learning Audits

As part of their technology initiative, Mid-Continent Research for Education and Learning (McREL, 2012) provides an audit procedure that will help schools to determine how technology is being used in a district, in a school, and by teachers. Including this audit or similar audits as part of a school's professional development plan adds a measurable element to the scheduled activities and provides essential information to help schools to be more efficient in their technology-learning efforts. As part of this approach, the audit includes a Teacher Technology Profile (TTP) survey and an Administrator Technology Profile (ATP) survey.

## Professional Development Cooperatives

Many school districts are realizing the benefits of developing technology cooperatives. This is especially true for small rural school districts. What cannot be achieved singularly can often be achieved through the collaboration of resources. With this in mind, some school districts are banding together and hiring technical coordinators and specialists who can provide professional development opportunities. Other school districts are partnering with colleges and universities to provide credit to experienced teachers who serve as instructors for professional development.

## Consortiums

Consortiums are proving to be an excellent way for small, frontier, or rural school districts to develop collaborative efforts with colleges, universities, and technology companies. Consortiums not only provide an opportunity to bring in technology specialists from other states and regions, but also provide teachers with an opportunity to obtain postgraduate credit.

## College and University Preservice Programs

Higher education is always looking for ways to extend learning and professional development beyond the campus. Recent restructuring efforts have led to major changes in preservice and student teaching programs. Additional core classes not only address educational technology but also include multicultural studies as well as professional leadership projects. Innovative programs involving moodling, e-learning, and m-learning help create mentor lines between student teachers, first-year teachers, and university professors.

## School, University, and College Partnerships

Colleges and universities are realizing the value of partnering with schools whether they are small or large. Professors are able to develop technology-based research projects that allow university students to receive credit for their experience. School districts, on the other hand, use the partnership as a way to obtain assistance, grants, and new ideas.

## Community Resources

School leaders are becoming more adept at recruiting individuals who have rich technological backgrounds and who actually live within the boundaries of the school district. These community members represent a great deal of technical experience and can provide direction and knowledge to school districts in numerous ways. A key is for school leaders and technology coordinators to seek out these individuals and involve them in the planning process.

Looking back in retrospect, each of the innovative professional development strategies noted above can be enormously helpful in inducing technological change and reform. This is especially true when innovative school administrators and technology coordinators want their students to embrace the gift of learning and be globally competitive in the future.

## Adult Education and Theory for Professional Development

In reflecting on the material presented in this particular chapter, it is important to remember that all of the discussion centered on viewing teachers as learners. A school leader should never create a professional development plan that is based on the premise that his or her teachers are deficient in educational matters related to technology. In this case, the school leader sends a message of the perceived inadequacy of the faculty. This is a very common approach to many professional development activities. The concern here is that this begins the whole process with a negative viewpoint of your teachers.

Instead, when the school leader develops a professional development plan based on adult learning principals, you show respect for teachers' ability to continue to learn and grow into their profession as it pertains to technology. This can be a challenging professional shift for many school principals because although they are educators, their primary professional shift has gone from working with children and youth to working mainly with adults. Principals have a tendency to incorporate pedagogical practices into their professional development thinking that is ineffective when working with adults (teachers) and their learning needs.

The principles of andragogy are quite different when compared to pedagogy. Andragogy, meaning the art and science of helping adults learn, has six main principles focused on looking at the needs of the adult learner:

1. Create a climate of respect.

2. Encourage active participation.

3. Build on experience.

4. Employ collaborative inquiry.

5. Learn for immediacy of application.

6. Empower participants.

The more that these components are built into the professional development plans, teachers will become more internally motivated to change or improve their instructional activities related to technology in the classroom.

## FUTURE CHALLENGES

In today's globally interconnected society, technology is becoming an increasingly integral part of cultural and educational change. And yet, schools by themselves cannot address the problem of educational equity and prosperity. The key then is linking quality professional development, along with new technology applications, as well as other community-based resources, to create a foundation for planning and implementation. It is through this process of effective technology planning, along with the creation of professional learning communities that school leaders can and will turn the corner on school reform.

## REFLECTIVE ACTIVITIES

1. Identify your school or district's technology coordinator or specialist. List the responsibilities he or she has in relation to professional development.

2. Formulate what percentage of your current technology budget is allocated toward professional development. What percentage would you like to get it up to, and why?

3. List what you do as a school leader or teacher leader to support professional development in your school. Evaluate some examples of your efforts.

4. Describe ways your school supports the integration of mobile technology in classrooms. How does your school rate in reference to other schools?

5. Chart the lines of communication for improving professional development in your school district. As an administrator, how would you improve these lines of communication?

6. Identify licensure requirements as per technology in regards to professional development for both school leaders and teachers in your state. Discuss how you might advocate a change or amendment to these requirements in order to best serve schools and students.

7. Reflecting on McREL's technology audit, consider what you perceive as the benefits of conducting such a survey of your technology staff development efforts.

# Teaching and Learning With Technology 4

## TECHNOLOGY LINKED WITH THE CONTEXT

When all is said and done, it will be teachers who determine the success or failure of a technology plan. They are the people who connect technology with curricular practice in a way that will enhance student achievement. It is the interaction between teacher and student that truly accentuates learning in a technological environment. Technology is a proven tool that can help lower dropout rates, enhance student achievement, provide access to information around the world, and raise students' self-esteem. In every classroom, teachers must contend with a variety of learners, such as the fast-paced learner, the less-motivated learner, students with learning difficulties, and the list could go on. With technology in the classroom, teachers have access to tools that have the potential for providing learning experiences relevant to each of these unique learners.

A classroom is a very complex setting to work in, and technology, for many teachers, only makes matters more complicated. In order to have a successful technology plan, technology coordinators and school leaders need to be conscious of the realities that can hinder the process of bringing technology into the 21st century classroom. Once school leaders seriously consider these realities, they will have the necessary knowledge to counter the negative impact of these barriers. There has been ample research in this area leading to the following variables negatively impacting technology integration (Hew & Brush, 2007).

- *Lack of Resources.* Teachers need the right technology that is linked with the vision and mission for technology in the local district and school.
- *Limited Knowledge and Skills.* This is where professional development is so important. Teachers need proper training and knowledge to help them take full advantage of the potential that technology has for reforming the educational experience for students. Readers can reflect back on the discussion from Chapter 3 to help in this matter.

- *Poor Visioning Institution.* Leaders in schools must have a desire to create 21st century schools. Technology change can happen in individual classrooms sparked by a progressive teacher, but meaningful school reform happens with school leaders who set the direction and support for a technologically literate school culture.
- *Negative Attitudes and Beliefs.* So many schools are plagued by outdated or defiant attitudes with people saying that it can't be done, that they don't want to change, or that they can't see the vision for technology. All school members must learn to see the vision and urgency for bringing technology into schools in meaningful and purposeful ways.
- *Weak Assessment Strategies.* Empirical assessment is such a huge driver of decisions related to educational reform. In this sense, some schools are nervous about the risks associated with giving technology a more dominant part in the learning experience of students with the fear that student achievement will go down during the integration phase. At the same time, empirical assessment can cause educators to use technology purely for data collection and assessment and lose sight of its ability to positively impact teaching and learning.
- *Inability to See Broad Application.* A dilemma within education is that there is a culture that says technology is only effective in certain subject areas and is not relevant across the entire curriculum.

The other big challenge facing schools is educators not having a clear understanding of what a 21st century school looks like and what kind of learning happens in it. This concern is so evident in our society that it was the cover story in the December 18, 2006, issue of *Time Magazine.*

Once educators catch the vision of this, then school reform linked with technology integration will be a natural path of school reform. Under this reality, the proper context will exist for the creative potential of technology to truly impact student achievement and curricular design.

## Competencies of the 21st Century Learner

The pedagogical concept of education is the art and science of helping students to learn. In helping students to learn, there is a societal philosophy that we are trying to provide young people with the necessary knowledge, skills, and dispositions that will help them to be healthy, informed, and productive citizens. In so doing, the work of education is to envision the future and see what learners will need 5, 10, or even 20 years into the future so that they can engage in their world. Educators must clearly understand that today's learning is in response to tomorrow's reality. In fact,

the OECD [Organisation for Economic Co-operation and Development], European Union, UNESCO [United Nations Educational, Scientific and Cultural Organization] and numerous other think tanks (Partnership for 21st Century Skills Framework) and authors (Dede, 2010) conclude that new realities demand people with different competencies than those considered appropriate for success in the agrarian and industrial era. Multi-literate, creative and innovative people are now seen as the drivers of the 21st Century and the prerequisites to economic success, social progress and personal empowerment. Organizations and authors have identified these competencies and call for a transformation of public education systems globally to meet current learning needs along with a shift in the way that we engage students in their own learning. (C21 Canada, 2012, p. 4)

The following material now discusses a few of these models for conceiving the 21st century educational experience and the dispositions viewed as essential within our educational enterprise. School administrators, technology coordinators, and curriculum leaders can consider these frameworks as they design technology plans based upon local contexts, teacher abilities, and student needs. Through this, it is hoped that educational leaders will develop a better understanding of how teaching, learning, and technology come together in the 21st century school and classroom. In each of the four models, the elements that directly bring technology into 21st century learning have been highlighted (bold and italicized) to bring these competencies to the forefront of the discussion.

The first model to consider is **Shifting Minds,** a 21st century inspired vision for Canada's public education systems.

| 21st CENTURY COMPETENCIES—Shifting Minds | | |
|---|---|---|
| **21st Century Competency** | **Targeted Outcomes** | **Rationale** |
| **Creativity and Innovation and Entrepreneurship** | Creativity: The ability to apply creative thought processes to create something of value<br><br>Innovation and Entrepreneurship: The capacity to create and apply new knowledge in innovative and entrepreneurial ways to create new products or solve complex problems<br><br>The capacity to invent new problem-solving heuristics when all standard protocols have failed (Dede, 2010) | Today's economic, social, environmental, and financial challenges are increasingly complex and require creative, innovative, and entrepreneurial thinking to solve problems and keep apace of the ongoing and escalating demand for new and innovative solutions and products. For success in school, work, and life, people must be able to use creativity in order to adapt and generate new ideas, theories, products, and knowledge. |
| **Critical Thinking** | A deep understanding of and capacity to apply the elements and processes associated with critical thinking and problem solving<br><br>*The ability to acquire, process, interpret, rationalize, and* | *The knowledge and digital era are demanding people with higher-order thinking skills;* the ability to think logically and to solve ill-defined problems by identifying and describing the problem, critically analyzing the information |

*(Continued)*

(Continued)

| 21st CENTURY COMPETENCIES—Shifting Minds | | |
|---|---|---|
| **21st Century Competency** | **Targeted Outcomes** | **Rationale** |
| | *critically analyze large volumes of often conflicting information to the point of making an informed decision and taking action in a timely fashion* | available or creating the knowledge required, framing and testing various hypotheses, formulating creative solutions, and taking action. |
| **Collaboration** | The ability to interact positively and respectfully with others in creating new ideas and developing products | Importance of interpersonal capabilities is higher and the skills involved are more sophisticated than in the industrial era. ***Social media have created a dominant impact on the collaboration dynamic that occurs outside schools.*** |
| | The ability to lead or work in a team and to relate to other people in varying contexts, including capacity to resolve and manage conflict | |
| | The capacity for sensitivity to the issues and processes associated with collaborating across cultures | |
| | *The ability to collaborate across networks, using various information and communication technologies* | |
| **Communication** | High-level literacy skills, including strength in a person's mother tongue with multilingual capacity a definite asset | ***Communication is more complex and sophisticated, and work is often occurring with peers located halfway around the world.*** |
| | *The ability to use technology to develop 21st century competencies in the context of core subjects* | Learning science reinforces constructivist models of building understanding and making meaning, which are built on human interactions. |
| | *The capacity to communicate using a variety of media and technologies* | |
| | *The ability to access, analyze, integrate, and manage large volumes of information* | |
| | *The capacity to effectively use social media to communicate and resolve challenges* | |
| | *The ability to critically interpret and evaluate ideas presented* | |

| 21st CENTURY COMPETENCIES—Shifting Minds | | |
|---|---|---|
| **21st Century Competency** | **Targeted Outcomes** | **Rationale** |
| | ***through a variety of media and technologies***<br><br>Highly developed cooperative interpersonal capabilities | |
| **Character** | Learners will develop 21st century *life skills,* such as<br><br>• Lifelong and learner<br>• Leadership, responsibility, and accountability<br>• Self-directed, adaptable, and resilient<br>• Tolerant, ethical, and fair<br>• Personal productivity<br>• Interpersonal (people) skills<br>• Mental and physical well being<br>• Proficiency in managing personal relationships | The knowledge economy and social environment are highly complex, fast paced, multicultural, and stressful in nature, demanding people with highly developed interpersonal traits and strength of character.<br><br>Collaborating to learn requires social emotional learning skills including self-awareness, social awareness, self-regulation, and relationship skills. |
| **Culture and Ethical Citizenship** | The capacity to comprehend Canada's political, social, economic, and financial systems in a global context<br><br>The ability to appreciate cultural and societal diversity at the local, national, and global levels<br><br>The ability to critically analyze the past and present and apply those understandings in planning for the future<br><br>The capacity to understand key ideas and concepts related to democracy, social justice, and human rights<br><br>Disposition and skills necessary for effective civic engagement<br><br>The ability to understand the dynamic interactions of Earth's systems, the dependence of our social and economic systems on | Canadians place value on the history and culture that shapes their country and its people. Aboriginal communities in particular wish to see their culture reflected in Canadian education policy, programs, and services. The increasingly global nature of the economic social, environmental, and financial sectors means cross-cultural interactions, creating both opportunities and challenges that require unique competencies and skill sets.<br><br>Canadians must be global citizens, with a clear identity of their own history and culture along with sensitivity and respect for diverse identities and cultures as impacted on their sustainability. |

*(Continued)*

(Continued)

| 21st CENTURY COMPETENCIES—Shifting Minds | | |
|---|---|---|
| **21st Century Competency** | **Targeted Outcomes** | **Rationale** |
| | these natural systems, our fundamental connection to all living things, and the impact of humans on the environment <br><br> The capacity to consider the impact of societal and environmental trends and issues | |
| **Computer and Digital Technologies** | *The capacity to use computers and digital resources to access information and create knowledge, solutions, products, and services* <br><br> *The capacity to use social media for learning* | *The 21st century is a technology- and media-driven environment, and digital literacy is an essential competency for both learners and teachers.* |

| SYSTEM REDESIGN PRIORITIES—Shifting Minds | |
|---|---|
| **System Element** | **Priorities for Action** |
| **Curriculum** | Learning outcomes and associated activities must be relevant to engage the 21st century digital learner. <br><br> The number of learning outcomes must be reduced substantially to increase instructional time and allow for depth of understanding. <br><br> Learning outcomes must be rationalized across subject areas to reduce redundancy while strengthening cross-curricular relationships. <br><br> Higher levels of learner performance in literacy and numeracy performance must be achieved. <br><br> 21st century competencies must be infused throughout all learning outcomes. <br><br> Assessment regime(s) must be complementary to 21st century learning outcomes and pedagogical practices. <br><br> Digital technology must be harnessed to ensure data generation dynamic and timely and able to be mined effectively and efficiently to allow timely adjustments and interventions. <br><br> Roles within education systems must be rationalized and clarified to enhance efficiency of program delivery. |
| **Pedagogy** | Teaching practices and assessment methods must change to align with 21st century models of learning. <br><br> Teachers must achieve fluency in using new technologies to engage and support student learning. |

| SYSTEM REDESIGN PRIORITIES—Shifting Minds | |
|---|---|
| **System Element** | **Priorities for Action** |
| | Personalized learning opportunities must be offered to all students. |
| | Learners must have individualized access to the Internet and digital resources. |
| | Teachers must offer project-based learning opportunities to students, reflecting the student's passion and interest areas. |
| | Teachers must embrace collaborative teaching models (e.g., professional learning communities). |
| | The application of social media to learning must be achieved. |
| | Complementary standards and assessments must be realized. |
| | Flexibility in instructional time allocations must be attained to support anytime-anywhere learning. |
| **Learning Environment** | Learning spaces must be flexible and offer opportunities for both personalized and collaborative learning. |
| | Mobile learning opportunities should be integrated with other learning delivery models, where appropriate. |
| | Learning environments must be information and communications technology (ICT) rich with adequate technical support and infrastructure. |
| | Design standards must support anytime-anywhere learning opportunities. |
| | Online learning, blended learning, and virtual schools must be pursued as viable and relevant options to meeting the needs of many learners. |
| | Networks must be designed to facilitate a seamless transition between digital devices to access the Internet. |
| | Assistive technologies to support the full range of learners, including gifted learners and learners with learning or physical disabilities must be ubiquitous. |
| **Governance** | Creating a 21st century model of learning requires a strategic and focused approach by governments and educators, and an alignment of purpose within the system. |
| | Leadership must be a shared responsibility of all education partners and stakeholders, demanding highly collaborative and communicative design and implementation processes. |
| | Creativity and innovation in the classroom are best promoted when central education agencies are responsible for policy (learning outcomes and resources) and schools are empowered and resourced to be creative and innovative in the delivery of learning (student performance and engagement). |
| | School leaders must model 21st century skills in daily decision making, develop school improvement plans reflecting 21st century learning goals, and support procedures and practices that promote the shift in mindset required to achieve 21st century learning in school. |

*(Continued)*

(Continued)

| SYSTEM REDESIGN PRIORITIES—Shifting Minds | |
|---|---|
| **System Element** | **Priorities for Action** |
| **Citizen Engagement** | Parental and community engagement in the transformation process are a prerequisite to success. |
| | Community engagement is essential to offer students both in-school learning supports and authentic learning opportunities outside the classroom. |
| | Societal awareness of and support for the return on investment benefits (economic, social, environmental, financial, and personal) of 21st century models of learning are essential for successful transformation. |

**Graphic 4.1** Conceptual Model of Shifting Minds

*Source:* C21 Canada. (2012). *A 21st Century Vision of Public Education for Canada.* Retrieved from http://www.c21canada.org/wp-content/uploads/2012/05/C21-Canada-Shifting-Version-2.0.pdf

The next model to consider is **Framework for 21st Century Learning** (Partnership for 21st Century Learning), a holistic view of 21st century teaching and learning that combines a focus on student outcomes and innovative support systems to help students master the multidimensional abilities required of them in the 21st century (see Graphic 4.2).

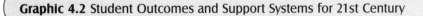

**Graphic 4.2** Student Outcomes and Support Systems for 21st Century

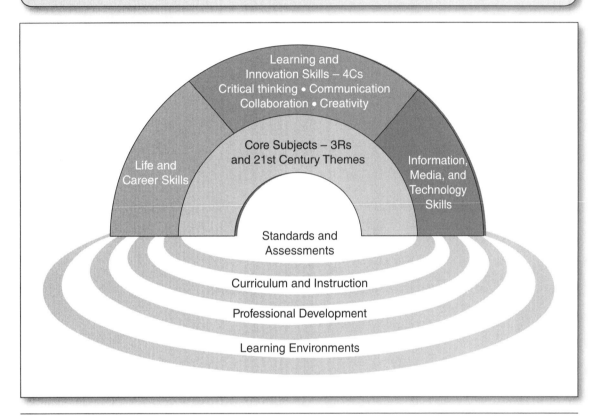

*Source:* Partnership for 21st Century Skills. Overview—Framework for 21st Century Learning. Retrieved from http://www.p21.org/overview/skills-framework

| Partnership for 21st Century Skills | |
|---|---|
| **21st Century Competency** | **Targeted Outcomes** |
| **Core Subjects** | The No Child Left Behind Act of 2001, which reauthorizes the Elementary and Secondary Education Act of 1965, identifies the core subjects as<br><br>• English<br>• Reading or Language Arts<br>• Mathematics<br>• Science<br>• Foreign languages<br>• Civics<br>• Government |

*(Continued)*

(Continued)

| Partnership for 21st Century Skills | |
|---|---|
| **21st Century Competency** | **Targeted Outcomes** |
| | • Economics<br>• Arts<br>• History<br>• Geography |
| **21st Century Content** | Several significant, emerging content areas are critical to success in communities and workplaces. These content areas typically are not emphasized in schools today:<br><br>• Global awareness<br>• Financial, economic, business, and entrepreneurial literacy<br>• Civic literacy<br>• Health and wellness awareness |
| **Learning and Thinking Skills** | As much as students need to learn academic content, they also need to know how to keep learning—and make effective and innovative use of what they know—throughout their lives. Learning and thinking skills are comprised of<br><br>• Critical-thinking and problem-solving skills<br>• Communication skills<br>• Creativity and innovation skills<br>• Collaboration skills<br>• Contextual learning skills<br>• Information and media literacy skills |
| **ICT Literacy** | Information and communications technology (ICT) literacy is the ability to use technology to develop 21st century content knowledge and skills, in the context of learning core subjects. Students must be able to use technology to learn content and skills so that they know how to learn, think critically, solve problems, use information, communicate, innovate, and collaborate. |
| **Life Skills** | Good teachers have always incorporated life skills into their pedagogy. The challenge today is to incorporate these essential skills into schools deliberately, strategically, and broadly. Life skills include<br><br>• Leadership<br>• Ethics<br>• Accountability<br>• Adaptability<br>• Personal productivity<br>• Personal responsibility<br>• People skills<br>• Self-direction<br>• Social responsibility |

| Partnership for 21st Century Skills | |
| --- | --- |
| **21st Century Competency** | **Targeted Outcomes** |
| **21st Century Assessments** | Authentic 21st century assessments are the essential foundation of a 21st century education. Assessments must measure all five results that matter: core subjects; 21st century content; learning and thinking skills; ICT literacy; and life skills. Assessment of 21st century skills should be integrated with assessments of core subjects. Separate assessments would defeat the purpose of infusing 21st century skills into core subjects. To be effective, sustainable, and affordable, assessments must use modern technologies to increase efficiency and timeliness. Standardized tests alone can measure only a few of the important skills and knowledge students should learn. A balance of assessments, including high-quality standardized testing along with effective classroom assessments, offers students and teachers a powerful tool to master the content and skills central to success. |

*Source:* Adapted from Partnership for 21st Century Skills. Overview—Framework for 21st Century Learning. Retrieved from http://www.p21.org/overview/skills-framework

Another model to consider is **Organisation for Economic Co-operation and Development (OECD) Framework** for 21st Century Skills and Competencies.

| OECD Framework | |
| --- | --- |
| **21st Century Competency** | **Targeted Outcomes** |
| **Information Dimension** | The information explosion triggered by information and communications technology (ICT) requires new skills for accessing, evaluating, and organizing information in digital environments. At the same time, in societies where knowledge has a central value, it is not enough to be able to process and organize information, but also to be able to model and transform it to create new knowledge or to use it as a source for new ideas.<br><br>• Research and problem solving skills<br>• Defining skills<br>• Evaluating skills<br>• Selecting skills<br>• Organizing skills<br>• Analyzing skills<br>• Interpreting information<br><br>Consistent with the processes of information and knowledge, this dimension includes two subdimensions listed below.<br>**Information as source: Searching, selecting, evaluating, and organizing information** |

*(Continued)*

(Continued)

| OECD Framework | |
|---|---|
| **21st Century Competency** | **Targeted Outcomes** |
| | The great bulk of available information on the Internet, as well as the proliferation of databases, makes the ability to find and organize information quickly and efficiently a critical skill. It presupposes that the student<br><br>• understands and then clearly defines the information needs on the basis of a question, issue, or task;<br>• knows how to identify digitally pertinent information sources; and<br>• knows how to look up for and select the digital information required in an effective and efficient way considering the problem to be solved.<br><br>Once the information has been found, it is fundamental that the student is capable of evaluating how valuable and useful the source and its contents are for the task at hand, as well as being able to store and organize the data or digital information efficiently so that it can be used again. Examples of skills and competencies belonging to this subdimension are<br><br>• Information literacy<br>• Research literacy<br>• Questioning literacy<br>• Media literacy<br><br>**Information as product: The restructuring and modeling of information and the development of own ideas (knowledge)**<br><br>This subdimension consists of what a student can do with digital information once it has been collected and organized. A student can transform and develop information in a variety of ways to understand it better, communicate it more effectively to others, and develop interpretations or one's own ideas on the basis of a question, issue, or task to be solved. Learners should have the following competencies:<br><br>• Integrating and summarizing information<br>• Analyzing and interpreting information<br>• Modeling information<br>• Observing how a model works and the relations between its elements<br>• Generating new information to develop new ideas<br><br>The process of developing one's own ideas is key, as it encourages students to develop their own thinking. Skills that belong mostly to this subdimension are creativity and innovation, problem solving, and decision making. |
| **Communication Dimension** | Communication plays an important role in the preparation of students to be not only lifelong learners, but also members of a larger community with voice and a sense of responsibility to others. Young people need to have the ability to communicate, exchange, criticize, and present information and ideas, including |

| OECD Framework | |
| --- | --- |
| **21st Century Competency** | **Targeted Outcomes** |
| | the use of ICT applications to participate in and make positive contributions to the digital culture. |
| | This dimension also has two subdimensions: |
| | *A) Effective Communication* |
| | Once the early stages of work with information and knowledge are complete, sharing and transmitting the results or outputs of information are very important for the impact of this work. In fact, this is a critical stage in the process that requires analytical work in itself, including processing, transforming, and formatting information and reflecting about the best way to present an idea to a particular audience. On the other hand, practical skills are needed to communicate effectively; these are linked to the use of the adequate available tools, use of correct language, and all other aspects that take the context into account to achieve an effective communication. Skills in this category include: |
| | <ul><li>Information and media literacy</li><li>Critical thinking</li><li>Communication skills</li><li>Collaboration and virtual interaction</li></ul> |
| | ICT supplies tools to support collaborative work among peers inside and outside school, for example providing constructive feedback through critical reflection on others' work or through the creation of spontaneous learning communities where some take the role of students and others of teachers. Today, participation in the digital culture depends on the ability to interact in virtual groups of friends and groups of interest, where young people are capable of using applications fluently and on a daily basis. Collaboration/team working and flexibility and adaptability are examples of skills that belong to this subdimension. |
| | *B) Ethics and Social Impact Dimension* |
| | Globalization, multiculturalism, and the rise in use of ICT also bring ethical challenges, so skills and competencies related to ethics and social impact are also important for the workers and citizens of the 21st century. |
| | **Social Responsibility** |
| | Social responsibility implies that individuals' actions may have an impact on society at large, both in a positive sense (i.e., there is a responsibility to act), but also in a negative one (i.e., there is a responsibility to refrain from certain actions). In terms of ICT for example, this refers to the ability to apply criteria for its responsible use at personal and social levels, acknowledging potential risks, as well as the use of rules of behavior that promote an adequate social exchange on the Web. Critical thinking, responsibility, and decision making are skills that are related to this subdimension. |

*(Continued)*

(Continued)

| OECD Framework | |
|---|---|
| **21st Century Competency** | **Targeted Outcomes** |
| | **Social Impact** |
| | This dimension refers to the development of a consciousness about the challenges in the new digital age. For example, there is consensus that the huge impact of ICT on social life is a matter that young people should reflect upon, considering the social, economic, and cultural implications for the individual and the society. These skills and competencies are often referred to as digital citizenship. The impact of young people's actions on the environment is another area that requires reflection and skills and related competencies also belong to this subdimension. |

*Source:* Ananiadou, K., & Claro, M. (2009). "21st Century Skills and Competences for New Millennium Learners in OECD Countries." *OECD Education Working Papers, No. 41*, OECD Publishing. Retrieved from http://dx.doi.org/10.1787/21 8525261154

The final model to consider in the context of understanding 21st century learning is the **NETS-T (National Educational Technology Standards for Teachers) Model** developed by the International Society for Technology in Education.

| NETS-T | |
|---|---|
| **21st Century Competency** | **Targeted Outcomes** |
| **Facilitate and Inspire Student Learning and Creativity** | Teachers use their knowledge of subject matter, teaching and learning, and technology to facilitate experiences that advance student learning, creativity, and innovation in both face-to-face and virtual environments. Teachers<br><br>• Promote, support, and model creative and innovative thinking and inventiveness<br>• Engage students in exploring real-world issues and solving authentic problems using digital tools and resources<br>• Promote student reflection using collaborative tools to reveal and clarify students' conceptual understanding and thinking, planning, and creative processes<br>• Model collaborative knowledge construction by engaging in learning with students, colleagues, and others in face-to-face and virtual environments |
| **Design and Develop Digital** | Teachers design, develop, and evaluate authentic learning experiences and assessment incorporating contemporary tools and resources to maximize |

| NETS-T | |
|---|---|
| **21st Century Competency** | **Targeted Outcomes** |
| **Age Learning Experiences and Assessments** | content learning in context and to develop the knowledge, skills, and attitudes identified in the NETS-S. Teachers<br><br>• Design or adapt relevant learning experiences that incorporate digital tools and resources to promote student learning and creativity<br>• Develop technology-enriched learning environments that enable all students to pursue their individual curiosities and become active participants in setting their own educational goals, managing their own learning, and assessing their own progress<br>• Customize and personalize learning activities to address students' diverse learning styles, working strategies, and abilities using digital tools and resources<br>• Provide students with multiple and varied formative and summative assessments aligned with content and technology standards and use resulting data to inform learning and teaching |
| **Model Digital Age Work and Learning** | Teachers exhibit knowledge, skills, and work processes representative of an innovative professional in a global and digital society. Teachers<br><br>• Demonstrate fluency in technology systems and the transfer of current knowledge to new technologies and situations<br>• Collaborate with students, peers, parents, and community members using digital tools and resources to support student success and innovation<br>• Communicate relevant information and ideas effectively to students, parents, and peers using a variety of digital age media and formats<br>• Model and facilitate effective use of current and emerging digital tools to locate, analyze, evaluate, and use information resources to support research and learning |
| **Promote and Model Digital Citizenship and Responsibility** | Teachers understand local and global societal issues and responsibilities in an evolving digital culture and exhibit legal and ethical behavior in their professional practices. Teachers<br><br>• Advocate, model, and teach safe, legal, and ethical use of digital information and technology, including respect for copyright, intellectual property, and the appropriate documentation of sources<br>• Address the diverse needs of all learners by using learner-centered strategies providing equitable access to appropriate digital tools and resources<br>• Promote and model digital etiquette and responsible social interactions related to the use of technology and information<br>• Develop and model cultural understanding and global awareness by engaging with colleagues and students of other cultures using digital age communication and collaboration tools |

*(Continued)*

(Continued)

| NETS-T | |
|---|---|
| **21st Century Competency** | **Targeted Outcomes** |
| **Engage in Professional Growth and Leadership** | Teachers continuously improve their professional practice, model lifelong learning, and exhibit leadership in their school and professional community by promoting and demonstrating the effective use of digital tools and resources. Teachers<br><br>• Participate in local and global learning communities to explore creative applications of technology to improve student learning<br>• Exhibit leadership by demonstrating a vision of technology infusion, participating in shared decision making and community building, and developing the leadership and technology skills of others<br>• Evaluate and reflect on current research and professional practice on a regular basis to make effective use of existing and emerging digital tools and resources in support of student learning<br>• Contribute to the effectiveness, vitality, and self-renewal of the teaching profession and of their school and community |

*Source:* NETS-T. (2013). Retrieved from http://www.iste.org/standards/nets-for-teachers

These are very interesting models that can help school leaders achieve an educational reality that is more closely linked with the lived experiences of the students we are educating. Further to this reality, it is clear that technology is not just a side educational endeavor. Technology and digital literacy are infused into how we communicate, create knowledge, understand our world, and build community. To build on this idea, it is important to remember that these models of 21st century schools don't exist in isolation as a purely educational concern. They are closely aligned with the skills, dispositions, and knowledge that the economy will need in the coming years, and this brings further meaning and purpose to this educational reform. Bridgstock (2009) conducted a study exploring the employability characteristics needed of graduates. Her research came up with an interesting conceptual model (see Graphic 4.3). In looking at this model, it is clear to see how 21st century learning is evident in the components of this model connecting learning to work.

On a global level, the OECD has responded to this educational and economic need by developing the OECD Skills Strategy in late 2012 (skills.oecd.org). In their research, they are indicating that there will be a continuing rise in the need for workers who have strong cognitive and interpersonal skills. The need for highly skilled workers will increase, and many of the OECD countries are going to be growing their service-based economies. Their work also looked closely at skills that are the most transferable from the education system to the

**Graphic 4.3** Graduate Attributes and Employability

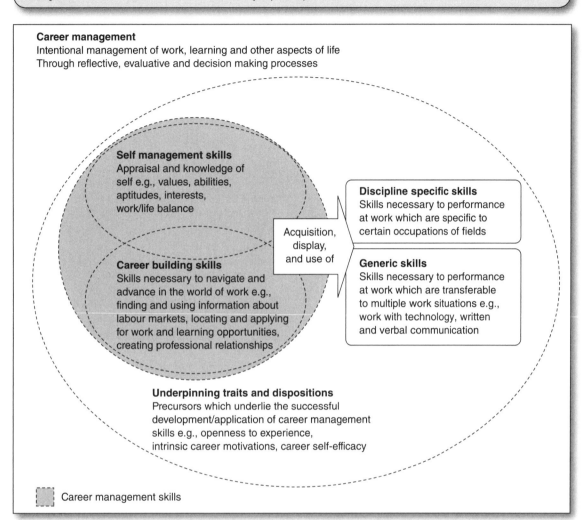

**Career management**
Intentional management of work, learning and other aspects of life
Through reflective, evaluative and decision making processes

**Self management skills**
Appraisal and knowledge of
self e.g., values, abilities,
aptitudes, interests,
work/life balance

**Discipline specific skills**
Skills necessary to performance
at work which are specific to
certain occupations of fields

Acquisition,
display,
and use of

**Career building skills**
Skills necessary to navigate and
advance in the world of work e.g.,
finding and using information about
labour markets, locating and applying
for work and learning opportunities,
creating professional relationships

**Generic skills**
Skills necessary to performance
at work which are transferable
to multiple work situations e.g.,
work with technology, written
and verbal communication

**Underpinning traits and dispositions**
Precursors which underlie the successful
development/application of career management
skills e.g., openness to experience,
intrinsic career motivations, career self-efficacy

Career management skills

*Source:* Bridgstock, R. (2009). The graduate attributes we've overlooked: Enhancing graduate employability through career management skills. *Higher Education Research & Development, 28*(1), 31–44.

economy. The following table describes the OECD findings. Looking closely, we can see the components of the 21st century learning competencies evident.

| Transferable Skills in the Workforce | |
|---|---|
| **Skill Competency** | **Associated Subskills** |
| Interpersonal skills | Teamwork |
| | Mentoring skills |
| | Negotiating skills |
| | Networking skills |

*(Continued)*

(Continued)

| Transferable Skills in the Workforce | |
| --- | --- |
| **Skill Competency** | **Associated Subskills** |
| Organizational skills | Time management skills |
| | Project management skills |
| Cognitive abilities | Creativity |
| | Abstract thought |
| | Problem solving |
| Communication skills | Presentation skills: Written and oral |
| Enterprise skills | Entrepreneurship |
| | Innovation |

*Source:* Organisation for Economic Co-operation and Development (OECD). (2012). *Transferable Skills Training for Researchers: Supporting Career Development and Research,* OECD Publishing. Retrieved from http://www.keepeek.com/Digital-Asset-Management/oecd/education/21st-century-skills-and-competences-for-new-millennium-learners-in-oecd-countries_218525261154

### Creating a 21st Century School Environment Activity

Reflect on the students in your school and rank the following competencies that are most needed by the students in your school. Rank from 1 to 16.

| | | | |
| --- | --- | --- | --- |
| Critical Thinking | _____ | Communication | _____ |
| Collaboration | _____ | Creativity | _____ |
| Innovation | _____ | Ethical Citizenship | _____ |
| Civic Engagement | _____ | Global Awareness | _____ |
| Leadership | _____ | People Skills | _____ |
| Social Responsibility | _____ | Problem Solving | _____ |
| Organization | _____ | Technology Fluency | _____ |
| Evaluate and Interpret Info | _____ | Internet Safety | _____ |

Rank the following literacies that are most needed by the students in your school. Rank from 1 to 9.

| | | | |
| --- | --- | --- | --- |
| Civic Literacy | _____ | Media Literacy | _____ |
| Information Literacy | _____ | Digital Literacy | _____ |
| Research Literacy | _____ | Cultural Literacy | _____ |
| Social Literacy | _____ | Economic Literacy | _____ |
| ICT Literacy | _____ | | |

Take the top four competencies and four literacies from #1 and #2 and reflect on ways that your school is currently incorporating 21st century learning into the curriculum. Try to list two specific ways that you are currently meeting this need. It could be happening at the school level, or it could be something a specific teacher/program is doing.

| Current Activities Showing You Are a 21st Century School | |
|---|---|
| **Competency** | **Example** |
| 1. | a. |
| | b. |
| 2. | a. |
| | b. |
| 3. | a. |
| | b. |
| 4. | a. |
| | b. |
| **Literacy** | **Example** |
| 1. | a. |
| | b. |
| 2. | a. |
| | b. |
| 3. | a. |
| | b. |
| 4. | a. |
| | b. |

Take the list of four competencies and four literacies and generate a list of two examples that you would like to see happening in your school that will help it develop more into a 21st century school.

| New Activities That Will Help You Move More Toward a 21st Century School | |
|---|---|
| **Competency** | **New Idea** |
| 1. | 1. |
| | 2. |
| 2. | 3. |
| | 4. |
| 3. | 5. |
| | 6. |
| 4. | 7. |
| | 8. |
| **Literacy** | **New Idea** |
| 1. | 1. |
| | 2. |
| 2. | 3. |
| | 4. |
| 3. | 5. |
| | 6. |
| 4. | 7. |
| | 8. |

Reflecting on the list you just created, are there any barriers in your school that could hinder the reforms or ideas you have for your 21st century school? Readers can look back at the discussion on barriers at the beginning of this chapter for a refresher on what each of the barriers mean.

## Lack of Resources

| | | |
|---|---|---|
| Competency New Idea #1 | Yes ❑ | No ❑ |
| Competency New Idea #2 | Yes ❑ | No ❑ |
| Competency New Idea #3 | Yes ❑ | No ❑ |
| Competency New Idea #4 | Yes ❑ | No ❑ |
| Competency New Idea #5 | Yes ❑ | No ❑ |
| Competency New Idea #6 | Yes ❑ | No ❑ |
| Competency New Idea #7 | Yes ❑ | No ❑ |
| Competency New Idea #8 | Yes ❑ | No ❑ |
| Literacy New Idea #1 | Yes ❑ | No ❑ |
| Literacy New Idea #2 | Yes ❑ | No ❑ |
| Literacy New Idea #3 | Yes ❑ | No ❑ |
| Literacy New Idea #4 | Yes ❑ | No ❑ |
| Literacy New Idea #5 | Yes ❑ | No ❑ |
| Literacy New Idea #6 | Yes ❑ | No ❑ |
| Literacy New Idea #7 | Yes ❑ | No ❑ |
| Literacy New Idea #8 | Yes ❑ | No ❑ |

## Limited Knowledge and Skills

| | | |
|---|---|---|
| Competency New Idea #1 | Yes ❑ | No ❑ |
| Competency New Idea #2 | Yes ❑ | No ❑ |
| Competency New Idea #3 | Yes ❑ | No ❑ |
| Competency New Idea #4 | Yes ❑ | No ❑ |
| Competency New Idea #5 | Yes ❑ | No ❑ |
| Competency New Idea #6 | Yes ❑ | No ❑ |
| Competency New Idea #7 | Yes ❑ | No ❑ |
| Competency New Idea #8 | Yes ❑ | No ❑ |
| Literacy New Idea #1 | Yes ❑ | No ❑ |
| Literacy New Idea #2 | Yes ❑ | No ❑ |
| Literacy New Idea #3 | Yes ❑ | No ❑ |

| | | |
|---|---|---|
| Literacy New Idea #4 | Yes ❑ | No ❑ |
| Literacy New Idea #5 | Yes ❑ | No ❑ |
| Literacy New Idea #6 | Yes ❑ | No ❑ |
| Literacy New Idea #7 | Yes ❑ | No ❑ |
| Literacy New Idea #8 | Yes ❑ | No ❑ |

## Poor Visioning

| | | |
|---|---|---|
| Competency New Idea #1 | Yes ❑ | No ❑ |
| Competency New Idea #2 | Yes ❑ | No ❑ |
| Competency New Idea #3 | Yes ❑ | No ❑ |
| Competency New Idea #4 | Yes ❑ | No ❑ |
| Competency New Idea #5 | Yes ❑ | No ❑ |
| Competency New Idea #6 | Yes ❑ | No ❑ |
| Competency New Idea #7 | Yes ❑ | No ❑ |
| Competency New Idea #8 | Yes ❑ | No ❑ |
| Literacy New Idea #1 | Yes ❑ | No ❑ |
| Literacy New Idea #2 | Yes ❑ | No ❑ |
| Literacy New Idea #3 | Yes ❑ | No ❑ |
| Literacy New Idea #4 | Yes ❑ | No ❑ |
| Literacy New Idea #5 | Yes ❑ | No ❑ |
| Literacy New Idea #6 | Yes ❑ | No ❑ |
| Literacy New Idea #7 | Yes ❑ | No ❑ |
| Literacy New Idea #8 | Yes ❑ | No ❑ |

## Negative Attitudes

| | | |
|---|---|---|
| Competency New Idea #1 | Yes ❑ | No ❑ |
| Competency New Idea #2 | Yes ❑ | No ❑ |
| Competency New Idea #3 | Yes ❑ | No ❑ |
| Competency New Idea #4 | Yes ❑ | No ❑ |
| Competency New Idea #5 | Yes ❑ | No ❑ |
| Competency New Idea #6 | Yes ❑ | No ❑ |
| Competency New Idea #7 | Yes ❑ | No ❑ |
| Competency New Idea #8 | Yes ❑ | No ❑ |

Literacy New Idea #1      Yes ❑      No ❑

Literacy New Idea #2      Yes ❑      No ❑

Literacy New Idea #3      Yes ❑      No ❑

Literacy New Idea #4      Yes ❑      No ❑

Literacy New Idea #5      Yes ❑      No ❑

Literacy New Idea #6      Yes ❑      No ❑

Literacy New Idea #7      Yes ❑      No ❑

Literacy New Idea #8      Yes ❑      No ❑

## Weak Assessment Strategies

Competency New Idea #1      Yes ❑      No ❑

Competency New Idea #2      Yes ❑      No ❑

Competency New Idea #3      Yes ❑      No ❑

Competency New Idea #4      Yes ❑      No ❑

Competency New Idea #5      Yes ❑      No ❑

Competency New Idea #6      Yes ❑      No ❑

Competency New Idea #7      Yes ❑      No ❑

Competency New Idea #8      Yes ❑      No ❑

Literacy New Idea #1      Yes ❑      No ❑

Literacy New Idea #2      Yes ❑      No ❑

Literacy New Idea #3      Yes ❑      No ❑

Literacy New Idea #4      Yes ❑      No ❑

Literacy New Idea #5      Yes ❑      No ❑

Literacy New Idea #6      Yes ❑      No ❑

Literacy New Idea #7      Yes ❑      No ❑

Literacy New Idea #8      Yes ❑      No ❑

## Inability to See Broad Application

Competency New Idea #1      Yes ❑      No ❑

Competency New Idea #2      Yes ❑      No ❑

Competency New Idea #3      Yes ❑      No ❑

Competency New Idea #4      Yes ❑      No ❑

Competency New Idea #5      Yes ❑      No ❑

| | | |
|---|---|---|
| Competency New Idea #6 | Yes ❑ | No ❑ |
| Competency New Idea #7 | Yes ❑ | No ❑ |
| Competency New Idea #8 | Yes ❑ | No ❑ |
| Literacy New Idea #1 | Yes ❑ | No ❑ |
| Literacy New Idea #2 | Yes ❑ | No ❑ |
| Literacy New Idea #3 | Yes ❑ | No ❑ |
| Literacy New Idea #4 | Yes ❑ | No ❑ |
| Literacy New Idea #5 | Yes ❑ | No ❑ |
| Literacy New Idea #6 | Yes ❑ | No ❑ |
| Literacy New Idea #7 | Yes ❑ | No ❑ |
| Literacy New Idea #8 | Yes ❑ | No ❑ |

For each item that you responded yes to, try to be creative and consider ways you could overcome the barrier. It might mean professional development, a shift in resources, or new technologies.

Barrier Breakdown #1:

Barrier Breakdown #2:

Barrier Breakdown #3:

Now select one to three of the items from question #4 (p. 100) that you would like to actually implement into your school activities or classroom curriculum.

21st Century Selection #1 _____

21st Century Selection #2 _____

21st Century Selection #3 _____

Once you have this list, reread through specific elements of the four 21st century models presented in this chapter related to your selections for supporting ideas. Remember this type of reform is not necessarily about throwing everything out and starting from scratch. As you probably saw from question #3 (p. 99), your school is perhaps already engaged in 21st century practices. Your job is to slowly continue to reform and transform by consistently incorporating new 21st century competencies and literacies into your school culture.

## GOING DEEPER INTO TEACHING AND LEARNING WITH TECHNOLOGY

The effort of this book is to bring to the attention of educators that we can no longer consider technology as a tool of educational practice. The reality is that technology has become the means through which we interact, engage, and create in our world. Consider

- How much technology has impacted the way you do your banking?
- How much technology has impacted your entertainment?
- How much technology has impacted the way you communicate with others?
- How much technology has impacted the way we receive news about our world?
- How much technology has impacted the way we learn?

In this sense, school administrators, technology coordinators, and curriculum leaders trying to create a 21st century classroom, where technology is infused into the teaching and learning experience, will need to reflect on the actual pedagogies used to create the learning context. It doesn't take much effort to look at the four models of 21st century learning presented in this chapter and come to the realization that the very nature of our philosophy of education is transitioning. The nature of our educational methodologies and theories are shifting to pedagogies that require learning in a technological space. On the Internet, it is easy to find research that explores specific instructional strategies, communication techniques, and learning methodologies related to bringing technology into the classroom, but there is limited discussion into how technology is actually challenging the educational pedagogies of the teaching and learning experience.

Pedagogy is the educational process that supports the desire of students to learn in an engaged and social manner where the teacher fosters and challenges this growth. There is also a strong connection between learning and the content of study. Learning happened when students could recite, memorize, and build upon content knowledge. This learning process is most connected to behaviorist theories related to the transmission of knowledge evolving out of the work of B. F. Skinner, John Watson, and Edward Thorndike. Also impacting educational practice, North American educators understand that education is not just about content knowledge but that our schools are places where the transmission of culture happens and where social processes occur. Schools are the sites where students learn how to act, behave, and socialize in their world. John Dewey (1916) referred to this as the Democratic Theory of Education, and Bandura (1977) classified it as social learning theory. Other theorists recognized that students could not be passive participants in the educational process but that they should be engaged in their learning and in the creation of knowledge. Jean Piaget and Jerome Bruner heavily influenced educational practice with the development of Constructivism. Here educators must clearly understand the cognitive development of their learners so that teachers can help students construct new knowledge based on an understanding of their existing experience and knowledge. On this front, Lev Vygotsky was influential in impacting pedagogy with the Zone of Proximal Development (ZPD). In this pedagogical reality, the teacher was instrumental in helping young learners to push into new learning capabilities and helping them to mature. Expanding this pedagogic reality, David Kolb built upon the concept of constructivism with his pedagogy of Experienced Based Learning. At the same time, it was not just about behaviors, experiences, or social engagement, but educational pedagogy practice could be improved through learning styles. Kolb called this Experiential Learning Theory. In this theory, teachers could improve student achievement when they understood how each individual child learned. Kolb classified learning styles into four categories: Converger, Diverger, Assimilator, and Accommodator. Other theories (VAK Model by Neil Fleming) looked at learning styles through the lens of whether or not the child was an auditory, visual, or kinesthetic learner. Teachers had a pedagogic responsibility to provide instruction and learning in a way that met the learning style of the different students that would be in any classroom.

Linked to learning styles, researchers impacted pedagogic theory through the introduction of the concept of *intelligences*. Here the idea is that students have distinct ways of processing and learning information. Howard Gardner developed the concept of multiple intelligences. Some of the intelligences impacting student learning include linguistic, logic-mathematical, musical, spatial, bodily/kinesthetic, interpersonal, intrapersonal, spiritual, and naturalistic. Emotional Intelligence is the ability to identify, assess, and control the emotions of oneself, of others, and of a group. It is further understood through Ability Emotional Intelligence and Trait Emotional Intelligence. We can see the influence of Wayne Payne, David Weschler, and Edward Thorndike in this pedagogic theory.

Pedagogy is the appropriate and relevant use of teaching strategies. Traditional pedagogy further places the teacher at the center of the learning process. Even student-centered learning theories require an articulate professional educator who uses a sound understanding of educational methodologies to create the student-centered educational space. Traditional pedagogy also places the teacher's philosophical beliefs on the experiences and background of the students. It is out of this realm where educators began to question the passive nature of these traditional pedagogies. From this, critical pedagogy began to emerge as an approach that emphasized habits of thought, reading, writing, and speaking on the part of the students and the teacher. Critical pedagogy involves interplay between the students and their teacher to reproduce and create knowledge. Within critical pedagogy is the formation of *problem-based learning* or *inquiry-based learning*. This is a student-centered pedagogy where students learn content knowledge through the experience of problem solving. This pedagogy recognizes the dynamic that occurs when teachers and students interact in the learning environment designed to explore and create knowledge. The question facing educators is whether or not these pedagogies are still relevant in the 21st century classroom.

## Linking Pedagogy to Technology: Two Examples From the Profession

### Example #1: Mobile Technology

*The following example is derived from Steven Puckett. He is a doctoral candidate in educational leadership at Georgia Southern University and is also a technology coordinator for his school district in Georgia. He is currently in the process of conducting research looking at teachers' perceptions of how mobile technology is impacting the teaching paradigm. In this material, Steven questions how mobile technology is changing learning and teaching. This work is excerpted with his permission.*

Educator and psychologist John Dewey (1916) stated that "not only is social life identical with communication, but all communication is educative. To be a recipient of a communication is to have an enlarged and changed experience" (p. 67). Many 21st century schools are engaging in new school reform called Bring Your Own Technology (BYOT). Within these programs, students are encouraged to bring their own technological devices into wireless classrooms where they can use them as part of the educational process. Smartphones, or mobile technology, are probably the main devices that students are bringing into the classroom. The infrastructure of traditional classrooms has not changed much throughout the ages, but the advent of mobile technology in the hands of students, both inside and outside of the classroom, is bringing about dramatic change both to society at large and to the formal education structures that have been in place for decades. In reviewing the literature, there is ample research in the area of student learning. From Piaget to Bruner, and from Dewey to Gardner, researchers have thoroughly discussed the theories, motivations, and patterns of student learning and achievement. However, in the area of mobile learning, there is a significant lack of research necessary to identify a framework for the many different theories that can factor in to a fuller understanding of learning through the lens of mobile technologies. Traditionally, most theories of learning have been grounded in the paradigm that learning occurs under the leadership of a trained teacher (Sharples, 2002). According to Sharples and other researchers in the area of mobile learning from the University of Birmingham in the United Kingdom, many educational theories factor in learning outside the standard teacher-student classroom model.

According to the U.S. National Research Council, effective learning builds on the skills and knowledge of students; is founded on knowledge, concepts, and methods that are taught efficiently; has assessment that is matched to the ability of the learner; and promotes a sense of community (National Research Council, 2000). For Piaget (1973), the basis of learning is discovery. Some first-time users of smartphones could perhaps attest to the discovery learning that takes place when the smartphone is initially activated beyond the walls of the sales desks where the phone was purchased. Jerome Bruner in the same year expanded Piaget's ideas to include the theory that learners create knowledge and concepts through social interactions (Bruner, 1973). Bruner's educational concepts about knowledge creation and communication take on new significance, in light of the advances in mobile technology. The view of learning as an active process of building knowledge and skills is most closely aligned to a social-constructivist approach to learning whereby learners create knowledge from their own experiences and their social interactions with others around them (Sharples, 2002).

In examining the impact of mobile technology on the modern classroom, it is important to realize that mobile telephone usage is becoming more ubiquitous among students as an increasing number of people are becoming technologically literate and are possessing mobile phones (Uden, 2007). Twenty years ago, the owners of mobile phones were relegated to carry large and unwieldy bag phones that could function only as a telephone. Now, students as young as elementary-school age are possessing sophisticated smartphones that can send and receive large amounts of data; access, create, and distribute media; and communicate with others through text, voice, e-mail, and video methods. Handheld mobile technologies are providing access to computing and information where student activities and learning are in progress, rather than in stand-alone desktop computers that historically were separate from other classroom activities (Uden, 2007). Vast numbers of students now have a phone, and most of them are using them as a regular, almost invisible function of their daily interactions with the world.

According to Uden (2007), mobile technology allows learning to occur in a process that is interactive and collaborative, but this collaborative learning only occurs if the technology is a close fit with the context in which it is used. With mobile technology becoming a regular component of the personal lives of students and teachers, the use of this mobile technology is naturally progressing into our educational realities. Where schools before were resisting the possession of mobile technology devices in the classroom, they are now either begrudgingly or willingly embracing its use in the classroom. From a teaching perspective, it is possible to take the theories behind most pedagogy and extrapolate them to include the use of mobile technology.

***Mobile Technology Ownership and Usage.*** Between 2002 and 2003, sales of mobile devices in the United States increased by 40% (Motiwalla, 2007). Further, by 2005, mobile phone sales outstripped personal computer sales. By 2008, the majority of companies in the United States had switched to wireless networks (Ellis, 2003). From the business world to the world of higher education, computers and similar electronic devices have become a staple of society. Laptop computers, smartphones, handheld electronic devices, and dramatically improved wireless Internet capabilities have rapidly changed the higher education environment (Green, 2000). The use of computer-assisted learning and online learning have increased rapidly in the past few decades, in large part due to heavy investment in Internet technology (Green, 1999). In 2000, a campus technology survey indicated that most college professors were using e-mail to communicate with students and a third of all college courses were using computer-assisted learning technology (Green, 1999). In 2002, 80% of students who owned computers or wireless devices indicated that the Internet had improved their educational experience (Jones, 2002).

From higher education down to secondary schools, the explosion of technology ownership and usage has dramatically increased. In 2009, the New York Department of Health and Mental Hygiene produced survey results indicating that 71% of New York teens aged 12 to 17 owned a cell phone, 60% owned either a desktop or a laptop computer, and 88% of their parents had mobile phones. They also documented that there was no significant difference in mobile phone ownership by race or ethnicity other than a slight increase in the highest income and education brackets. Additionally, boys were just as likely as girls to own cell phones (Lenhart, 2009).

Technology is here to stay. While the theories behind much of what takes place in the classroom are well grounded in a firmly established body of literature, the theories behind how to best utilize mobile technology in the classroom are still to be determined. Just as instructional and educational technology programs are grappling with a rapid infusion of new devices, so too are researchers coming to terms with a rapidly changing social-cultural revolution when it comes to mobile technology in the classroom. However, by building upon the founders of modern education, it is evident that there is a strong case to be made that the utilization of mobile technology is a 21st century manifestation of a social constructivist view of education.

***Mobile Technology and Mobile Learning.*** Not only are the theoretical foundations for the use of mobile technology not fully examined, but there is also a lack of clarity when it comes to defining mobile technology and mobile learning. While the case can be made that there is support for mobile learning from an educational theory perspective, it is imperative that mobile technology and mobile learning be adequately defined. The definition of mobile learning has expanded to include learning that occurs on a mobile device such as a personal data assistant, mobile phone, iPod, tablet PC, or laptop (Traxler, 2009).

While formal education is often discussed as a face-to-face, lecture-format instructional setting, there is a growing body of research that links mobile learning to the individual experiences of the students involved (Traxler, 2009). In other words, learning occurs when the learner is not at a fixed, predetermined location, or learning that happens when the learner takes advantage of learning opportunities offered by mobile technologies (O'Malley et al., 2003). While there is research indicating that mobile technology is being piloted and implemented in the classroom, it is important to clarify what is mobile learning. According to Traxler, mobile learning is more consistently defined in terms of the technology being used in the hands of students, rather than in terms of the learners' experiences with these devices. Historically, the actual learning that is taking place with mobile devices would have been characterized as informal learning rather than formal learning (Traxler, 2009).

In 2004, Georgieva identified the main types of mobile devices being used in the classroom as notebook computers, tablet PCs, Personal Digital Assistants (PDA), and cellular phones. While PDAs and notebook computers tend to have more functionality, Georgieva (2004) pointed out that cell phones and their modern incarnation as smartphones provided more usefulness to students, while also being much lower in price.

Just as defining mobile technology and mobile learning is challenging and often conflicting, Traxler (2009) indicated that the pervasive use of these devices is both changing the nature of knowledge and communication and is also a result of other social and economic forces. An important distinction must be made between finding information and knowing information.

Traxler (2009) pointed out that mobile technologies are changing the nature of work that is founded on knowledge as these mobile devices simultaneously create and distribute new methods of performance, commerce, learning, and activity. The major difference highlighted in Traxler's research is that mobile technology is no longer merely a way to enhance or support learning, but it is also impacting the actual knowledge and learning process at the same time.

In Cobcroft's *Mobile Learning in Review* (2006), the question is raised as to whether the increasing availability of mobile technology and its application merely support the curriculum, or if it is becoming the core business of education. The environments have implications for learners, teachers, technology planning, and sustainability (McGovern & Gray, 2005).

Educational technology is defined as the hardware, media, and application of technology within the process of instructional design (Nichols & Allen-Brown, 1996). Using technology is a result of greater cultural phenomena within education. In addition to defining mobile learning and mobile technology in the context of the appropriate pedagogical theory, educators must also understand that today's mobile learners are digitally literate, mobile oriented, experimental in nature, and always on, with a constant focus on social media connectedness (Oblinger, 2003). Teachers, students, and parents now have in their hands the skills and technology to stay in contact through mobile phones, the Internet, and computers (McMahon & Pospisil, 2005).

In addition to being consumers of information, current students are now also creating their own content. Just having technology in the hands of students is not enough. In 2005, Wagner stated that the success of mobile learning will involve the convergence of multiple experiences. While the classroom and the learners' themselves are changing, in order to examine how mobile learning is implemented, it is helpful to consider five broad categories of technology: portability, platform, delivery, media technologies, and development languages (Attewell, 2005). Not only do educators need to define what is mobile technology, how this technology is manifesting itself in the hands of learners, how it is being implemented, but also the theoretical support for allowing and even encouraging this manifestation.

In addition to examining several theories highlighted in the literature such as social constructivist theory, action learning theory, critical theory, other broad theories were repeatedly referenced when examining mobile technology. Behaviorist theories where activities result in a change in a learner's behavior are evident in mobile classroom response systems commonly found in classes today (Dufresne, Martial, Ramstein, & Mabilleau, 1996), as well as text messaging to mobile phones (Thornton & Houser, 2004).

The constructivist belief that learning is an active process where new ideas and knowledge are constructed is evident when students participate in simulations games. Collaborative learning through social interaction as well as activity theory is evident in computer supportive learning (Engeström, 1987). All of these various usages of mobile technology can be firmly supported by Vygotsky's social-cultural theories of knowledge acquisition through social interaction (Vygotsky, 1978).

After examining what is mobile technology, how prolific it is in today's classrooms, and how it is an extension of other theoretically sound pedagogical strategies, the research next leads to the question as to why mobile technology is and should be so prevalent in the classroom. Six possible reasons for utilizing mobile technology in the classroom are identified: freedom to set individual goals, ownership, fun, communication, learning in context, and continuity (Kember, 1997). From a theoretical perspective, mobile learning can support a range of teaching concepts and methodologies, as different content area disciplines and different teachers will approach teaching in their own unique ways (Kember, 1997). Mobile learning technologies in some classrooms will lead in delivering content, while in others it will be used to support the discussion of concepts covered in the classroom (Traxler, 2009). Students and teachers are better able to personalize instruction according to their own learning styles (Coffield et al., 2005).

With the understanding that technology and especially mobile technology can support engagement of students by increasing the effectiveness of interactions between teachers and students, in 2006 researchers observed that the use of mobile communications technology had a significant impact on student learning motivation, pressure, and performance (Rau, Gao, & Wu, 2006). The use of text messaging, e-mail, and online forums were examined with 45 students, and the results showed that instant messaging helped merge the roles of the student and the instructor effectively by significantly increasing student motivation without causing higher pressure. The implications from this research pointed out that the use of public expression through media should be carefully considered, as they dramatically increase student pressure when juxtaposed with the lower student pressure created by the use of text messaging.

In 2009, Chinese classrooms that were struggling with interactivity between students and students with the instructor made significant positive gains in student interactivity by incorporating mobile text messaging with real-time instruction (Wang, Wu, & Wang, 2009). Instant polls, short text messages, and instructor responses in real time dramatically increase student interaction and levels of engagement. The use of mobile technology in the classroom can engage students and change their thoughts, feelings, and actions and has significant results in the area of student engagement (Wang et al., 2009).

Classrooms that incorporate technology-rich experiences can provide learners with greater opportunities to develop skills that are needed for the 21st century workforce (Leh, Kouba, & Davis, 2005). The advent of mobile technology provides new opportunities for students to develop higher-order thinking skills. The trends for modern classrooms to utilize computers, Internet, social networks, and mobile technology continue to increase the emphasis on cutting edge technology (Keane, 2010). With today's learners storing information in the Internet cloud, sending and receiving text messages, streaming audio and video, and creating applications on handheld devices, there are significant challenges for teachers to keep up with these changes, including lack of time, training, and support. Even with the dramatic increase of technology in school, more attention must be focused on teachers' perceptions of how these technological advances are challenging the teaching paradigm.

### Example #2: Technological Pedagogical Content Knowledge (TPACK)

The original concept of this pedagogical approach grew out of the work of Lee Shulman (1986). In his article, Shulman begins with the infamous quote of George Bernard Shaw, "He who can, does. He who cannot, teaches." Shulman is most concerned with the fact that this seeming professional insult "appears to underlie the policies concerning the occupation and activities of teaching" (p. 4). In tracing the historical roots of teacher evaluation practices, he revealed that the education profession had gone from assessments based solely on content knowledge (early 1900s) to an assessment of the teaching practice. For example, teacher evaluation measures in the 1980s considered organization in preparing and presenting instructional plans, evaluation, recognition of individual differences, cultural awareness, understanding of youth, management, and educational policies and procedures. Shulman was concerned that content was lost in the measurement of teacher effectiveness. In this sense, he laments that Shaw was correct in his assessment of the teaching practice even into the 1980s, and Shulman changes the quote to "He who knows, does. He who cannot, but knows some teaching procedures, teaches" (p. 6). Going through a discussion about research into teacher effectiveness of the time and its justification to focus more on teacher behavior as a means of measuring teacher effectiveness, Shulman concluded that "in their necessary simplification of the complexities of classroom teaching, investigators ignored one central aspect of classroom life: the subject matter" (p. 6). In this educational reality, the pedagogical process superseded a serious discussion into whether or not students were actually learning the content and if teachers had a sound understanding of the content they were responsible for teaching:

> From the perspective of teacher development and teacher education, a host of questions arise. Where do teachers' explanations come from? How do teachers decide what to teach, how to represent it, how to question students about it and how to deal with problems of misunderstanding? What are the sources of teacher knowledge? What does a teacher know and when did he or she come to know it? How is new knowledge acquired, old knowledge retrieved, and both combined to form a new knowledge base? (Shulman, 1986, p. 8)

Shulman (1986) affirmed that the intent is not to denigrate pedagogy at the cost of content, but to realign pedagogy with content knowledge so as to bring out the full potential of a teacher's capacity to teach and aid in student achievement. Based on his research of teachers and their practice, Shulman classified the relationship between pedagogy and content as *Content Knowledge.*

From this, Content Knowledge was divided into three subcategories: (a) *subject matter content knowledge,* (b) *pedagogical content knowledge,* and (c) *curricular knowledge.*

Subject matter content knowledge relates to the amount and organization of knowledge in the mind of the teacher. For example, Bloom's Taxonomy is a way we can organize content knowledge from the lower-order thinking skills of being able to remember the facts of a subject to the higher-order thinking skills of the ability to create new understandings of the subject matter. Related to this, teachers must understand and be able to convey the syntax of their subject. The syntax is the processes and procedures each subject area uses to determine truth, falsehood, validity, or invalidity. Also, when there are competing claims regarding an issue in the discipline, subject syntax provides the rules for determining which claim has greater warrant. According to Shulman (1986),

> teachers must not only be capable of defining for students accepted truths in a domain. They must also be able to explain why a particular position is deemed warranted, why it is worth knowing, and how it relates to other propositions, both within the discipline and without, both in theory and in practice. (p. 9)

Pedagogical Content Knowledge accesses the dimension of knowledge about a subject area for the purposes of teaching it. This knowledge focuses on the ways of representing and formulating the subject that make it comprehensible to others. In this sense, a sound understanding of educational methodologies is central in helping the teacher represent the subject through relevant and appropriate instructional activities based on research as well as those derived from wisdom and experience with the subject matter as a teacher. Teachers must understand what makes learning the subject area easy or difficult at different ages and maturity and what conceptions and misconceptions students will most likely bring to the subject area. Teachers need knowledge of the strategies most likely to be fruitful in the (re)organizing of a student's understanding of the subject area (Shulman, 1986).

Curricular Knowledge is the full range of programs designed for the teaching of particular subjects and topics to be covered at a given level, the variety of instructional materials available in relation to those programs, the indicators used to determine advancement in the subject area, and the variety of approaches and resources available for teaching the subject area.

In reflecting on the expertise of the teachers involved in his study and the knowledge and professionalism they displayed, Shulman ends with a further refining of Shaw's original quote, "Those who can, do. Those who understand, teach."

Bringing the topic back to the focus of this book, Koehler and Mishra (2009) introduced educators to Technological Pedagogical Content Knowledge building upon the work of Shulman and specifically bringing technology into the pedagogical discussion. They set forth the model presented in Graphic 4.4.

**Graphic 4.4** The TPACK Framework

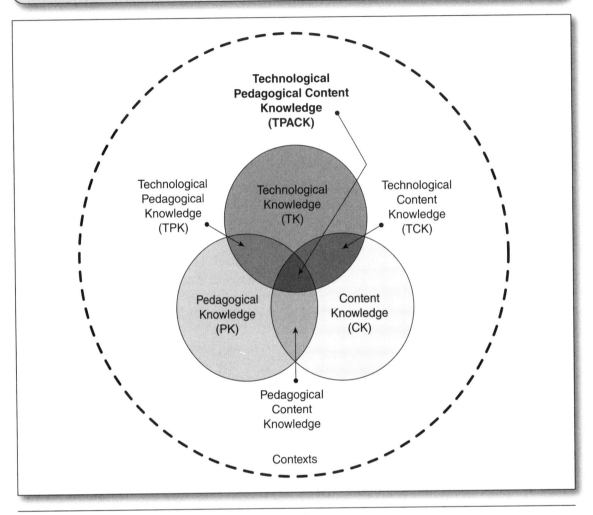

In the middle of the conceptual model are three concentric circles. Content Knowledge (CK) refers to a teacher's knowledge about the subject matter he or she is responsible for teaching students. This is directly linked with the concept of Subject Matter Content Knowledge as espoused by Shulman. Pedagogical Knowledge (PK) is the teacher's deep knowledge about the processes and methods of teaching and learning. This is consistent with a teacher's knowledge of educational realities such as how students learn, cognitive development, classroom management skills, lesson planning, and student assessment. As noted by Koehler and Mishra (2009), teachers should be aware of

how students construct knowledge and acquire skills and how they develop habits of mind and positive dispositions toward learning. As such, pedagogical knowledge requires an understanding of cognitive, social, and developmental theories of learning and how they apply to students in the classroom. (p. 64)

Overlapping these two constructs is Pedagogical Content Knowledge (PCK). This relates to the teachers' ability to interpret the subject matter, find multiple ways to represent it, and adapts and tailors the instructional materials to alternative conceptions and students' prior knowledge. This area covers the "core business of teaching, learning, curriculum, assessment, and reporting student achievement" (p. 64).

Technological Knowledge (TK) relates to the teachers' ability to understand technology broadly enough to apply it productively at work and in the educational process to help in the growth and development of their students. It is about not seeing computer literacy as an end state but something that is developmental and adaptable regardless of the actual technology device. In this sense, it is an evolving, lifetime effort. Intersecting CK and TK is Technological Content Knowledge (TCK).

> This is an understanding of the manner in which technology and content influence and constrain one another. Teachers need to master more than the subject matter they teach; they must also have a deep understanding of the manner in which the subject matter can be changed by the application of specific technologies. (Koehler & Mishra, 2009, p. 65)

It is about visioning the relationship between technology and the content area and how one improves the other and challenges the other. Between PK and TK is Technological Pedagogical Knowledge (TPK). This relates to the ability of the teacher to see beyond the actual design of the technology and understand it within the pedagogical realm of advancing student learning and understanding. For example, most technology is not specifically designed for educational use such as word processing or blogs or video recording. It becomes the responsibility of the educator to see its educational application within the curriculum. This is TPK.

At the core of the model and intersecting all the concentric circles is Technological Pedagogical Content Knowledge (TPACK). This is an understanding that emerges from the interactions among content, pedagogy, and technology knowledge. This is the basis of effective teaching with technology, requiring an understanding of the representation of concepts using technologies; pedagogical techniques that use technology in constructive ways to teach content; knowledge of what makes concepts difficult or easy to learn and how technology can help redress some of the problems that students face; knowledge of student's prior knowledge and theories of epistemology; and knowledge of how technologies can be used to build on existing knowledge to develop new understandings and conceptions of their world (Koehler & Mishra, 2009, p. 66).

In this pedagogical reality, there is no single technological solution for any given curricular situation, and there is no right pedagogy whether it is teacher-centered, critical pedagogy, behaviorism, or learning style theory. The focus is more about understanding the context and seeing how technology, pedagogy, and content knowledge can interplay to advance student growth and achievement. This allows the curriculum to be timeless regardless of the technology of the day. It is more dependent on an articulate teacher who sees the potential of various technologies to solve the learning needs of 21st century students and their learning. This is the teaching and learning environment most responsive to 21st century schools.

## FUTURE CHALLENGES

The context and reality of the educational process is changing. Within this change, states, provinces, and federal governments are recognizing that the very nature of learning in the 21st century is different. Much of this reenvisioning is happening as a direct result of the way that technology has impacted the way we think, understand, and create in our world. This educational change is also sparked by a changing business reality that requires entrepreneurs, industry, and workers who conceptualize the work world in 21st century ways. Educators must respond to these changes by preparing students who are at a minimum technologically literate. Among other sources, school leaders need to review Shifting Minds out of Canada and the Partnership for 21st Century Skills Framework as possible guides for bringing this new culture of learning into their curriculums.

## REFLECTIVE ACTIVITIES

1. In creating a 21st century school, which of the four models presented in this chapter is most related to the vision you have for your school and students? Why?

2. How would you describe the link between content, technology, and pedagogy?

3. Write down your personal thoughts on the TPACK model. Is this something you would like to share with your faculty? Why or Why not? If you do, describe the ways you would do this.

# The Culture of Technology 5

## THE PRINCIPAL AS THE BUILDER OF TECHNOLOGY CULTURE

Beyond the reality of having the actual technological devices and systems in public schools, school administrators should be aware of a new educational culture and responsibility that come with 21st century learning and schools. As was discussed in Chapter 4, one of the core realities associated with 21st century learning is that technology is interwoven into the educational experience and that there is a close relationship among technology, pedagogy, and the content. Consequently, if school administrators get too focused on the "tools" of technology, they will be missing out on the essence of 21st century learning. In this new educational paradigm, educators are helping their students with developing essential competencies, dispositions, and literacies that will enable students to navigate an increasingly technological and changing world. Further considering the discussion in Chapter 8, we come to realize that we should not be basing our school infrastructure around a specific piece of technology but should instead be future-proofing our schools. This means that the actual infrastructure of the school is adaptable to changing devices and concepts of teaching, learning, and processing information. So too is the reality with students and technology. Twenty-first century learning is about helping young learners be adaptable and literate in the cultural, societal, and technological aspects of their world. It is not about the device itself, but more about the ability to be responsive, responsible, and innovative in technological use, no matter the device. This is the culture of technology, and school administrators, technology coordinators, and curriculum leaders have an integral responsibility in its creation.

- Be responsive
- Be responsible
- Be innovative
No matter the device!

*Embrace the opportunities, Be creative, work through frustration!*

*How to incorporate tech into daily learning?*

*How to incorporate tech to being used in the classroom?*

*★ 21st century learning is really not a choice.*

The reality for schools that are integrating technology into school practices and educational activities is that the process is going to impact administrators, teachers, students, and families in both positive and negative ways. There is going to be excitement over the educational opportunities and the potential for real learning change. There is also going to be frustration over just how to incorporate technology into daily learning and how technology is actually going to be used in the classroom. It is one thing to have the vision for one-to-one learning, and it is another thing to plan it and do it. Educators need to embrace the opportunities and try to be creative in working through the frustrations because the educational reality is that 21st century learning is really not a choice. It is educational reform that needs to happen. Take a moment to reflect on Figure 5.1 from "The Digital Learning Imperative: How Technology and Teaching Meet Today's Education Challenges."

As a society, we cannot continue to lose this many students and have this many students ill-prepared for the needs of a 21st century economy. At the same time, students, as well as teachers, are genuinely excited about the learning opportunities that digital learning can bring. Research conducted by iTEC (Oldfield, 2012) found that there was a significant cultural and pedagogic change happening in the more than 1,200 classrooms surveyed across Europe. In the study, 85% of teachers reported that they felt confident in their digital technology skills. With this confidence, there was a solid connection established to the amount of time that technology was used in the classroom with 44% of the teachers reporting digital technology being used in 41% to 100% of their lessons. In addition, 56% of the teachers reported an increase in technology usage from their previous year of teaching. Of this increase in technology usage, teachers reported computer projection; digital resources such as e-books, databases; digital media tools such as video cameras, YouTube, Flickr; and text communication such as e-mail as their most used technologies. Of the most used technologies, 30.5% of teachers reported that computer projection technologies were very useful in aiding learning. Interactive whiteboards were rated second at 16.6%. Within this study, some 280,000 students were also surveyed about their ideas on technology in the classroom. The following list represents how students want to see technology in the classroom:

1. Schools provide students with netbooks.

2. Teachers focus on developing 21st century skills such as collaborative and social skills.

3. Schools provide students with digital exercise books and digital paper.

4. There is an increased focus on new media literacies.

**Figure 5.1** The Leaking Pipeline

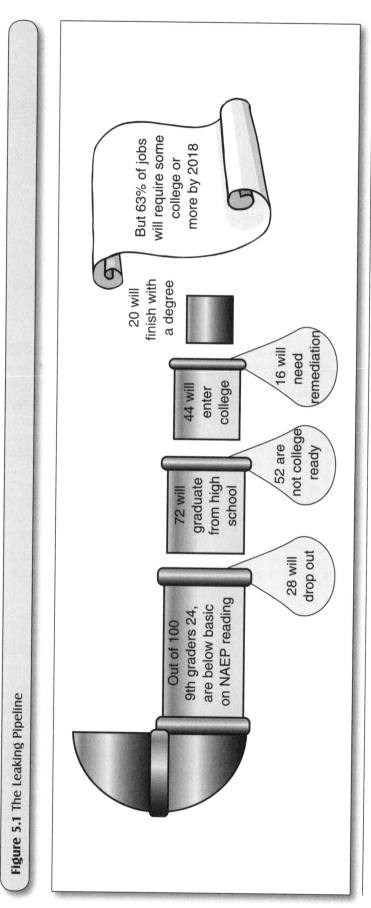

Out of 100 9th graders 24, are below basic on NAEP reading

28 will drop out

72 will graduate from high school

52 are not college ready

44 will enter college

16 will need remediation

20 will finish with a degree

But 63% of jobs will require some college or more by 2018

*Source:* Alliance for Excellent Education. (2012). The Digital Learning Imperative: How Technology and Teaching Meet Today's Education Challenges. Retrieved from http://www.all4ed.org/files/DigitalLearningImperative.pdf

5. Schools increasingly teach specialist skills for specific jobs.

6. Schools provide unlimited access to the Internet when using a computer on school premises.

7. Pedagogies based on game design principles and play are increasingly seen as a tool for enjoying teaching and learning.

8. Learners work on projects, doing authentic tasks, and using technology creatively to tackle real challenges; this includes discovery-based learning.

9. Teachers use whole bodies of connected evidence from a variety of media to assess students.

10. Computers don't just present information but begin to understand its meaning. Intelligent systems learn what students are interested in and help them get what they want.

Notice in this list that it is not necessarily about the technology, but more about how they see the culture of learning in the classroom differently. Table 5.1 from the iTEC study portrays a real cultural shift in how the educational process is conceptualized when we bring technology, content, and pedagogy together.

**Table 5.1** Taxonomy of Technology

| Taxonomy | Category | Top Results |
|---|---|---|
| Activities and interactions (including pedagogy) | Curriculum and Assessment Knowledge and Skills | 1. Teachers focus on developing 21st century skills such as collaborative and social skills.<br><br>2. There is an increased focus on new media literacies.<br><br>3. Schools increasingly teach specialist skills for specific jobs.<br><br>4. Pedagogies based on game design principles and play are increasingly seen as a tool for enjoying teaching and learning.<br><br>5. Learners work on projects, doing authentic tasks and using technology creatively to tackle real challenges; this includes discovery-based learning.<br><br>6. Teachers use whole bodies of connected evidence from a variety of media to assess students. |
| Environment | Learning Spaces | 1. Learning spaces are designed to accommodate different learning activities. |

| Taxonomy | Category | Top Results |
|---|---|---|
| | | 2. Areas are set-up so that students can work as a team. The seating and table arrangement can be reconfigured to allow everyone to see and talk to each other. |
| | | 3. Schools have a variety of areas that can be used for lessons or study, including small spaces for individual work, small group working, and whole class teaching. |
| People and roles | Changing Roles | 1. All learners have opportunities to work with other learners and to collaborate locally, nationally, and internationally. |
| | | 2. Learners are able to access formal education at any time of the day (people, resources, courses). |
| | | 3. There is an increase in child-centered learning with the teacher building links between children's interests and curricula. |
| Resources (including technology) | Technology | 1. Schools provide students with netbooks. |
| | | 2. Schools provide students with digital exercise books and digital paper. |
| | | 3. Schools provide unlimited access to the Internet when using a computer on school premises. |

When it comes to technology and learning, the researchers determined that students prefer more learner-centered and collaborative opportunities. Flexibility is also central in this learning cultural shift where students want flexibility in their learning spaces and also in terms of the how, when, and with whom learning can happen.

Drawing on this changing reality that both teachers and students are wanting and experiencing, principals will be integral in setting the direction for this technological cultural shift happening in schools around the world. The following material from *Leadership and Effectively Integrating Educational Technology* by Chris Toy (2008) describes 10 ways that principals can be instrumental in creating a 21st century culture of technology in their schools.

1. *Principals must effectively and consistently model the use of the same technology tools they expect teachers to use in their classrooms with students.* A powerful way for a principal to model the use of technology is to integrate it into staff meetings in the same way that teachers might in their classrooms.

*integrate it into staff meetings.*

2. *Principals must be consistent in their decisions and expectations about integrating learning technology in the school.* If a school faculty and administration agree to 21st century learning frameworks, there can be few exceptions to this integration. People will always be able to come up with excuses or rationalizations as to why they can't do it or need more time. Don't waiver in the vision

and the timeline. Granting exceptions just give justification that the previous way of doing things is still acceptable.

*Clear expectations*

3. *The principal's communication about the pace and process of integrating learning technology needs to be clear and reasonable.* In your technology plan, make sure you are clear with your staff about just what you mean by "integrating technology" or by "digital learning." Clarity makes it much easier to set measurable and achievable goals for technology. This clarity also makes it easier for teachers to meet the technological targets you set.

4. *The principal must provide appropriate professional development time and resources to support effective classroom implementation technology.* Appropriate professional development sends a message to faculty that technology and 21st century learning are essential to the school reform process.

5. *The principal must support early adopters and risk takers.* You should be showing enthusiasm toward teachers who are genuinely interested in digital learning or one-to-one learning. This is the type of culture you want to encourage and support in your school. Get these teachers to share their efforts in staff meetings, or provide them with opportunities to attend technology workshops together.

6. *The principal must do whatever it takes to ensure that all staff has early access to the very same digital tools that students will be using in their classrooms.* The general guideline here is that teachers should have opportunities to use the new technology about 1 year to 6 months prior to integrating it into the classroom.

7. *As the educational leader, the principal must make it crystal clear to the technology coordinator that all decisions relating to learning technology will be made by the educational leaders with input from the technology leaders. Not the other way around. In the balance between control of the technology and access for learning, the more important consideration must be access for learning.* If, in the interest of safety and control, students are blocked from the technology and Internet access they need to truly change their learning, students and teachers will see little value in bringing technology into the classroom. In this sense, acceptable use policies are more important than extensive blocks and controls. The principal should establish a culture where staff and students know how to use technology responsibly.

8. *The principal must set and support the expectation that student work will be done and stored using technology.* Technology must be seen within the school as an integral component of how the work of education gets done. Principals must bring technology into the school culture in a way that makes education easier, more effective, or more engaging. If technology doesn't serve this role, then it will just be another burden placed on the shoulders of students and teachers.

9. *Principals must ensure that families and the public are kept informed about the school's goals and progress relating to its use of technology.* The promotional role of principals is essential in creating and establishing 21st century learning culture.

10. *The principal must be an active and public champion for all students, staff members, and the school in moving the vision of fully integrating learning technology*

*for 21st century schools.* Principals must continually articulate how technology integration and digital learning will benefit students and the learning process. Spotlight teachers who are exemplifying best practices and students who have used technology in meaningful and creative ways to improve their learning and achievement.

## Rethinking the Concept of Technology Control

As technology becomes integrated into the 21st century learning experience, educational leaders are beginning to realize that we can no longer exist within a culture of technology control. The scope and variety of ways that technology is entering the learning process is just making this reality of technology control incredibly complex to manage and limits schools from reaching the full potential that new and innovative technologies can have on student achievement. The traditional approach for technology in schools was based on the paradigm of controlling where, when, and how students had access to technology. The computer lab is a prime example of this. On the other end of the spectrum, consider a program of Bring Your Own Device (BYOD) where students can use their own mobile devices to access the Internet through wireless systems in each classroom. In this educational paradigm, there is limited control, and students have anytime-anywhere access to technology and their learning.

The reason that control with technology exists in schools is because there is both a legal and philosophical responsibility to make sure our students are safe. Heavy protection features existed on computers to make sure that students did not use technology in inappropriate and possibly malicious ways. Teachers and administrators wanted to make sure that students stayed on task and focused on only using technology for purely academic purposes. This is called protection, or safety, and will be discussed in the section on culture of responsible use later in this chapter.

Reflecting back on many of the discussions in this book about technology, it is near to impossible to have the same culture of technology control. Twenty-first century learning requires a dramatic shift in how we conceptualize technology culture and how schools should be controlling it. Think closely as to why so many district and local school leaders are hesitant of bringing wireless technology into their schools and then allowing students to access the Internet in their classes through their own mobile devices? Why does this fear exist? Most readers would get the sense that educators are giving up a control feature that was inextricably linked to the culture of technology in schools. The culture was that we couldn't trust students to be responsible in how they used technology, what they were accessing on the mobile devices, and how they would be using these wireless devices in the classroom. Since educators couldn't trust students on the vast and expansive World Wide Web with all its dangers, we had to control students in how they used and accessed technology. This culture of technology presents itself in policies that prohibit broad categories of behavior and access: banning cell phones, blocking social networking sites, filtering certain topics or words. Taken to an extreme, these polices can lead to results ranging from humorous (one student was unable to do a report on his Congressman, Dick Armey, due to a keyword filter) to truly restrictive (where in some districts, teachers and students can only use online services that have been approved with the district) (Massachusetts Educational Technology Advisory Council, 2010, p. 2).

Now this is not necessarily a bad thing because the intent behind this technology control has noble purposes. The issue at hand is that technological advances and the changing culture inherent in 21st century learning are demanding a shift in how educators conceptualize control and what it should look like.

In order to develop young learners who are inventive, inspired, and independent, educators need to create a culture of technology that gives them the freedom and respect to use technology and develop a digital literacy that is meaningful to them—not a culture that is derived from a limited technology perspective grounded in fear and control. So what would this 21st century concept of technology control look like?

- We can and should allow students to manage their own devices. Help them learn the relevant technical and organizational skills, especially as this has become a vital part of life outside school.
- Loosen the Parental Controls. Allow them the freedom and responsibility to manage their school apps, set up their school e-mail, and more. Have someone instruct them on best practices.
- Allow them the freedom to find and use other apps as appropriate to their activities in class.
- You can purchase some apps centrally but otherwise ask parents to purchase the apps. There is an abundance of inexpensive choices.
- A Responsible Use policy should clearly state what is allowed and disallowed. Child and parent alike should sign the policy.
- Freedom and responsibility come with consequence. Define a clear outcome for inappropriate use and act upon it as required.
- Use a Web filter but set restrictions loosely and only block categories of sites that are potentially harmful. Ensure you have monitoring in place so you can track Web usage if needed. Rather than acting as Big Brother, set an expectation of personal responsibility and take action when the standards are not met.
- Allow students the latitude to express their knowledge in different ways and with different tools wherever possible and subject to your prior approval. The process of learning should be more personally meaningful and motivational.
- Let them find and bring tools that they are most comfortable using.
- Give them the latitude to be teachers as well as learners: when they invent, discover, or master something new, have them teach others and create tutorials that you post online. (Gliksman, 2012)

Regardless of the varying level of controls that schools are setting regarding technology use, students are using technology extensively in both their educational and personal lives. We have moved out of the era where, for most students, the only access they had to technology was in the school. Take a look at Graphs 5.1 and 5.2 and the revealing data (n = 330,117 K–12 students) regarding student access to technology in our current context.

**Graphic 5.1** High School Internet Access Outside of School

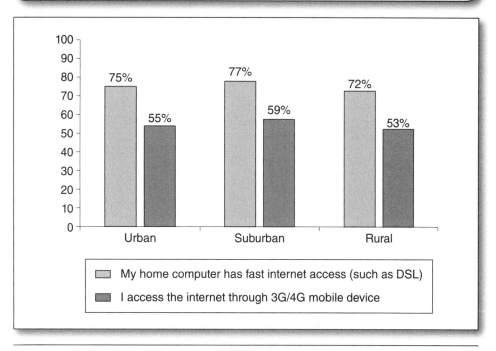

*Source:* Speak Up 2012. (2012). Mapping a personalized Learning Journey: K–12 students and parents connect the dots with digital learning. Retrieved from http://www.tomorrow.org/speakup/pdfs/SU11_PersonalizedLearning_Students.pdf

**Graphic 5.2** Students' Personal Access to Mobile Devices

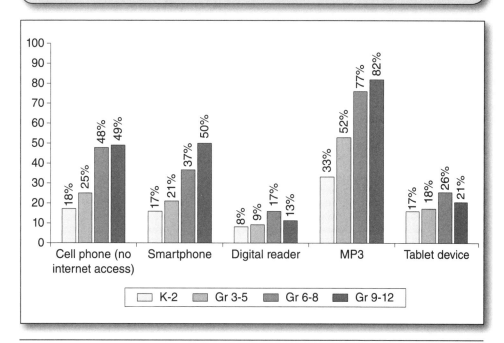

*Source:* Speak Up 2012. (2012). Mapping a personalized Learning Journey: K–12 students and parents connect the dots with digital learning. Retrieved from http://www.tomorrow.org/speakup/pdfs/SU11_PersonalizedLearning_Students.pdf

Students are not only using technology for personal use but also for educational purposes outside of school. In the study cited from the tables just presented, students indicated the following information.

- One in 10 students in Grades 6–12 have sent out a tweet about an academic topic that interests them.
- 15% have informally tutored other students online or found an expert to help them with their own questions.
- 18% have taken an online assessment to evaluate their own self-knowledge.
- One-fifth has used a mobile app to organize their schoolwork.
- One in four has used a video that they found online to help with homework.
- 30% of middle school students and 46% of high school students have used Facebook as a way to collaborate on classroom group projects.
- Almost half of high school students have sought out information online to help them better understand a topic that is being studied in class.

Students are showing educators that they can use technology as a part of their self-directed learning. In order for schools to provide that rich, digital experience that students need, the concept of control has to synchronize with the technological requirements of 21st century learning and to be more in line with how students are actually acting out their learning. Table 5.2 lists the areas of technology control that students saw as a problem, as presented in the Project Tomorrow study (Speak Up 2012, 2012).

**Table 5.2** Student Perceived Barriers to Technology Use in Schools

| Obstacles to Tech Use at School | Students: Grade 6–8 | Students: Grade 9–12 |
| --- | --- | --- |
| I cannot use my own mobile devices. | 57% | 55% |
| I cannot access my social networking site. | 50% | 51% |
| Websites I need for learning are blocked. | 49% | 59% |
| I cannot use my communications tools. | 42% | 39% |
| Teachers limit how I can use technology. | 40% | 42% |

These students are telling educators that in setting up restrictive controls on technology usage, educators are limiting their learning potential. The students were also questioned about what would be their wish list regarding technology use at school. The suggestions were the following:

- 47% of students wanted unlimited Wi-Fi Internet access throughout the school.
- 38% would like technological tools to help organize their schoolwork.
- 37% asked for access to the school network from home, school, or wherever they were with their mobile device.
- 36% of students wanted communications tools to support their interactions with other students and their teachers.
- 32% would like collaboration tools to work with their classmates on schoolwork projects.

Within this study, there was a great deal of discussion about mobile learning and digital learning through access with mobile devices. The students in this study want to bring mobile devices into the school and classroom and recognize that there will be many benefits to their learning due to the ease of access to content information, collaboration opportunities, and organizational infrastructures. The question for educators is whether or not we are ready to operate under a new concept of technological control that would open up these kinds of learning opportunities for students and teachers. Graph 5.3 presents a picture of how students would use mobile devices in their learning.

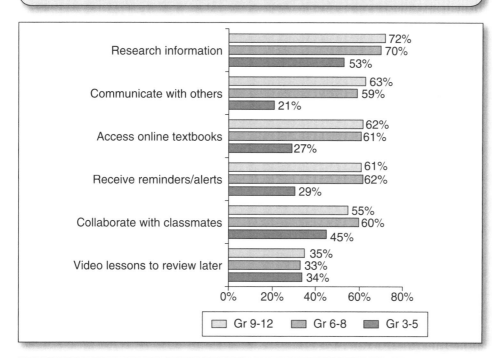

**Graphic 5.3** Personalized Learning Through Mobile Devices at School

*Source:* Speak Up 2012. (2012). Mapping a personalized Learning Journey: K–12 students and parents connect the dots with digital learning. Retrieved from http://www.tomorrow.org/speakup/pdfs/SU11_PersonalizedLearning_Students.pdf

As a final picture of this changing culture of technology control in schools, the researchers in the Project Tomorrow study asked parents, students, and principals to conceptualize their ideal model for bringing technology into the school. In looking at Graph 5.4, readers will begin to see that due to the digital, wireless, and social network realities of this technology, traditional forms of technology control would make this technology reality near to impossible. In this sense, educators need to ask themselves about how they can rethink the way technology is controlled in their school so that 21st century learning can happen.

## A New Culture of Digital Citizens

Reflecting on the discussion in the previous section, it is apparent that technology safety and control is shifting from being the sole responsibility of school administrators, teachers, and technology coordinators to a model of shared

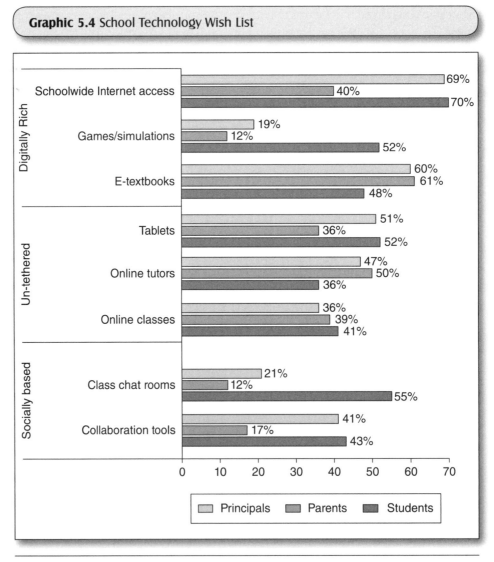

**Graphic 5.4** School Technology Wish List

*Source:* Speak Up 2012. (2012). Mapping a personalized Learning Journey: K–12 students and parents connect the dots with digital learning. Retrieved from http://www.tomorrow.org/speakup/pdfs/SU11_PersonalizedLearning_Students.pdf

responsibility among educators, students, and families. This is directly in line with the philosophical basis of 21st century learning where the educational focus is on helping students to become digitally literate. In one sense, they become digital learners who are aware of and understand the norms of appropriate and responsible technology use. Taking it further, technology and academic plans in schools should address helping young learners to become digital citizens. The authors of this book have done extensive reading and discussion with colleagues on this topic. The following information represents a solid framework and guide for creating a culture of digital citizenry with the students in your school.

## Nine Themes of Digital Citizenship (digitalcitizenship.net)

1. *Digital Access: Full Electronic Participation in Society.* Technology users need to be aware of and support electronic access for all to create a foundation for digital citizenship. Digital exclusion of any kind does not enhance the growth of users in an electronic society. All people should have fair access to technology no matter who they are. Places or organizations with limited connectivity need to be addressed as well. To become productive citizens, we need to be committed to equal digital access.

2. *Digital Commerce: Electronic Buying and Selling of Goods.* Technology users need to understand that a large share of market economy is being done electronically. Legitimate and legal exchanges are occurring, but the buyer or seller needs to be aware of the issues associated with it. The mainstream availability of Internet purchases of toys, clothing, cars, food, etc. has become commonplace to many users. At the same time, an equal amount of goods and services that are in conflict with the laws or morals of some countries are surfacing (which might include activities such as illegal downloading, pornography, and gambling). Users need to learn about how to be effective consumers in a new digital economy.

3. *Digital Communication: Electronic Exchange of Information.* One of the significant changes within the digital revolution is a person's ability to communicate with other people. In the 19th century, forms of communication were limited. In the 21st century, communication options have exploded to offer a wide variety of choices (e.g., e-mail, cellular phones, instant messaging). The expanding digital communication options have changed everything because people are able to keep in constant communication with anyone else. Now everyone has the opportunity to communicate and collaborate with anyone from anywhere and anytime. Unfortunately, many users have not been taught how to make appropriate decisions when faced with so many different digital communication options.

4. *Digital Literacy: Process of Teaching and Learning About Technology and the Use of Technology.* While schools have made great progress in the area of technology infusion, much remains to be done. A renewed focus must be made on what technologies must be taught as well as how they should be

used. New technologies are finding their way into the workplace that are not being used in schools (e.g., videoconferencing, online sharing spaces such as wikis). In addition, workers in many different occupations need immediate information (just-in-time information). This process requires sophisticated searching and processing skills (i.e., information literacy). Learners must be taught how to learn in a digital society. In other words, learners must be taught to learn anything, anytime, anywhere. Business, military, and medicine are excellent examples of how technology is being used differently in the 21st century. As new technologies emerge, learners need to learn how to use that technology quickly and appropriately. Digital citizenship involves educating people in a new way—these individuals need a high degree of information literacy skills.

5. *Digital Etiquette: Electronic Standards of Conduct or Procedure.* Technology users often see this area as one of the most pressing problems when dealing with digital citizenship. We recognize inappropriate behavior when we see it, but before people use technology, they do not learn digital etiquette (i.e., appropriate conduct). Many people feel uncomfortable talking to others about their digital etiquette. Often rules and regulations are created or the technology is simply banned to stop inappropriate use. It is not enough to create rules and policy, we must teach everyone to become responsible digital citizens in this new society.

6. *Digital Law: Electronic Responsibility for Actions and Deeds.* Digital law deals with the ethics of technology within a society. Unethical use manifests itself in the form of theft and/or crime. Ethical use manifests itself in the form of abiding by the laws of society. Users need to understand that stealing or causing damage to other people's work, identity, or property online is a crime. There are certain rules of society that users need to be aware of in an ethical society. These laws apply to anyone who works or plays online. Hacking into others' information, downloading illegal music, plagiarizing, creating destructive worms, viruses or creating Trojan Horses, sending spam, or stealing anyone's identify or property is unethical.

7. *Digital Rights and Responsibilities: Those Freedoms Extended to Everyone in a Digital World.* Just as in the American Constitution where there is a Bill of Rights, there is a basic set of rights extended to every digital citizen. Digital citizens have the right to privacy, free speech, etc. Basic digital rights must be addressed, discussed, and understood in the digital world. With these rights also come responsibilities as well. Users must help define how the technology is to be used in an appropriate manner. In a digital society, these two areas must work together for everyone to be productive.

8. *Digital Health and Wellness: Physical and Psychological Well-Being in a Digital Technology World.* Eye safety, repetitive stress syndrome, and sound ergonomic practices are issues that need to be addressed in a new technological world. Beyond the physical issues are those of the psychological issues that are becoming more prevalent such as Internet addiction. Users need to be taught that there inherent dangers of technology. Digital citizenship includes a culture

where technology users are taught how to protect themselves through education and training.

9. *Digital Security (Self-Protection): Electronic Precautions to Guarantee Safety.* In any society, there are individuals who steal, deface, or disrupt other people. The same is true for the digital community. It is not enough to trust other members in the community for our own safety. In our own homes, we put locks on our doors and fire alarms in our houses to provide some level of protection. The same must be true for the digital security. We need to have virus protection, backups of data, and surge control of our equipment. As responsible citizens, we must protect our information from outside forces that might cause disruption or harm.

## Calgary Board of Education (CBE) Policy on Digital Learning

The following material represents how one school district is handling digital citizenry based on the nine themes of digital citizenship in their technology plan.

The following activities are prohibited and will be addressed on an individual basis as needed:

- Use of someone else's CBE account or access to the Learner Accessible Wireless Network (LAWN)
- Sharing of usernames and passwords for other people to use
- Sending, posting, displaying or using obscene language/messages or pictures or information about oneself or others
- Harassing, insulting, or attacking another person or their reputation
- Viewing websites through a proxy server
- Plagiarism of online content
- Texting or gaming
- Tampering with any computer accessories, hardware, or software
- Use of technology or accessing sites not approved by staff
- Trespassing in others' folders, work areas, or files
- Utilizing another student's device without permission
- The following sites are prohibited from use:
  - Vulgar or lewd depictions of the human body
  - Any adult content
  - Violent act
  - Online gambling
  - Social networking sites (such as Facebook, Nexopia, etc.)
  - Sites that encourage the use of illicit or illegal substances
  - Sites that advocate hatred or violence against an identifiable group
  - Sites promoting criminal activity
  - Noneducational games
  - And many more (see the link below for the complete list)

This is the specific CBE filter Level 2 (www.innovativelearning.ca/sec-learntech/POD/f2.html).

Our expectation is that our students will become educated and responsible digital citizens. If, however, students breach any of the above, each situation will be dealt with on an individual basis and may result in

- Restriction or loss of technology privileges
- Restriction of use or confiscation of personal device
- School based disciplinary consequences
- Police intervention and/or legal action

Lastly, it is important that parents/guardians and students remember the following as we begin this new educational opportunity:

- The school is not responsible for the loss, damage, or theft of student electronic devices.
- The school is not able to provide technical support for student devices.
- Devices can only be utilized when students are under the direct supervision of a teacher in an approved area of the school.
- Devices can only be utilized for educational purposes.
- Misuse will be determined by the staff and administration.

We view digital citizenship as a shared responsibility between students, their families, and the school. We appreciate families taking time to discuss this new opportunity with their children and supporting the work of the school in moving it forward. In discussing this matter at the family level, all students and families are to sign a Digital Citizenship Plan and return it to the appropriate school administrator. Each local school within CBE can adapt this based on specific local needs and student population variations.

## Calgary Board of Education (CBE) Digital Citizenship Plan

In reviewing local digital citizenship plans, readers of this book can use this as a guide or a starting point for developing their own digital contract between students, families, and the school. Readers can also refer to Resource A at the end of this chapter for a graphic of a wireless network that is responsive to digital citizenry.

- ☐  I will make a plan with my parent(s)/guardian(s) around technology use (time, location, turning my phone off or leaving it in the kitchen at bedtime, online purchasing, etc.) at home.

  Plan Details:

  _____

- ☐  I understand that my phone and/or other tech device will be turned off at bedtime and I will not use it.

- ☐  I understand that we have an "open phone/technology" policy. That means my parent(s)/guardian(s) can review my calls, texts, e-mails, and/or _____ whenever they want.

☐ In my family, we always use passwords and we change them often. I will not give out my passwords to anyone—even best friends—other than my parent(s)/guardian (s).

☐ If a stranger ever contacts me or texts me, I will show my parents.

☐ I will not fight, swear, or gossip in e-mails or instant messages. I never respond to inflammatory, obscene, or insulting e-mails or to messages that are mean or in any way make me feel uncomfortable.

☐ If someone is mean to me online, I won't respond. I'll tell my trusted adult so we can make a plan to work together to solve the issue.

☐ If I see someone being mean to another person online, I will tell a trusted adult to get help.

☐ I will speak up and tell someone if I see something on the Internet that is wrong, inappropriate, or criminal in nature. I will be a good online citizen and not do anything that hurts other people or is against the law.

☐ I will not post or share personal pictures of myself or others on the Internet, by phone or

_____.

☐ We do not give out personal indentifying information such as our name, address, date of birth, school name, and/or phone number on a website or to people we meet online.

☐ If someone asks me something inappropriate when I am online, I understand that I need to tell my parent(s)/guardian(s). I also know I will not get in trouble and that telling my parent(s)/guardian(s) helps keep me safe and builds trust.

☐ I will not lie about my age to join any website and understand that the rules are designed to help keep me safe.

☐ I never download pictures, freeware, shareware, or text from unknown sources or websites we don't trust. I understand that plagiarism is cheating and pirating music, movies, and games is stealing.

☐ I will never open e-mail attachments from an unknown person or company. I do not follow links to websites through e-mail or click on pop-ups.

☐ I never respond to spam or junk mail. I keep my primary e-mail address only for use by my friends and family.

☐ I understand that there are consequences for not following these rules. Those consequences may include things like losing the privilege to use my phone or computer.

☐ I understand this digital citizenship plan is for my well-being and safety because my parent(s)/caregiver(s) love me.

☐ _____

☐ _____

☐ _____

☐ _____

☐ _____

☐ _____

_____         _____

Child's Signature                Parent's Signature

_____         _____

Date                             Date

As part of this new initiative, the CBE has provided students and educators with a variety of resources to help in the integration of digital citizenry into the school culture. Readers can refer to the website listed for a complete list of their resources and their relevant URL links (www.cbe.ab.ca/learninginnovation/digitalsafety-digitalcitizenship-mediaawareness.asp).

For the purposes of this book, some of the resources include:

*Nine Elements of Digital Citizenship:* a free Internet resource to support understanding of digital citizenship.

*Privacy Pirates:* Licensed website that is a game-based platform addressing concepts related to privacy and the Internet.

*Passport to the Internet:* Licensed website that is an interactive, role-playing resource to help in issues related to digital citizenship.

*My World:* Licensed website for high school students that includes Internet safety lessons, resources, activities, and games related to digital citizenship.

*The Association for Media Literacy:* A free Canadian resource for media literacy in education for teachers, parents, and students.

## A Culture of Responsibility

As the shift of responsibility for safety and proper use of technology moves into a shared framework among educators, students, and families, school administrators have a variety of constructs they need to address in their schools. The following sections describe some of these cultural educational realities.

### Cyberbullying

Cyberbullying is a growing concern among educators and parents. Cyberbullying is bullying that takes place using electronic technology. Electronic technology includes devices such as cell phones, computers, and iPads. It usually happens on communication tools such as social media sites, text messages, and information uploading sites like YouTube. Cyberbullying can take the form of mean/threatening text messages or e-mails, rumors, or gossip posted on social media sites, and/or embarrassing pictures or videos posted on websites. Graphs 5.5a and 5.5b describe the reality of cyberbullying among students.

**Graphic 5.5a** Cyberbullying by Gender

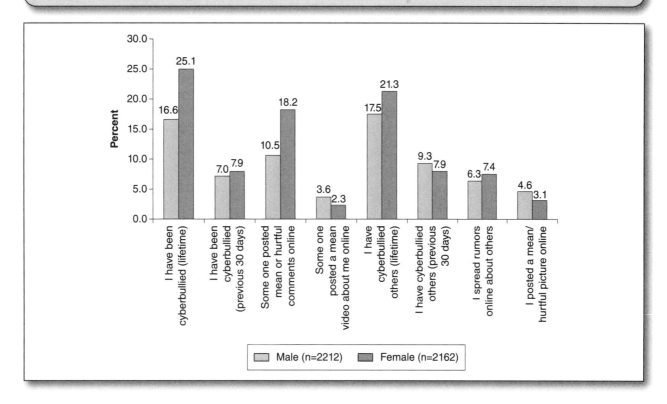

**Graphic 5.5b** Cyberbullying by Offense

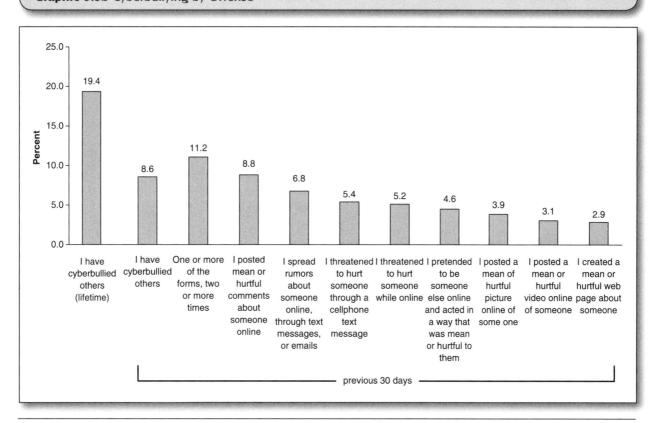

*Source:* Cyberbullying Research Center (2013).

Cyberbullying is real, and educators have a responsibility to create a culture of zero tolerance. There is a variety of resources available to help school administrators address this matter and develop a culture of respect and responsible technology usage among students. A great place to start is the website available at www.stopbullying.gov/cyberbullying/index.html or the National School Boards Association website. As an aid to principals and district leaders, the stopbullying.gov group conducted a review of state educational laws as they pertain to bullying. Their research indicated the following as core elements in a cyberbullying initiative. As a beginning point in establishing a culture of zero tolerance as it relates to cyberbullying, principals and educational leaders would benefit from making sure their current policies align with this infrastructure.

## Cyber- and Antibullying Policy Framework

1. Purpose Statement

    a. Outlines the range of detrimental effects bullying has on students, including impacts on student learning, school safety, student engagement, and the school environment.

    b. Declares that any form, type, or level of bullying is unacceptable and that every incident needs to be taken seriously by school administrators, school staff (including teachers), students, and students' families.

    *Example Statement:*

    **Oklahoma**: Okla. Stat. Ann. Tit. 70, § 24–100.3 (2009): "The Legislature finds that bullying has a negative effect on the social environment of schools, creates a climate of fear among students, inhibits their ability to learn, and leads to other antisocial behavior. Bullying behavior has been linked to other forms of antisocial behavior, such as vandalism, shoplifting, skipping and dropping out of school, fighting, and the use of drugs and alcohol . . . Successful programs to recognize, prevent, and effectively intervene in bullying behavior have been developed and replicated in schools across the country. These schools send the message that bullying behavior is not tolerated and, as a result, have improved safety and created a more inclusive learning environment."

2. Statement of Scope: *Covers conduct that occurs on the school campus, at school-sponsored activities or events (regardless of the location), on school-provided transportation, or through school-owned technology, or that otherwise creates a significant disruption to the school environment.*

    *Example Statement:*

    **Indiana**: Ind. Code Ann. § 20–33–8-13.5 (b) (2010), Disciplinary Rule Requirements: "The discipline rules [related to bullying] . . . must apply when a student is: (1) on school grounds immediately before or during school hours, immediately after school hours, or at any other time when the school is being used by a school group; (2) off school grounds at a school activity, function, or event; (3) traveling to or from school or a school activity, function or event; or (4) using property or equipment provided by the school."

3. Specification of Prohibited Conduct

   a. Provides a specific definition of bullying that includes a clear definition of cyberbullying. The definition of bullying includes a nonexclusive list of specific behaviors that constitute bullying and specifies that bullying includes intentional efforts to harm one or more individuals, may be direct or indirect, is not limited to behaviors that cause physical harm, and may be verbal (including oral and written language) or nonverbal. The definition of bullying can be easily understood and interpreted by school boards, policymakers, school administrators, school staff, students, students' families, and the community.

   b. Is consistent with other federal, state, and local laws.

   c. Prohibited conduct also includes

      i  Retaliation for asserting or alleging an act of bullying.

      ii Perpetuating bullying or harassing conduct by spreading hurtful or demeaning material even if the material was created by another person (e.g., forwarding offensive e-mails or text messages).

   ***Example Statement:***

   **Kansas**: Kan. Stat. Ann. § 72–8256.C.2 (2009): "'Cyberbullying' means bullying by use of any electronic communication device through means including, but not limited to, e-mail, instant messaging, text messages, blogs, mobile phones, pagers, online games and websites."

4. Enumeration of Specific Characteristics

   a. Explains that bullying may include, but is not limited to, acts based on actual or perceived characteristics of students who have historically been targets of bullying and provides examples of such characteristics.

   b. Makes clear that bullying does not have to be based on any particular characteristic.

   ***Example Statement:***

   **North Carolina**: N.C. Gen. Stat. § 115C-407.15(a) (2010): "Bullying or harassing behavior includes, but is not limited to, acts reasonably perceived as being motivated by any actual or perceived differentiating characteristic, such as race, color, religion, ancestry, national origin, gender, socioeconomic status, academic status, gender identity, physical appearance, sexual orientation, or mental, physical, developmental, or sensory disability, or by association with a person who has or is perceived to have one or more of these characteristics."

5. Development and Implementation of Local Education Agencies (LEA): *Directs every LEA to develop and implement a policy prohibiting bullying through a collaborative process with all interested stakeholders, including school administrators, staff, students, students' families, and the community, in order to best address local conditions.*

*Example Statement:*

**Maryland**: Md. Code Ann., Educ. § 7–424.1(c) (2010): "[1] Each county board shall establish a policy prohibiting bullying, harassment, or intimidation. . . . [3] A county board shall develop the policy in consultation with representatives of the following groups: (i) Parents or guardians of students; (ii) School employees and administrators; (iii) School volunteers; (iv) Students; and (v) Members of the community."

6. Components of LEA

   a. *Reporting of Bullying*

   iii Includes a procedure for students, students' families, staff, and others to report incidents of bullying, including a process to submit such information anonymously and with protection from retaliation. The procedure identifies and provides contact information for the appropriate school personnel responsible for receiving the report and investigating the incident.

   iv Requires that school personnel report, in a timely and responsive manner, incidents of bullying they witness or are aware of to a designated official.

   *Example Statement:*

   **Wisconsin**: Wis. Stat. § 118.46.1(a) (2009): "The [policy on bullying] shall include all of the following: . . . (6) A requirement that school district officials and employees report incidents of bullying and identify the persons to whom the reports must be made."

   b. *Investigating and Responding to Bullying:* Includes a procedure for promptly investigating and responding to any report of an incident of bullying, including immediate intervention strategies for protecting the victim from additional bullying or retaliation, and includes notification to parents of the victim, or reported victim, of bullying and the parents of the alleged perpetrator, and if appropriate, notification to law enforcement officials.

   *Example Statement:*

   **Massachusetts**: 2010 Mass. Adv. Legis. Serv. Ch. No. 71.370(g) (2010): "Upon receipt of such a report, the school principal or a designee shall promptly conduct an investigation. If the school principal or a designee determines that bullying or retaliation has occurred, the school principal or designee shall (i) notify the local law enforcement

THE CULTURE OF TECHNOLOGY

agency if the school principal or designee believes that criminal charges may be pursued against a perpetrator; (ii) take appropriate disciplinary action; (iii) notify the parents or guardians of a perpetrator; and (iv) notify the parents or guardians of the victim, and to the extent consistent with state and federal law, notify them of the action taken to prevent any further acts of bullying or retaliation."

c. **Written Records:** Include a procedure for maintaining written records of all incidents of bullying and their resolution.

**Example Statement:**

**California**: Cal. Educ. Code § 234.1 (2010): "The department shall assess whether local educational agencies have done all of the following: . . . (e) Maintained documentation of complaints and their resolution for a minimum of one review cycle."

d. **Sanctions:** Include a detailed description of a graduated range of consequences and sanctions for bullying.

**Example Statement:**

**Alabama**: Ala. Code § 16.28B.5 (2010): "The model policy, at a minimum, shall contain all of the following components: . . . [4] A series of graduated consequences for any student who commits an act of intimidation, harassment, violence or threats of violence. Punishment shall conform with applicable federal and state disability, antidiscrimination, and education laws and school discipline policies."

e. **Referrals:** Includes a procedure for referring the victim, perpetrator, and other to counseling and mental or other health services, as appropriate.

**Example Statement:**

**Maryland**: Md. Code. Ann., Educ. § 7–424.1.b (2010): "[2] The model policy . . . shall include: . . . (viii) Information about the types of support services available to the student bully, victim, and any bystanders . . . "

7. Review of Local Policies: ***Includes a provision for the state to review local policies on a regular basis to ensure the goals of the state laws are met.***

**Example Statement:**

**Illinois**: 105 Ill. Comp. Stat. Ann. 5/27–23.7(d) (2010): "The policy must be updated every 2 years and filed with the State Board of Education after being updated. The State Board of Education shall monitor the implementation of policies created under [this subsection of the statute]."

8. Communication Plan: ***Includes a plan for notifying students, students' families, and staff of policies related to bullying, including the consequences for engaging in bullying.***

*Example Statement:*

**Arkansas**: Ark. Code Ann. § 6–18–514(b) (2009): "The policies shall: [6] Require that notice of what constitutes bullying, that bullying is prohibited, and the consequences of engaging in bullying be conspicuously posted in every classroom, cafeteria, restroom, gymnasium, auditorium, and school bus in the district; and [7] Require that copies of the notice ... be provided to parents, students, school volunteers, and employees."

9. Training and Preventative Education

   a. Includes a provision for school districts to provide training for all school staff, including, but not limited to, teachers, aides, support staff, and school bus drivers, on preventing, identifying, and responding to bullying.

   b. Encourages school districts to implement age-appropriate school- and community-wide bullying prevention programs.

*Example Statement:*

**South Carolina**: S.C. Code Ann. § 59–63–140 (F) (2009): "Schools and school districts are encouraged to establish bullying prevention programs and other initiatives involving school staff, students, administrators, volunteers, parents, law enforcement, and community members."

10. Transparency and Monitoring

    a. Includes a provision for LEAs to report annually to the state on the number of reported bullying incidents, and any responsive actions taken.

    b. Includes a provision for LEAs to make data regarding bullying incidence publicly available in aggregate with appropriate privacy protections to ensure students are protected.

*Example Statement:*

**Ohio**: Ohio Rev. Code Ann. § 3313.666.10 (2010): "the district administration ... [shall] provide ... a written summary of all reported incidents and post the summary on its website."

11. Statement of Rights to Other Legal Recourse: *Includes a statement that the policy does not preclude victims from seeking other legal remedies.*

*Example Statement:*

**Oregon**: Or. Rev. Stat. Ann. § 339.364 (2009): "Victim may seek redress under other laws. ... [This statute] may not be interpreted to prevent a victim of harassment, intimidation, or bullying or a victim of cyberbullying from seeking redress under any other available law, whether civil or criminal."

*Source:* "Key Components in State Anti-bullying Laws" (2013).

## Cybersafety and Security

The Internet is an amazing place. It is also a dangerous place. Local and national news regularly cover stories related to hackers stealing personal information from computers and databases, or kids being lured into dangerous situations as a result of "meeting" someone in a chat room. Schools have always been responsible for the safety of students while they are in the care of educators. It is a social responsibility that teachers and school administrators take very seriously. In an environment of digital learning and regular technology usage, keeping students safe and secure while online is a very real concern. To this end, cybersafety is the ability to act in a safe and responsible manner when interacting online. It also includes digital behaviors that help students to protect their reputation and to protect their personal information. In establishing a culture of cybersafety in their schools, school administrators should engage their staff and students in a dialogue about cybersafety. School administrators and teachers can focus their discussion within the following areas:

- Talk with students about how to recognize online risks, make informed decisions, and take appropriate actions to protect themselves. This includes helping students know how to identify potentially dangerous online situations and how to appropriately avoid or report them: for example, posting offensive material, "friending" strangers, posting private information, and engaging in or failing to report cyberbullying.
- Talk with students about how to make informed decisions about appropriate protection methods and safe practices in a variety of online situations. This includes helping children understand the importance of following Terms of Use guidelines, disciplined and productive use of Internet time, safely exiting an inappropriate site, protection of passwords, and avoiding cyberbullying.
- Show students how to demonstrate and be an advocate for safe behaviors among peers, family, and community.

*Source:* Internet Keep Safe Coalition (2009).

## Acceptable Use

Twenty-first century digital learning is going to naturally see students increase the amount of time accessing online resources and using school technology for their learning. Digital citizenship is so important because it helps students understand acceptable and responsible ways to use the technology. Acceptable use is basically a policy and a contract between the students and the school that the students will respect district and school technology resources.

The Department of Education in the State of Victoria in Australia has put together a sound template that school administrators can use in establishing necessary agreements between students and schools as it relates to acceptable use. School leaders can use this as a guide to establishing acceptable use practices in their school.

At [INSERT SCHOOL NAME] we

- Support the rights of all members of the school community to engage in and promote a safe, inclusive and supportive learning environment
- Have a Student Engagement Policy that clearly states our school's values and the expected standards of student behavior, including actions and consequences for inappropriate behavior
- Educate our students to be safe and responsible users of digital technologies
- Raise our students' awareness of issues such as online privacy, intellectual property, and copyright
- Supervise students when using digital technologies for educational purposes
- Provide a filtered Internet service but acknowledge that full protection from inappropriate content can never be guaranteed
- Respond to issues or incidents that have the potential to impact on the well-being of our students
- Know that some online activities are illegal, and as such, we are required to report this to the police
- Provide parents/guardians with a copy of this agreement
- Support parents/guardians to understand the importance of safe and responsible use of digital technologies, the potential issues that surround their use and strategies that they can implement at home to support their child

## Acceptable Use Agreement: Upper Primary and Secondary Students

Cybersafety is an important issue for all students. By the time students arrive at secondary school, most will already be regular and active users of digital technologies including social media tools such as Facebook.

Schools that want to support students to behave safely and responsibly online, both inside and out of school, can use this agreement template. Schools can add and/or delete information to make them relevant to the school environment.

Students can work through the behaviors described in Part B at school with their teacher and take it home to share and discuss with their parents.

Part C is for schools that received funding to purchase devices through the National Secondary School Computer Fund (NSSCF). If the school did not receive funding, this section can be deleted.

## Part A: School Profile Statement

[INSERT SCHOOL NAME] recognizes the need for students to be safe and responsible users of digital technologies. We believe that explicitly teaching students about safe and responsible online behaviors is essential and is best taught in partnership with parents/guardians. We request that parents/guardians work with us and encourage this behavior at home.

The school profile statement should focus on programs and procedures that are in place to support safe and responsible use of digital technologies. This statement can define how the school demonstrates their duty of care for students working in online spaces. This statement should be revised regularly to reflect a detailed understanding of the school's relevant programs and procedures as well as online needs of their students.

## Part B: Student Declaration

When I use digital technologies I agree to be a safe, responsible, and ethical user at all times, by

- Respecting others and communicating with them in a supportive manner; never writing or participating in online bullying (for example, forwarding messages and supporting others in harmful, inappropriate, or hurtful online behaviors)

- Protecting my privacy; not giving out personal details, including my full name, telephone number, address, passwords, and images
- Protecting the privacy of others; never posting or forwarding their personal details or images without their consent
- Talking to a teacher if I personally feel uncomfortable or unsafe online, or if I see others participating in unsafe, inappropriate, or hurtful online behaviors
- Carefully considering the content that I upload or post online; this is often viewed as a personal reflection of who I am
- Investigating the terms and conditions (e.g., age restrictions, parental consent requirements). If my understanding is unclear, I will seek further explanation from a trusted adult.
- Confirming that I meet the stated terms and conditions; completing the required registration processes with factual responses about my personal details
- Handling information and communications technology devices with care and notifying a teacher if they are damaged or require attention
- Abiding by copyright and intellectual property regulations. If necessary, I will request permission to use images, text, audio, and video and cite references.
- Not interfering with network systems and security, the data of another user or attempting to log into the network with a user name or password of another student
- Not bringing to school or downloading unauthorized programs, including games

In addition, when I use my personal mobile phone, I agree to be a safe, responsible, and ethical user at all times, by

- Respecting others and communicating with them in a supportive manner; never verbally or in writing participating in bullying (for example, harassing phone calls/text messages, supporting others in harmful, inappropriate, or hurtful online behaviors by forwarding messages)
- Keeping the device on silent during class times; only making or answering calls or messages outside of lesson times (except for approved learning purposes)
- Respecting the privacy of others; only taking photos or recording sound or video at school when I have formal consent or it is part of an approved lesson
- Obtaining appropriate (written) consent from individuals who appear in images or sound and video recordings before forwarding them to other people or posting/uploading them to online spaces

## Part C: Conditions of Use for School-Owned Devices

## Equipment

### Ownership

- If taken home, the student must bring portable devices fully charged to school every day.
- The school retains ownership of the device until the student completes Year 12. At this time ownership of the device will be determined by the school.
- Parents/guardians and students should be aware that files stored on the device, or on the school's server, are not private.
- If the student leaves the school prior to completing Year 12 or moves to another government or nongovernment school, interstate or overseas, the device must be returned to the school.

### Damage or Loss of Equipment

- All devices and batteries are covered by a manufacturer's warranty. The warranty covers manufacturer's defects and normal use of the device. It does not cover negligence, abuse, or malicious damage.
- Any problems, vandalism, damage, loss or theft of the device must be reported immediately to the school.
- In the case of suspected theft, a police report must be made by the family and a copy of the report provided to the school.
- In the case of loss or accidental damage, a statement should be signed by a parent/caregiver and provided to the school.
- Students may be required to replace lost or damaged chargers.
- If a device is damaged or lost, the principal or their nominee will determine whether replacement is appropriate and/or whether the student retains access to a device for home use.
- If a device is damaged and the damage is not covered by the manufacturer's warranty or any of the school's insurance arrangements, the principal may determine that the student will pay the costs of repairing the damage or, if necessary, the costs of replacing the device.

### Standards for Device

The student is responsible for

- Adhering to the school's Acceptable Use Agreement or Student Engagement Policy when using the machine, both at home and school
- Backing up data securely
- Maintaining settings for virus protection, spam, and filtering that have been set as a departmental standard

## Part D: Student Commitment

### Definition of Digital Technologies

This Acceptable Use Agreement applies to digital technologies, social media tools, and learning environments established by our school or accessed using school-owned networks or systems, including (although are not limited to)

- School-owned information and communications technology devices (e.g., desktops, laptops, printers, scanners)
- Mobile phones
- E-mail and instant messaging
- Internet, Intranet, and Ultranet
- Social networking sites (e.g., Facebook, SuperClubsPLUS)
- Video and photo sharing websites (e.g., Picasa, YouTube)
- Blogs
- Microblogs (e.g., Twitter)
- Forums, discussion boards, and groups (e.g., Google groups, Whirlpool)
- Wikis (e.g., Wikipedia)
- Vod and podcasts
- Video conferences and Web conferences.

This Acceptable Use Agreement applies when I am using any of the above digital technologies at school, at home, during school excursions, camps, and extracurricular activities.

I understand and agree to comply with the terms of acceptable use and expected standards of behavior set out within this agreement. I understand that there are actions and consequences established within the [INSERT SCHOOL NAME] Student Engagement Policy if I do not behave appropriately.

Date: _____

Student Name: _____

Name of School Contact: _____

Phone Number of School Contact: _____

Parent/Guardian A Signature: _____

Name of Parent/Guardian A: _____

Parent/Guardian B Signature: _____

Name of Parent/Guardian B: _____

© State of Victoria 2012

Source: Victoria Department of Education and Early Childhood Development (2013).

## FUTURE CHALLENGES

An important part of 21st century learning and schools is recognizing that we are trying to develop a new culture as it relates to technology. This technology culture happens through an articulate principle that creates it at the school level. This culture is about conceptualizing a new relationship between technology and school control. As the level of technology control shifts to a more free and open access to technology and information, a culture of digital citizenship will emerge. From here, digital citizenship requires that students learn to use technology and online activities in safe and responsible ways. As such, a culture of responsible use needs to be stipulated within technology school reform plans. The key concept here is that school administrators, technology coordinators, and curriculum leaders have to be careful that they don't just focus on the devices of technology plans. For 21st century schools and digital learning to be a success, the future challenge for educators is to blend the technology devices and infrastructures with an appropriately aligned technology culture.

## REFLECTIVE ACTIVITIES

1. Describe how your school/district currently understands control as it relates to technology use.

2. Most educators have taken the time to write an educational/teaching philosophy statement. Write a technology philosophy statement. Readers may want to try the survey by Jason Ohler titled "Knowing your school's technology culture" (available at www.jasonohler.com/pdfs/anthro-tech-assess.pdf) to help you formulate your philosophy of technology as it relates to your school.

3. Assess your current Acceptable Use document. Is it meeting the current needs of your school and students based on your technology plan?

4. List three things you have done in the past 6 months to address cyberbullying in your school.

5. Look ahead and write down one new thing you can do in the next month to respond to a cybersafety issue with your students.

6. After reading this chapter, write down three things you are doing to help your students to become stronger digital citizens. Now describe two new things you would like to do in your school to help your students to be better digital citizens.

# Wireless Infrastructure (Calgary Board of Education)

## Calgary Board of Education

## Using CBE School Wireless

## Guest Network

### Allowing Schools to Control Who Uses Their Wireless Network

Web access has become fundamental to not only our students and staff, but to visiting guests at the schools. The CBE recognizes that guests such as parents, presenters, or private contractors may require Web access in order to enrich the learning environment we provide to our students. To this end, we have created a "Captive Portal" system similar to those you see when you go to a coffee shop or free access Wireless location.

### Setting Up Guest Accounts:

The school Principal will be responsible for delegating individuals to administer wireless guest accounts. An administrator will log into the wireless system from a desktop computer, and will create a username and password for a guest user that requires access.

### Using CBE Guest Accounts:

Once a guest account has been created, guests:
1. need to enable their wireless cards,
2. connect to the "CBE GuestNet" network,
3. will have to open a web browser,
4. browse to any website they wish,
5. will be presented with a login page.
6. will log in using their guest account information as set up by the school's assigned Administrator.

### How Long and Where Do They Work?

Guest accounts can be valid from a minute to five days, and can only be used at the school which created the account. Accounts will automatically be disabled and removed from the system.

It is important to note that this guest accounts have less network access than the CBE Owned Devices network, and as such students/staff are discouraged from using this network for their web surfing requirements.

## Network Overview

### Three Networks

The CBE is deploying three networks

* one for CBE Owned Equipment,
* one for CBE Learners
* one for CBE Guests.

Each of these networks has different features and services. Some of these features are detailed in the chart below:

| | CBE Owned Devices | CBE LAWN | CBE GuestNet |
|---|---|---|---|
| Internet Access | Standard | Limited | Limited |
| Content Filtering Level | School + Teacher level filtering | School level filtering only | School level filtering only |
| School LAN access | YES | NO | NO |
| Login Method | Automatic | Captive Portal using CBE login credentials | Captive portal using credentials created by school |
| Locations Usable | Every CBE School | Every CBE School | Only at the school where the account is created |
| Equipment | All CBE wireless devices | Staff and Student Devices only | Guest devices only |

## What if I need help?

If you have questions or require further information about your new Wireless infrastructure, please contact the HELP DESK. If you experience technical or performance problems with your new equipment, please contact the HELP DESK or have your School Tech raise a HEAT ticket that outlines the problem you are experiencing. We are committed to resolving your issues promptly.

(Continued)

# Why Use CBE Wi-Fi?

## Available at all CBE Schools

The CBE recognizes the need to provide its digital citizens easy access to wireless connectivity for every one of our schools. Wireless access to the CBE network and to the Internet is a critical component of our three year education plan.

## Simple

The CBE's Wireless eliminates the need to learn or share complex network passwords, and allows CBE equipment to easily connect to the network from any location. Using their existing CBE username and passwords Students and teachers will be able to connect their personal devices to the CBE Learner Accessible Wireless Network (CBE LAWN) at any site. In addition CBE guests such as contractors and parents will be able to access the Internet from accounts that the school will create and control.

## Fast

The CBE's Wireless network infrastructure used legacy technologies, but has been expanded to include newer and faster 5Ghz 802.11n technologies.

## Getting Started

All you need to get started is a device that has Wireless capability. This could be a laptop, netbook, iPod/iPhone, or any other device. Just check your owner's manual or look for the wi-fi logo on your device:

# CBE Owned Devices

## Secure Network Access to the CBE Network From Every School

The new network allows you to take your **CBE issued device** to any school and access all the network facilities at the location including printers, scanners, and file-shares/servers.

It is important to note that this level of access is only available to CBE equipment. Your personal computer or computers that your guests bring in will have to connect to either the CBE LAWN or the CBE Guest-Net networks.

In order to connect wirelessly, you need to complete this **one time procedure. Your school tech will be able to assist you if required:**

- Power down your device, and connect it to the school network using a blue cable.
- Boot up your device, and once it has fully booted, unplug it from the school network.
- Surf Wirelessly

# CBE LAWN

(CBE Learner Accessible Wireless Network)

### Wireless Internet to Every CBE Digital Citizen at Every School

In keeping with the philosophy of student lead learning at the CBE, **students and staff** will now be able to bring their own wireless devices to the school and access the Internet. The network will work with any wireless device that supports 802.11b/g/n technology.

## Connecting to the Network:

1. enable your wireless card.
2. look for the "CBE LAWN" Network connect to it.
3. open your web browser browse to any website you wish. You will be presented with a login page.
4. Simply login using your CBE username and password.
5. You will then be able to surf the web on that device.

## When should I use this network?

You should use this network for your own personal devices only, and must not connect CBE owned computers to it. For example, the network will be content filtered to the level of the school you are at. Some websites may be blocked that would be accessible from with a CBE owned device. This network only allows for Web surfing, whereas the CBE Owned Devices network allows access to a broader range of services on the Internet.

After completing these steps **once**, you will be able to use the wireless CBE Owned Devices network at every school.

Please note that during the initial few months of this network rollout, Macintosh computers will require the school tech to configure the Mac before it will work on the LAWN.

# Public Relations and Technology 6

The development of a strong public relations program is at the core of educational change and reform. According to Jetter (2012), creative communication strategies are one of the most important ways to reimage schools and make meaningful connections between school and community. That said, one of the best ways to enhance communication strategies both within the school and with the community is the use of advanced technology applications as well as the implementation of a top-notch public relations (PR) program. Keeping with this perspective, this chapter focuses on the importance of developing a high-quality PR plan that allows school leaders to shift from old ideas to new ideas, and more importantly, to create exciting ways to make every school successful.

## ADMINISTRATIVE ROLES IN PUBLIC RELATIONS

Since school leaders play such a pivotal social role in their local communities, they are in an excellent position to encourage positive progress and meaningful change. According to James Kielsmeier (2010), founder and chief executive officer of the National Youth Council, it will be administrators who will be expected to create a bridge of interaction and shared purpose with others to best formulate stronger communities in the future. Taken together, the importance of these school leaders as supporters of technology and leaders in the community cannot be underestimated. Due to the increasing need for better communication relations, more school officials are demonstrating higher levels of involvement in community work, professional development, instructional supervision, and school climate improvement. Without a doubt, these new-age administrators are personally committed to using innovations in technology to increase student achievement as well as to communicate with the public. Thus, for school administrators, joining organizations and working directly with the community as "movers and shakers" is fast becoming common practice (Portin, 2010). Readers can refer to Box 6.1 for how technology coordinators can be involved in linking school technology efforts with the community.

## BOX 6.1. TOP 10 TIPS FOR TECHNOLOGY COORDINATORS

- *Keep first things first.* Always ask yourself if your technology activities align with the school's core mission.
- *Sell on strategy, spend on tactics.* The marketing of your technology plan should articulate the high-level aims of the plan, but internally, you are focused on addressing the specific steps to meet the high-level aims.
- *Think open.* Be on the lookout for ways to make your technology plan as open and flexible as possible.
- *Leave room for risk.* You want security in your technology purchases and plan, but leave room in your budget to pilot new technologies that show you appreciate innovation.
- *Think fast.* Make advancing your school's connection to the Internet a top priority.
- *Get smart about data.* In your plan, make sure you find ways to consolidate and use as much school and student data as possible to achieve your core mission and use this to sell technology to the community and your school.
- *Invest in your wetware.* This is your teaching staff and your technology support team. Nothing pays off more in a technology plan than properly funded technology training.
- *Keep an eye on "total cost of ownership."* Remember that a technology plan is a complex entity with a wide spectrum of costs associated. Make sure you remain cognizant of the real price tag for technology.
- *Share the risk.* Technology companies want your business and you want their innovation. Be creative in these business relationships where they let you experiment before buying and you offer them advertising or longer contracts.
- *Learn from a kid.* Remember that a sixth grader might be able to show you more of what is happening now and will be happening in the future with technology than any collection of experts. Don't be afraid to talk to your students about technology and what the school needs.

*Source:* Ravenaugh (2013).

The association between educational leaders and their communities is no surprise. Likewise, school officials are not surprised that their roles are expanding and broadening by the moment. But, what they find surprising is the need for a wide range of PR skills. As a result, educational leaders of past decades are now becoming the reimaging specialists of today. With the need for greater communication skills, the list of administrative roles in PR continues to grow—and grow fast. In fact, the demands on school administrators seem endless. The key is enlisting the help of essential staff, faculty, and community leaders in the PR process. Everyone benefits when the entire community and staff are fully informed about successful technology programs and activities. That said, a little community relations can go a long way, especially in the successful implementation of technology initiatives—and certainly when everyone is included. In light of these developments, as well as new demands being placed on school leaders, Box 6.2 lists a series of PR roles found in schools today (Whitehead, Boschee, & Decker, 2013).

> ### BOX 6.2. COMMON PUBLIC RELATIONS ROLES
>
> - Developing a sense of what the public needs to hear, being able to write journalistically, and knowing how to deal with the press
> - Developing a public relations advisory board to address technology curriculum issues
> - Responding to local and state legislation as it relates to technology
> - Improving administrative and staff relations as well as increasing staff morale
> - Preparing communication vehicles to inform the public about changes in technology curriculum
> - Developing school and business partnerships as they relate to technology

## Barriers to Quality Schools

Many schools are experiencing academic success; yet, some schools are more successful than others. This can be attributed to barriers that inhibit growth and change. For example, by not involving the community and gaining support for technology changes, school districts diminish their chances for financial and educational support of the technology plan. Levies and special bond issues for technology can be difficult to pass, because a community lacks a basic understanding and awareness as to the importance of technology to teaching and learning. Thus, without community financial and moral support, school leaders often falter in their attempt to plan and implement an effective technology program such as the one outlined in this book. In the end, school districts must craft a powerful improvement strategy as well as a plan of action to be successful (Odden, 2012). This is why public relations programs are so critical in promoting successful change. With increased external commitment in school district planning and infrastructure, local school leaders can hone their skills on how to effectively communicate with teachers, parents, board members, community leaders, and the general public. More specifically, with the development of a quality public relations program, consistent goals, latest technology, and well-planned strategies, school leaders can literally improve their schools.

In the current context of continual school improvement, school leaders will be wise to improve their public relations skills. Additionally, these same leaders will benefit from sharing with the community new applications and developments, such as mobile technology, informational data retrieval systems, and data-driven instruction. Equally important, these leaders will need to deal with controversial issues and be able to take negative situations and turn them into positive ones.

Making sure community members not only support schools, but also understand and support school technology, means both school leaders and technology coordinators are going to have to become expert external communicators. This involves basing school-community relations on visionary goals and well-planned strategies. Before this can be accomplished, however, it is necessary to determine what PR program the district already has in place. One approach is to ask questions about how technology is being used from a school-community standpoint.

The following is a list of possible findings that could come from this exercise:

- Determine that there is an excellent technology program, but no one knows about it
- Realize that parents want to work with technology in the school as volunteers, but there is no parent aide program
- Find that only 60% of parents know about the school's technology program
- Notice that some teachers are hesitant about having parents work with technology in classrooms
- Want to pass a mill levy or building reserve for technology but suspect the voters will vote it down
- Discover that an opportunity for a technology media event was missed because a local reporter became lost trying to locate your school
- Find that students are making great strides in using technology effectively, and yet teachers are not being recognized for their efforts

Given the circumstances of today's challenges, many school leaders and technology coordinators are often too busy to think about PR opportunities. Even though administrators are rightfully concerned with these problems, it is paramount they rearrange priorities. First and foremost, they must begin formulating a PR program to ensure the success of their technology initiative as well as to ensure it stays focused on student achievement.

One of the first steps in developing a technology-based public relations program is to ask the following questions:

- What is the role of the administrator in PR, and how does that role apply to technology?
- Why do we need to promote public relations in the field of technology?
- What key components make up the PR process?
- What are some specific communication strategies school leaders can use?
- What are the future challenges?

## Public Relations and Technology

Planning and implementing a technology initiative is not an easy task. One of the difficulties can be a lack of societal support. This lack of support has created a pressure cooker of sorts for school leaders and technology coordinators alike, especially with much of the pressure coming primarily from external stakeholders. Clearly, this is a major concern and has both school leaders and technology coordinators scrambling to find better ways to improve school-community relations.

In order to develop more effective PR programs, school administrators and technology coordinators should

- Reassess what principals and supervisors can do to help promote their technology programs
- Create and implement strategic-technology PR plans for their schools
- Establish professional relationships with businesses

- Learn how to handle conflict and criticism involving technology issues
- Build trust
- Establish clear and open communications with parents and community members regarding the technology program
- Respond to reform by creating, adopting, and implementing strong board policies on how technology applications are to be used in schools
- Establish clear and concise communications on how coordinating technology with the curriculum enhances student achievement

By and large, the public is considered to perceive school change and reform as being difficult to achieve. The best example of this is The Commission on Excellence Report that found American Education at risk but noted little or nothing about the thousands of successful schools in the United States (Whitehead, Boschee, & Decker, 2013). To counter these perceptions, school leaders are now developing proactive PR programs as a method of self-protection and self-promotion. The idea is not to avoid bad news but to address problems as well as spotlight success stories in education. The good news is that positive PR programs help highlight the advancement of schools with increases in student achievement, note advances in educational technology and instruction, and begin moving schools toward a process of change.

Involving and mobilizing the community in schools means responding to community interests. The initial step for a successful school district public relations (PR) program is to support a school-level supplemental plan. The purpose for a school-level supplemental plan is to allow for flexibility, making it more probable challenges and problems will be addressed. The supplemental school-level public relations plans should extend rather than nullify a district PR plan. Therefore, according to Kowalski (2011), these documents should identify how and why the district plan is extended and how district-level and school-level activities will be coordinated. To help ensure that PR is a viable school function, the principal should establish a school PR committee. This group might include the district PR director or other district-level administrator (serving as a liaison to the superintendent), at least one community stakeholder, and several school employees including the principal or an assistant principal.

The relationship between a district-level PR plan and a supplemental school-level PR plan is illustrated in Figure 6.1.

## THE PUBLIC RELATIONS PROCESS

In the process of bridging communication gaps, school leaders and technology coordinators are realizing that public relations programs should emphasize planning, research, communication, and evaluation. These components may not be necessary in every project, but they do reflect all of the essential components. With this in mind, the following section reveals how effective PR programs have been successfully developed in many schools across the United States.

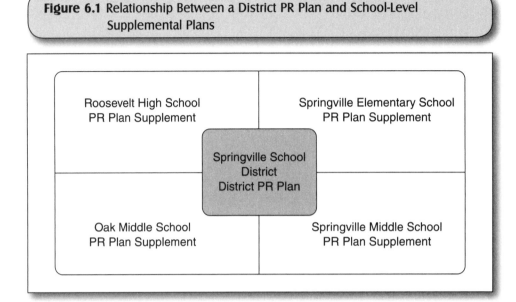

**Figure 6.1** Relationship Between a District PR Plan and School-Level Supplemental Plans

*Source:* Adapted from *Public relations in schools* (5th ed.) by T. J. Kowalski, 2011, Upper Saddle River, NJ: Pearson Education, Inc., p. 123.

## Public Relations Plan

Building community support is crucial in creating supportive learning environments (Vollmer, 2011). Moreover, to build community support, school leaders need to start conversations through the development of detailed public relations plans. In this regard, a public relations plan should include a goal and mission statement, internal and external analyses, objectives and strategies, action plans, and research, using a tried-and-true model as noted below is important. In addition, keeping the focus squarely on people helps schools smoothly introduce a technology initiative (Overbay, Mollette, & Vasu, 2011),

### Goal and Mission Statements

A PR advisory board consisting of administrators, teachers, parents, and community members need to meet and formulate a philosophy and mission statement. The philosophy statement should reveal a general understanding of the beliefs, concepts, and attitudes of a group as well as align with the school district's overall goal and mission statement.

> The goal and mission statements must clearly address the need to increase school-community relations. For example, our school will provide an educational learning environment that supports and sustains academic achievement, academic excellence, and lifelong learning for all students. This learning environment is child-centered in its focus and is supported by a caring and involved community.

The entire community should be informed about all aspects of the technology program. Chapter 2 elucidates the vision, mission, and goal-setting exercise as a means to coordinate a public relations plan with a technology plan.

### Mapping the Community

One of the first steps for school leaders developing a PR plan is to map out their communities and identify groups via internal and external analysis. Mapping not only provides needed information as to groups and resources, but it also provides a sense of direction. For example, a great resource here is the Map Builder feature in MapQuest (www.mapquest.com/tools/mapbuilder). This feature allows you to draw boxes and different shapes on the map that you can use to label "zones" related to groups, communities, business regions, public regions, and high/low population density zones, or whatever is relevant to your PR needs. This can give you a good picture of what is in your community and how zones overlap. You can also place pins on the map. You can use this for example to pin the locations of all the families who attend your school or all the businesses that are within a 5-mile radius of the school. Looking at maps like this can help you visualize what is around your school.

### Internal and External Analysis

Internal and external analyses involve viewing variables from both school-based (internal) and community-based (external) positions. The PR advisory board discusses both school and community strengths and weaknesses. For example, the PR advisory board might address a basic delineation of educational responsibilities as they relate to technology on the part of students, parents, educators, and the public.

### Objectives and Strategies

At this point, the PR advisory board develops objectives and strategies, which should relate to the philosophy as well as the goal and mission statement to improve school-community relations. A possible objective might stress the need to develop an online or traditional newsletter about the technology program.

### Action Plans

Following the development of a philosophically based goal and mission statement, as well as objectives, an action team composed of both members of the original PR advisory board and of new participants should be selected to address each strategy. This team later reports to the original board regarding the completion and success of specific objectives.

An action committee assigned to develop a strategy for creating a newsletter or community message begins by drawing a set of guidelines. Topics are then researched and data are collected. Next, calendar deadlines are set, assignments are made, and materials and resources are acquired. After a proof with a layout is made, revisions and adjustments are addressed, and the message (either online or hardcopy) goes operational. More importantly, the communication is distributed to target groups.

PR plans, such as the one outlined above, allow school leaders to anticipate problems. As a result, both administrators and technology coordinators begin to research and to think through problems in strategic ways.

## Research

Research is a major element in the PR process; however, this component is rarely used. To be effective, school leaders and teacher leaders need to target messages for specific audiences. This means having access to research data without requiring professional researchers. Many effective school leaders can find accessible research data right in their own schools. Data simply need to be collected, organized, and clearly presented. A partial list of local data sources might include

- Data retrieval systems
- Former publications of the school district
- Test scores (assessment data)
- Classroom student assessment data
- Online, On Demand, professional development programs
- High school and college dropout statistics
- Superintendent and principal reports
- Special education and Title I reports
- Official student records
- Former single-purpose surveys and questionnaires
- Interviews with staff members
- Interviews with parents and students

A partial list of nonschool data resources might include

- State departments of education
- State agencies
- U.S. Department of Education
- Federal agencies
- Community and business leaders
- Area resource councils
- Colleges and universities
- Professional organizations like the International Technology Association

Data sources such as those listed above provide school leaders with quality information about their technology program. For example, a school leader reviews a single-purpose survey on school technology and finds

- an analysis of achievement test scores revealing students who are making two-year gains in nine months;
- teachers on staff who have been using technology with such strategies as collaborative learning, writing across the curriculum, and mobile device learning (m-learning);
- a staff member whose work has been recognized by a technology association;
- several teachers on staff who have discovered a new application and wish to share it with staff members; and
- students who have indicated a desire to participate in the local technology fair.

Special projects, such as technology conferences and fairs, can provide a wealth of data about students, curricula, and schools. Materials displayed reveal writing abilities, understanding, special skills that can be shared quickly and universally via Skype, moodling, and other multimedia applications. School leaders and technology coordinators who want to develop projects such as technology nights and technology conferences need to work collaboratively with staff and community members to formulate a management plan for the program implementation. Technology coordinators can be especially helpful with PR projects due to their knowledge of programming techniques.

Innovative public relations projects provide school leaders with information about their schools, as well as provide a plethora of ideas for online and hardcopy newspaper articles, mobile device applications, media stories, and common newsletters. Nonetheless, school leaders and PR advisory groups still have to set priorities as to what should be highlighted in PR projects. As a result, school leaders and teacher leaders planning a PR project need the proper communication tools to be successful.

## Communication Tools

As school leaders work to employ research-based practices, they need to use as many communication tools as possible. With this in mind, John Wherry (2009), president of the Parent Institute in Fairfax, Virginia, formulated an easy-to-read chart (see Exhibit 6.1) summarizing two basic kinds of communication—*mass media* and *interpersonal skills*—and the strengths and weaknesses principals need to know about each.

**Exhibit 6.1** Communication Tools

| Communication type | Strengths | Weaknesses |
|---|---|---|
| *Mass media.* Designed to reach many people at once impersonally.<br><br>• Newsletters, fliers, memos, meetings, handbooks, form letters<br>• Group e-mail<br>• Bulletin boards<br>• Radio/TV | • Excellent for providing information<br>• Help reinforce existing attitudes | • Poor for creating attitudes where none already exist<br>• Nearly worthless for changing attitudes |
| *Interpersonal.* Designed to personally reach one person or a group of people.<br><br>• Meetings<br>• Parent conversations and telephone calls | • Excellent for creating attitudes where none already exist | • Poor for providing information |

*(Continued)*

**Exhibit 6.1** (Continued)

| Communication type | Strengths | Weaknesses |
|---|---|---|
| • Handwritten notes<br>• Individual e-mail<br>• Home visits | • Excellent for changing attitudes people already have | |

*Source:* Using the Right Communication Tool by J. H. Wherry, 2009, *Principal, 88*(3), 6. Reprinted with permission.

As noted above, innovative communication tools can provide school leaders with information about a school as well as provide a bevy of ideas for public relations projects. Nonetheless, administrators must work toward setting priorities as to what should be targeted and not targeted as they relate to various communication strategies. The need then is for school officials and directors who are planning public relations projects to address the following questions:

- Is the public relations project exemplary?
- How does the public relations project focus on student learning?
- Is the public relations project unique to school and community?
- What aspects of the public relations can be easily identified?
- Is the public relations project timely?
- Are financial resources available for the public relations project?
- Does commitment exist from staff and community to complete the public relations project?
- Is there enough time to complete the public relations project for the school?
- Is the public relations project feasible administratively?

## COMMUNICATION STRATEGIES

The strength of any public relations program lies with effective communication strategies. PR strategies are sometimes referred to as PR survival skills. This is especially true with increasing societal pressures as well as advances in cloud computing and video-sharing websites. Thus, a good PR program is paramount in maintaining as well as improving a positive school climate. With this in mind, effective school leaders quickly learn to adapt and hone their communication skills by using tried-and-true tenets of PR: meaningfulness, timeliness, interesting people, exciting events, as well as the accessibility of reporting (Whitehead, Boschee, & Decker, 2013).

### Communication Tenets

- **Meaningfulness** often determines how parents and community members receive PR messages. Articles involving technology and national schools are usually not as popular as stories involving the local school or community.

For example, parents and community members are more interested in finding out about a local technology program than about one in a national magazine.

- **Timeliness** can make the difference in successful PR programs. The media does not want yesterday's news. This is especially the case with bloggers. When promoting an event, school leaders must always remember a fundamental rule: "Publicize an event before it happens and not after." Information about a new school technology program is more interesting than information about a program developed several years ago.

- **Interesting people** usually attract media coverage. If administrators really want to get their stories out to the public, they should invite recognizable personalities to their school. Sports figures, politicians, and authors are good choices. For example, one school annually invites a famous children's author who shares her experiences in writing via the use of technology applications. It has been a huge media success. Unfortunately, there are times when special people are not available due to distances. This is where Web-based applications can also prove useful in providing students with access to special personalities. In all cases of providing special presenters, school leaders should contact the media early, because editorial decisions on story selection must be made as soon as possible.

- **Exciting events** often generate "media play." The more controversial the stories, the greater the chance of having reporters arrive at schools. For example, if a school district decides to place restrictions on students using mobile devices then reporters might be more inclined to visit.

- **If the situation is extremely controversial,** which is sometimes the case with technology, school leaders should try to put a positive edge on the situation. The key then is to get a story out as quickly as possible before bloggers and/or sensationalists cover it first. Once a story is out—it's out—and quickly becomes viral, a rule of thumb when covering a controversial topic is to say as little as possible, to be honest, and to hope community members, reporters, and bloggers hear what you say. If in doubt, school leaders should write a statement and give it to reporters or media representatives. Written documents in any format help minimize the chance of miscommunication.

- **Accessibility of reporting** can be a factor in the success of a PR program. When media people are under the gun, they become increasingly selective about stories. For example, becoming aware of the time of day in which reporters like to cover a story is important. Newspaper reporters doing hard-copy sometimes meet with editors in the morning and thus prefer to cover stories in the afternoon or evening if possible. Television reporters, on the other hand, have a real crunch time just before the evening and late news. They often prefer stories earlier in the day that allow more set-up time than in the afternoon or evening. If school leaders are out of sync with reporters and their time frames, they are not likely to get their story out. In addition, school leaders can make reporters' lives a whole lot easier, and increase the chance of coverage, if they submit written information to the media about the event. Using online capabilities speeds up the process and gives reporters a chance to check details they might have missed.

When dealing with online and/or hardcopy newspapers, school leaders should try to send digital pictures or ask editors to send a photographer. This is largely due to the general public desiring pictures and visual images. In addition, the editor is more likely to cover or print the story due to the expense of time gathering photos and videos on the project. Another important step in the communication process is to identify internal or external target groups. Internal target groups include individuals directly associated with the school, such as administrators, teachers, staff, board members, and students. External groups consist of individuals outside the school, such as parents, business and community leaders, and the general public.

## Communication Strategies for Internal Groups

A positive connection appears to exist between high staff morale and the development of successful school technology programs.

### Classroom Teachers

An old saying applies: "If classroom teachers are happy, students are happy. If students are happy, parents are happy. If parents are happy, school board members are happy. If school board members are happy, superintendents and principals are happy." The bottom line is that if teachers are happy, everyone is happy. This may sound too simple, but it is true.

Many educators believe that fostering pride in schools and acknowledging teachers for their work helps increase staff morale. If this is true, then administrators wanting to promote technology need to focus on motivational approaches. Thus, school leaders and technology leaders wanting to increase staff morale should incorporate the following motivational strategies into the PR plan.

### Improving Communication via Instructional Leadership

As instructional leaders, school leaders should remain knowledgeable about current trends in schools and technology. Administrators should review professional journals and other Web-based sources for ideas. For example, a partial list of sources might include *eSchool News, Tech Trends, Tech & Learning, Fast Company, and Electronic Learning.* Regardless of what resources are used, it is critical for school leaders to remain up-to-date as to the latest in technological innovations. With this in mind, the authors have noticed the following to be integral elements in the communication process that should be addressed:

- Using walk-about supervision approaches for teacher improvement with technology. Many teachers need supervision via guidance, knowledge, and understanding rather than just a formal evaluation. Much of this can be done with administrators using mobile devices and applications.
- Working to keep schools small, enabling administrators to know all the children by name and many of the parents as well. The research base on the relative effects of large and small schools is vast and quite consistent.

According to Linebarger (2011), researchers have found that media-based classroom instruction combined with professional development for teachers led to substantial progress in early reading skills for students. It is for this reason school leaders need to

- Offer to provide technology classes. A little time taken by a teacher to work with a student on a multimedia project often pays big dividends in enhancing a positive school climate.
- Work to maintain class size at 12 to 17 students at K–3 level, and classes of 20 or fewer at the fourth- to eighth-grade level, regardless of economics.
- Ensure that appropriate planning time is scheduled for teachers.
- Involve teachers in technology planning. The more ideas presented generally mean more options for school leaders and technology coordinators if they are willing to take the risk and listen.
- Act as a resource person for materials and equipment used in technology. When a problem with technology materials or resources surfaces, most school leaders can get in touch with other administrators and find what is available—fast.
- Set budget priorities to assist classroom teachers with special technology projects.

**TECHNOLOGY THOUGHT**

Creating positive change is a great way to shift and redirect negative attitudes.

### Improving Staff Morale

School leaders can improve communication and increase staff morale.

- Visit with teachers individually and informally about technology programs as well as student needs. Personalizing the process helps teachers feel more inclined to take risks and set higher professional technology goals.
- Acknowledge teachers' roles as per integrating successful technology programs, either verbally or publicly. A well-written and sincere note or e-mail of thanks to a staff member for their work involving technology generates a lot of positive feelings.
- Create links on websites for substitutes, informing them about the school's unique technology program.
- Recognize in weekly or monthly e-memos teachers who have had success with the technology programs and applications. Good administrators take advantage of every opportunity to highlight the achievements of their school and staff.
- Promote leaves of absence, conferences, summer workshops, and professional seminars. Teachers, administrators, and board members who have an opportunity to attend special programs, immerse themselves in

new material, and develop new ideas that add a new dimension and depth to the school and enrich the lives of its students.

- Promote staff digital communication and links allowing staff members to share new information about technology successes in the school.
- Organize cabinet meetings or videoconferences, before school or after school, to air any concerns that are not negotiable. All grade levels should be represented. Cabinet meetings provide good opportunities to discuss problems. One staff member from each grade level provides representation, but any individual should be able to attend or participate.
- Assist the parent-teacher association/organization (PTA/PTO) in providing special luncheons honoring teachers using technology effectively.
- Organize a potluck for Technology Awareness Week. The first 10 minutes can be used for allowing staff members to report on positive or interesting ideas in technology.
- Develop an in-school task force committee whose purpose is to generate ideas regarding how to promote educational technology.

### Involving Noncertified Staff Members

Successful school leaders and technology coordinators quickly learn the importance of noncertified staff. Day-to-day operations in the classroom would not run smoothly without the help of administrative assistants, secretaries, clerks, custodians, and other support staff. A positive secretary often sets the tone for the entire school. A cheerful custodian or maintenance officer makes children feel secure and comfortable. To be sure, these individuals are a tremendous resource for our schools.

### Using Noncertified Staff

School leaders should

- Ensure that noncertified staff members' efforts do not go unnoticed. Children could use technology and writing skills to make unique cards or e-mail messages acknowledging positive contributions of noncertified individuals. For example, students can use technology applications to make special cards acknowledging the contributions of the custodians to the school.
- Encourage noncertified staff members to share their special skills with students. Keeping with this perspective, school secretaries and administrative assistants can share word-processing and organizational skills with children in the classroom.
- Organize a career day. Students are encouraged to read about various careers of their choice. As part of career awareness, students can visit and work with specific noncertified school staff for a period of time. Information about their experiences can be shared on a school website.
- Acknowledge noncertified staff members as much as possible. Students can generate an app or write articles about contributions of noncertified staff members. These can be submitted to the school paper or linked to a school website. Student leaders can also provide staff members with special awards during assemblies.

## Board Members

Successful schools have positive and progressive board members. Trustees often reflect the political, economic, and social commitment of the community. Without their support, administrators will have a difficult time developing an effective PR program. Board support is vital.

## Board Member Communication

Communication with board members can be improved in a number of ways:

- Board members should be encouraged to attend the National School Board's International Technology Conference. This conference provides board members with a positive experience about technology. In some states, board members receive no remuneration for their services and thus feel more appreciated and knowledgeable when able to attend state or national meetings.
- Administrators should make sure that board members are aware of successful school activities using technology effectively. Teachers and staff can make presentations using up-to-date applications highlighting successful programs. Moreover, school board members should be invited into classrooms to work directly with students currently using technology. The kids love to show off, and board members enjoy interacting with the students.
- Board members should be provided with copies of all PR communications—either online or hardcopy. Digital copies of all notices, newsletters, and other forms of communication can be given to board members each month as part of an electronic information packet.

## Students

Since students will be the most active users of technology in schools, it is essential that they have news and information directed specifically to them. Surveying students via Survey Monkey and other online survey programs helps set the tone for any school. It gives school leaders and teachers a better perspective and understanding of school climate and culture.

## Student Communication

Successful school leaders can improve communication with students in the following ways:

- Keep an open door and allow students to discuss problems.
- Monitor technology groups to make sure students are being challenged with appropriate material.
- Reward students who excel in technology with honor passes. Electronic passes provide freedom of movement for the students within the building. Students love them!
- Allow students to form a technology club.
- Support special mini courses or electives that relate to technology. Mini courses allow students to investigate and explore new technology

applications. Special funds can be set aside for teachers to set up technology clubs as well as special technology sessions for parents.

- Encourage teachers to display stories produced with multimedia technology. Student work can be displayed on the school website, in hallways, display cases, or in area businesses.
- Encourage teachers to provide positive reinforcement. Students and parents enjoy having teachers communicate positive news. Some administrators use their mobile devices to call, e-mail, or text parents on the spot when a child has finished a book or written a story. Parents and students greatly appreciate and honor this recognition.

## Communication Strategies for External Groups

Being aware of parent feelings about technology can make the difference between a positive program and an ineffective one.

### Parents and the School

Parents are a critical component of the school technology process. Children learn more and often like school better if parents are part of the school process. As a result of research, educators in technology are now realizing the importance of involving parents in their child's education. With this in mind, school leaders and technology coordinators need to ask the following questions:

- What are some ways that school administrators and supervisors can involve parents in technology?
- How can administrators increase communication between home and school?

The answers can be found within the following communication strategies.

- The first step is developing a parent aide program. Successful parent partnership programs should have at least one enthusiastic parent and teacher willing to coordinate the program jointly. The parent coordinator organizes and administers the program while the teacher acts as a liaison for the staff.
- Encourage parents working in parent-aide volunteer programs to accept assignments to a grade level not occupied by their children. Some parents working with their children in classrooms can cause problems due to a lack of objectivity. Procedures for a successful program include encouraging parents to choose a level above their child's grade. This procedure enables parents to learn more about the curriculum as well as allow parents to become better able to assist their children for the coming year. This process also enables parents to develop a more positive attitude toward school.
- Set up an open house, and use programs such as Schools Wanting to Acknowledge Parents (SWAP). Parents are able to swap places with students for a demonstration of a technology lesson. Administrators need to use care in developing a SWAP program because some parents will feel insecure about being asked questions. Being aware of parent feelings can make the difference between having a positive or an ineffective program.

- Develop a technology advisory board that encourages parents to discuss problems and allows parents to provide input into the technology program. Such meetings are becoming more pronounced due to the advent of site-based management strategies.

### Increasing Communication With Parents

School leaders can increase communication with parents:

- Have special PTA/PTO Parent Nights. Display new technology programs and applications.
- Encourage teachers to report student progress on a regular basis through school network PASS systems. In addition, teachers can make personal calls, e-mails, text, or write notes. With an abundance of readily accessible mobile devices in classrooms, teachers are finding it easy to contact parents at any moment. Parents simply check messages with a precoded extension and wait for a message describing the day's homework assignment. Unfortunately, some students do not always like this innovation.
- Develop a summer technology program. YMCAs and other youth organizations have sponsored summer technology programs in schools across the United States.
- Set up coffee meetings and gatherings in parents' homes. Many parents enjoy having a school administrator meet with them in a setting away from the school. The coffee klatch concept is an old idea that is being rediscovered by school leaders all across the country.

### Business and Community Leaders

It is also essential to involve business and community leaders in our PR projects. Business involvement in education is becoming even more important, and a major development has been the growth of school and business partnerships. Business leaders now recognize that they can play a fundamental role in improving education. For instance, corporate executives are assisting school administrators with PR and marketing ideas. Executives are also opening businesses to students exploring career options and completing research.

Other community leaders can be helpful as well. Mayors, commissioners, police chiefs, and fire marshals enjoy working with children and are usually willing to come to schools and take part in a video conference. What matters most is that many people in our communities want to help schools—they just need to be asked.

### Communicating With Business and Community Leaders

The following are examples of how business and community leaders can work with schools.

- School administrators can invite community and business leaders as well as their employees to share ideas about technology.
- Community and business leaders and their employees can communicate with teachers and students via innovative technology applications and programs.

- Business and community leaders can provide virtual and/or conventional field trips for children allowing them to see firsthand how technology is used in various careers and job-related activities.

The above examples are just a few of the many ways school and businesses can collaborate and communicate using educational technology. A basic reality is that more schools are working with business and community leaders to expand students' horizons in how technology will be used in the future. This mobilization of community-wide relations has provided some dramatic improvements in school PR reform.

## SCHOOL-COMMUNITY RELATIONS

Problems in schools usually need to be addressed with alacrity. Accessible school leaders solve problems—whereas *inaccessible* school leaders do not. Building and maintaining trust, however, implies two-way communications and involves parents and community members working with school leaders and technology coordinators to create successful school technology programs. With this in mind, school-community relations are noted in this section as being directed by either teachers or administrators.

---

**TECHNOLOGY THOUGHT**

When you encourage everyone's involvement—everyone has a chance to be a part of the solution.

---

### Teacher-Directed Community Relations

Successful teachers who use technology with the curriculum can improve school-community relations by providing special community programs that include multimedia productions by students. Examples include

- Providing student publications that are produced via technology applications for communities
- Formulating a Bring Your Boss to a Technology Breakfast program encourages businesses and schools to have their administrators participate in an activity where students share multimedia presentations and discuss issues. Many technology councils and schools have developed this program.
- Helping students develop multimedia presentations and website links for homeless centers and nursing homes
- Providing a no-books day that directs students to use technology rather than books in all aspects of the curricula
- Giving away T-shirts promoting Technology With Books
- Providing special apps and website links relating to early child education for new mothers in hospitals

## Administrator-Directed Community Relations

School administrators can improve school-community relations by

- Encouraging staff members to submit articles to media about their successful technology programs or activities. Using websites, applications, local media, and newspapers to share school technology ideas is common in most states.
- Being visible and available on a daily basis to work with parents or community members regarding technology programs or other activities. Problems in schools usually need to be addressed with alacrity.
- Arranging for a distinguished-visitor tour of the school by community, civic, business, media, and political leaders. Some visitors may want to spend more time observing students working with technology in the classroom, whereas others like to visit with students about their school experience.
- Providing a school technology award to an outstanding volunteer helping with technology.
- Working with PTA/PTO parent groups to develop online applications and links as well as a reader board or newspaper advertisement listing the names of community members supporting technology.
- Planning special banquets for students excelling in the use of school technology. Parents are especially pleased to have their children honored. Some vocational centers cater the whole event, considering it excellent online training for vocational students.
- Designating a community I Love Technology Day,
- Developing weekly electronic calendars and newsletters given to faculty, parents, and key community leaders. Specific dates of technology events as well as anecdotal stories about students and faculty are popular with community members.
- Speaking to local community organizations. Various groups need to hear and to understand what is happening in technology at individual schools as well as across the nation. Toast Masters, Kiwanis, Lions, Chamber of Commerce, and Rotary are a few examples of organizations that welcome presentations on educational issues.
- Volunteering to work on community projects. Involvement in the civic organizations reveals an interest in the community. For example, a principal may work with a local service club to provide additional technology funding for schools.
- Developing a text, video, podcast, or recorded message service. Parents can check in for information on special events, school activities, and student and faculty accomplishments. Technology activities can be highlighted in the message.

It is through the development of these types of activities that school leaders and technology coordinators can best develop a successful public relations plan. The key is to watch, listen, and sort out the good from the not so good and determine the scope of a plan that best formulates an effective communication strategy.

## Building Consensus

It is critical for school leaders to build consensus and improve school-community relations. As we have seen, some obvious ways school leaders and technology coordinators can improve school-community relations are

- Setting PR awareness as the number one priority
- Formulating a PR advisory committee
- Establishing a PR plan
- Determining internal and external target groups
- Increasing parent participation in schools
- Improving staff morale through effective communication
- Tying PR campaigns to measurable student success outcomes

Each of the public relations concepts put forth in this chapter help build consensus, and they do work. Each has proven effective in numerous schools. If school leaders and technology coordinators need more information about any of the strategies discussed in this chapter, they should consult a PR professional or media specialist. In addition, they can obtain information from any number of national and international educational professional organizations. Developing a quality and effective PR program is crucial if school leaders are to promote the overall understanding of how technology is used successfully in schools. Educational reform in the 21st century will not happen without support for technology and technological innovations. It is therefore critical for all school leaders to begin the process of building a national and international consensus for educational technology. Only through awareness is it possible to fully appreciate the tremendous impact that technology has had on teaching and learning.

## FUTURE CHALLENGES

Engaging in a collective process of school reform is critical to success. As part of this process, it is paramount for educational leaders to create and develop an effective public relations program. In this chapter, the authors discussed the importance of public relations as a format for introducing new technology initiatives. Also discussed was the role of administrators in the PR process. In our search, we found that technology coordinators as a whole continue to play a pivotal part in promoting technology as well as promoting school change. Keeping with this perspective, these leaders have the responsibility to get the word out about successful educational programs, especially technology programs. Why? Because parents and community members want to know how schools are readying their children for a new digitally interconnected world. Even more importantly, however, is that through the development of quality public relations programs, school leaders and coordinators are helping give schools and communities across the world a chance to secure a better future for everyone.

# REFLECTIVE ACTIVITIES

1. List the basic characteristics of your current technology PR plan.

2. Identify how much time you currently spend on PR initiatives in relation to the technology programs you have at your school.

3. Assess what ways you currently interact with the external community from a PR standpoint.

4. Write a goal and mission statement for your technology plan.

5. List your school and community's strengths and weaknesses in relation to technology.

6. Formulate at least five objectives for your PR plan.

7. List some viable ways that your school can share information about your technology program. In addition, list some creative ways that, at first, appear difficult for your school to implement.

8. Note examples of how a PR plan can impact a school's technology program.

9. Plan how you think you would go about evaluating your PR activities.

# 7

# Financial Management

Understanding the value of educational technology is a major step toward developing 21st century learning in our public and private schools. Likewise, once technology is deemed a financial priority, school leaders can work toward encouraging relevant support from local communities. By accessing community sources of funding, such as special levies, bond issues, building reserves, and grant support, local schools and districts can secure the funding necessary to develop progressive technology plans. Further, a strategic financial plan will open up nontraditional sources of external funding such as gifts, donations, fundraising opportunities, and the ability to forge new partnerships with local businesses desiring to assist schools. Thus, even in an age of tight budgets, school administrators and technology coordinators are finding that by saving money and addressing educational problems early, schools can foster more independent learning (Levin, 2012). Subsequently, more administrators are realizing that appropriately financing school technology is a key to reforming and improving schools. With each passing day, there are more demands to garner must-have technology tools needed to transform classrooms and increase student achievement. As most educational leaders already know, technology innovations can be expensive and represent a huge investment.

Today's school leaders have minimal guidance when facing harsh budgets. Decisions dealing with economic conditions are generally represented by two distinct lines of thought. First, there is *the response to cutback leadership or management.* Second, there is *a move toward crisis management* such as advocating slashing budgets, reducing programs, and eliminating teachers and staff. Given these two limited options, school leaders need to explore all possibilities if they are to accommodate tomorrow's technology. Thus, with more generations of digital natives on the way, school leaders are scrambling to find creative ways to finance and budget educational technology. This is of paramount importance and is clearly critical if future generations of children are to remain educationally, socially, and economically competitive on a global level.

# FUNDING PUBLIC EDUCATION

The following information describes the most current data at the time of writing this book as they relate to the funding of public education in the United States. This is essential to help school administrators better understand the overall financial context in which they operate. This will also help educational leaders to make more informed choices about funding and supporting their technology plans.

Under the Constitution, the responsibility for K–12 education happens at the state level, but this does not preclude the federal government from being involved in the nation's educational system. In this sense, the federal government provides assistance to the state school systems as a means to support school success and student achievement. This first happens through the 1965 Elementary and Secondary Education Act (ESEA). The act authorizes grants for elementary and secondary school programs for children from low-income families; school library resources, textbooks, and other instructional materials; supplemental education centers and services; strengthening state education agencies; education research and professional development for teachers. In 2001, ESEA was reauthorized under the No Child Left Behind Act. This reform had expressed federal purposes

**Graphic 7.1** Annual Expenditure per Student by Educational Institutions From Primary Through Tertiary Education by Type of Services (2008)

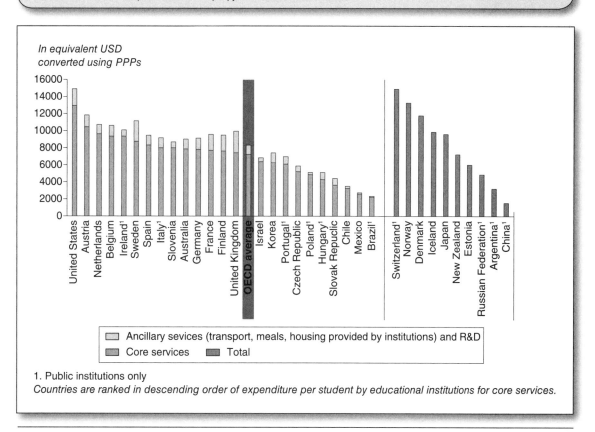

*Source:* Organization for Economic Co-operation and Development (2011).

to raise the achievement for all students and to close the achievement gap. The federal government mandated that they would do this through accountability, research-based instruction, and flexibility and options for parents.

**Graphic 7.2** Annual Expenditure per Student in Primary and Secondary Education for All Services (2008)

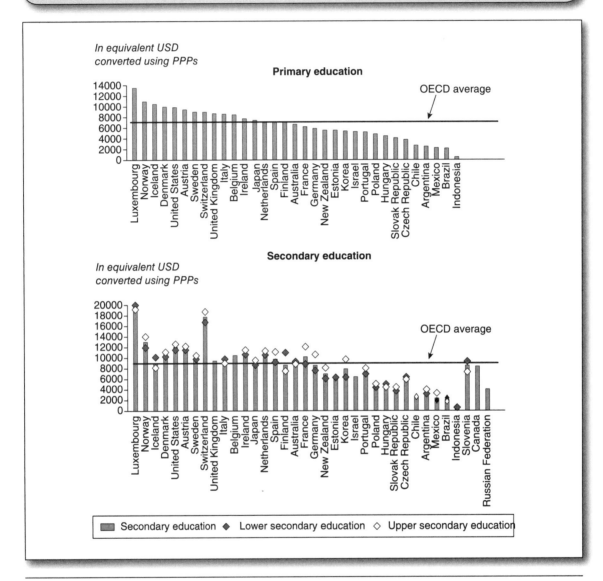

*Source:* Organization for Economic Co-operation and Development (2011).

Compared with other OECD (Organization for Economic Co-operation and Development) countries (Graph 7.1), it is clear that the federal government invests heavily into public education in the United States (Graph 7.2). Interesting to note here is that under the OECD statistics, the United States directs 81.1% of all education funds in the K–12 system toward compensation of all staff, leaving 18.9% to support all other education expenditures. Further, 2008/2009 data indicate that per-pupil expenditures on public K–12 education had a national average of $10,591, with Utah on the low end at $6,612 per pupil and the District of Columbia maxing out at $19,698 per pupil.

To look more specifically at the American context, it shows that the federal government has continued to invest heavily in the system of public education.

**Graphic 7.3** Federal Spending Under the Elementary and Secondary Education Act

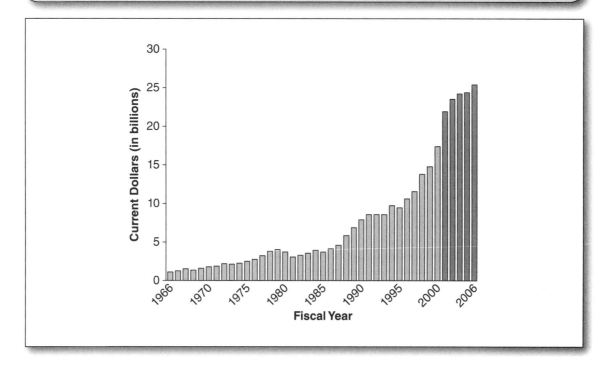

**Graphic 7.4** Total Expenditures for Elementary and Secondary Education

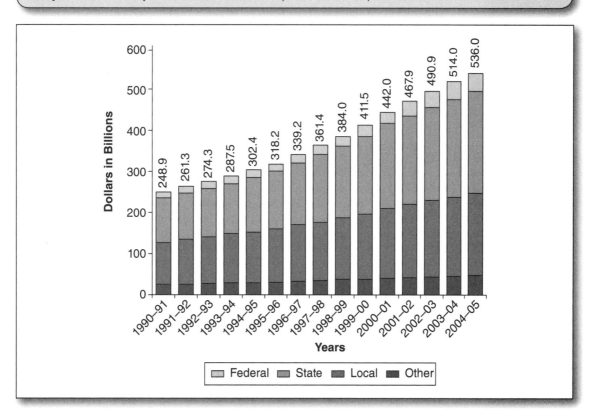

Graph 7.3 shows that federal allocations toward public education have risen from $2 billion in 1966 to $25 billion in 2006. Graph 7.4 shows the breakdown of public support for education. What this chart describes is that for the last year's data, 83 cents out of every dollar spent on education comes from the state and local level: 45.6% from state governments, 37.1% from local governments, 8.3% from the federal government, and 8.9% from private sources.

The following data describes some of the elements of the Federal Education Budget Fiscal Year 2012 to give readers a further sense of the current financial context under which they operate. In here might be some of the areas you can access funding to support the technology initiatives you are planning for your local school.

- $900 million for Race to the Top Awards to encourage local leaders to work together to develop comprehensive plans involving ambitious reforms designed to produce rapid educational change and improvement.
- $300 million for Title I Rewards to provide financial and other rewards to staff, students, and schools that are making the most progress in improving student achievement and turning around low-performing schools.
- $300 million for Investing in Innovation (i3) program to develop, evaluate, and scale up promising and effective models and interventions to improve the outcomes for students. The request includes priorities for Science, Technology, Engineering, and Mathematics (STEM) education.
- $90 million for a new Advanced Research Projects Agency: Education (ARPA-ED) initiative that would pursue breakthrough developments in educational technology and learning systems and support systems for educators.
- $3.25 billion for the Excellent Instructional Teams initiative to help states promote and enhance the education profession and increase effectiveness of teachers and school leaders to improve learning for students.
- $185 million in mandatory funding for a new Presidential Teaching Fellows program that allows states to provide scholarships up to $10,000 to talented individuals who commit to teaching for at least 3 years in a high-need school.
- $835 million for the Effective Teaching and Learning for a Complete Education Initiative to support educators in delivering instruction designed to help all students reach college- and career-ready standards. The program should support the use of technology and interdisciplinary approaches that lead to more effective instruction.
- $150 million for Promise Neighborhoods to provide grants for comprehensive approaches to meeting the full range of student needs, drawing on a spectrum of resources available in the local communities around the school.
- $1.3 billion for a reauthorized 21st Century Community Learning Centers program for grants that provide students with additional time for academic and enrichment activities and that coordinate access to comprehensive services.
- $365 million for Successful, Safe, and Healthy students to carry out strategies designed to improve physical and mental health of students.

- $206 million to improve the teaching and learning of STEM subjects aligned with college- and career-ready standards.
- $14.8 billion for a reauthorized and strengthened Title I, Part A College- and Career-Ready Students program to (1) support statewide accountability systems to ensure that all students graduate high school and are ready for college and a career; (2) measure schools based on progress toward this goal; (3) reward schools for closing achievement gaps; and (4) carry out interventions in the lowest-performing schools.
- $420 million for a reauthorized Assessing Achievement program to help states improve the quality of their assessment systems.
- $11.7 billion for special education grants to states to continue paying a significant share of state and local costs of improving educational outcomes for children with disabilities.

*Source:* Fiscal Year 2012 Budget Summary and Background Information (n.d.).

Looking at the overall picture, the following lists some of the various funding sources that support public education.

## Federal Government

- Title I
- Reading First Funds
- English Language Acquisition
- No Child Left Behind
- The Individuals with Disabilities Education Act (IDEA)
- Other government agencies like the National School Lunch Program

## State and Local Government

- Taxes
- Levies/Bonds
- Lotteries

## Private Funding

- Fundraising events
- Increased parent costs
- Teachers putting their own money into classrooms
- District or school education foundations
- Philanthropy
- Private and public grants/foundations

## Federal Allocations

Times are difficult, but there are federal funds and grants available to schools via the U.S. Department of Education, the National Science Foundation, and the National Endowment for the Humanities, as well as other agencies. More likely, however, these funds are channeled to local educational agencies

(LEAs) allowing for state-level technical assistance. The bottom line is to get federal funds to schools, teachers, and students—early. Unfortunately, with requirements for transparency, this is not always the case. According to Tynan (2011), some budgeted money has been locked up in controversy over provisions that tie the disbursement of funds to student performance on standardized tests. To avoid these types of conflicts and pitfalls, it is essential administrators develop structured application plans to successfully access and distribute funds. For further information on federal educational funding and programs, one can contact the Department of Education, local educational agencies, as well as local community school districts.

## State Financial Support

Sources of technology funding from states are varied and are becoming more creative in nature. Many states now include one-time legislated allotments, competitive grants, state lotteries, and other forms of gambling, while other states use revenue from resources such as gas, coal, and oil to support local technological initiatives. What is interesting is that more states are turning to an assortment of revenue options as a way to fund technology. These might include: taxation, license plate fees, developer fees, special levies, fines, and forfeitures to fund technology. States are also developing technology trusts to cope with the pressures of financing school technology. With this in mind, state legislative bodies are allocating large sums of money to help with digitally related programs and applications. At the same time, states are finding it prudent to place these funds in designated trusts. State trusts allow initial technology monies to possibly earn higher rates of interest until such time as leaders agree as to how it should be spent. The following is a partial list of funding strategies used by a number of states across the country:

- State educational agencies are working with both private and public agencies as well as school districts to seek funding sources for technology. Experts in school technology are serving in advisory capacities to state and federal agencies in all matters pertaining to technological implications and opportunities in education.
- State legislatures are funding respective educational agencies in launching alliances, partnerships, and public awareness initiatives that gain broad-based public and private financial support for technology development.
- States are assisting school districts in securing affordable access to telecommunications services and equipment. These acquisitions are made through aggregated purchasing; support for education, community, and business partnerships that maximize resources; establishment of tax incentives for the high-tech industry to assist schools in securing affordable access; and legislative action to ensure school districts access to channel capacity and production support through existing cable systems.
- State legislatures are ensuring that any financial development, adoption, revision, or restructuring of education reflects current technological requirements for learning.

- State legislatures are enacting legislation to revise current constitutional and statutory language regarding bonds and levies to give school districts increased flexibility to effectively purchase, operate, upgrade, and maintain technology and telecommunications.
- State legislatures are establishing ongoing technology and telecommunications grant programs through state agencies to provide funds to school districts to equitably support student learning.
- State legislatures are increasing technology funding to state educational agencies in the areas of increasing and expanding services in technology networking and working with institutions of higher learning.
- State legislatures are appropriating funds to state educational agencies to develop, implement, and assess technology-based curriculum projects.

# SUCCESSFUL GRANT WRITING FOR TECHNOLOGY

Grants are one of the most common ways to fund technology, but they can be difficult to attain without an in-depth knowledge of the varied processes involved. Preparing a successful technology grant for school districts now requires careful research and planning. The following represent some practical suggestions for school leaders and technology coordinators regarding how to develop a successful grant-writing plan.

## Grant Proposal

A grant proposal is a request from a private or government source to fund a specific project. Preparing a grant application form demands careful research, study, and planning. The quality and integrity of a grant often tests the value of the project for which a school is seeking funds. Matching the needs of a school district to the philosophy, interests, and regulations of a funding source is crucial to the process. A large percentage of technology grant proposals are rejected simply because the proposal did not align with the foundation's or the government agency's philosophy. This can easily be countered by contacting the organization through an e-mail or letter (hardcopy or electronic version) of inquiry to determine if your school's interests identify with the funding agency's requirements. You may also be able to determine whether or not funds are presently available for projects such as yours.

By carefully going through the following activities, administrators can ensure that all the essential elements of any grant proposal are met.

## Special Grant-Writing Strategies

Grant writers will generally increase the overall chance of having a project approved by following a prescribed set of strategies listed below:

- Research the background of the funding agency or foundation.
- Find out what types of projects have been approved in the past by the funding source.

- Obtain a copy of other grants accepted by the funding source and analyze them for style and content.
- Personalize the proposal to fit the funding source. One proposal should not fit all.
- Note statistics and document special references.
- Include visuals, such as graphs and charts, in the proposal.
- Proofread proposals carefully before submission. At least five people should proofread a proposal.
- Reflect a feeling of confidence and success in writing the proposal.
- Highlight measurable outcomes that will derive from the project.
- Link measurable outcomes to the budget and funding allotment.
- Focus on evaluation and follow-up that will be made at various points during the project.

## Grant Configuration

The overall organization and configuration of the grant should

- Identify and address a special educational problem or need that will be addressed by the grant
- Focus on district technology goals and mission statement
- Provide a review of the literature
- Follow guidelines and requirements established by the funding source
- Highlight key words and phrases in the proposal that were originally used in literature provided by the funding source
- Attempt to place the grant in perspective. Why should the funding source approve your request and not another?

## Writing the Grant

1. Clarify the problem and establish supporting needs assessment data. Answer the question of how the grant will solve the problem and address the needs of the school district. If possible, the grant should always, indirectly or directly, focus on benefiting students and the community. Also make efforts to link your school needs with the needs the granting agency is trying to fulfill. You want to connect your grant request with what the needs the grant is trying to meet.

2. State clear, measurable indicators of success related to the problem. The objectives and outcomes need to be realistic.

3. Focus on the strength of your leadership in ensuring project completion.

4. Establish commitment from the board, staff, and community for the technology project.

5. Develop your plan of action.

6. Develop the evaluation component.

7. Link successful outcomes to initial budget and grant allocation.

8. Complete Grant Proposal form below to help in your preparation of the grant proposal.

## Funding Sources

### District

- Innovative Teacher grants
- Title I
- Title II
- Parent-teacher organizations

### Community

- Local businesses
- Community organizations
- Service organizations

### State

- State Department of Education
- State professional organizations
- Colleges and universities

# GRANT PROPOSAL

The following material can help readers as they configure their grant proposal to be organized and to make sure they have completed all the necessary steps toward a successful grant application. Consider this a worksheet and complete each of the following components as described.

## Initial Contact

Prepare a letter of inquiry requesting written guidelines from the potential funding source. Initial correspondence should be no longer than three pages in length and should reflect essential elements of the project. From this process, you should be able to determine if your project generally matches the mandates of the funding agency and warrants a complete application on your school's part.

Done ❏

### 1. COVER LETTER

Write a letter that represents the best possible image of the district and school. The cover letter should have the name and purpose of the project, amount requested, length of project, and the name of the project director. Special references should be made to community relations and benefits of the project. The letter should also convey a feeling that the district will remain committed to the project even after the grant timeline expires. The letter should be signed and dated by the board chair.

Done ❏

### 2. INTRODUCTION

   (a) Origins of the Project                                 Done ❏

   (b) Statement of Purpose                             Done ❏

(c) Project Philosophy                                               Done ❑

(d) Relevant School Highlights                                       Done ❑

(e) School's Opening Date: _____                         Done ❑

School Demographics and Community Socioeconomic Status:

_____

_____

_____

_____

Student Population: _____

Faculty and Staff Numbers: _____

                                                                     Done ❑

School Special Projects Linked With the Grant Proposal:              Done ❑
Current Technology Status:

_____

_____

_____

_____

_____

_____

_____

                                                                     Done ❑

School Technology Awards and Recognition:                            Done ❑

Organizational Affiliations:                                         Done ❑

Articles Published by School Faculty and Administration:             Done ❑

Quotes and Comments of Support From Community
Members and Experts:                                                 Done ❑

### 3. NEEDS ASSESSMENT STATEMENT

This is a statement of why the technology project is necessary and why funding is needed. In order to establish the benefits of receiving the funding, the needs, goals, and problems of the technology project should be stated in measurable terms. Try to avoid the use of jargon and always focus your discussion on the needs of students, faculty, and parents. *Consider the following questions:*

What is the problem being faced by the school in relation to technology and student achievement?

_____

_____

_____

_____

_____

_____

Done ❑

How is this project a response to district technological missions?

_____

_____

_____

_____

_____

_____

Done ❑

How are your needs correlated with needs of other schools in the community? Provide data or information indicating similar needs of other schools in the district.

_____

_____

_____

_____

_____

_____

Done ❑

What statistical or anecdotal evidence do you have in support of your technology efforts? Focus on student achievement and professional development.

_____

_____

_____

_____

_____

_____

Done ❑

What are the experts saying? Cite influential writers and researchers in the field who give support to your technology initiative.

_____

_____

_____

_____

_____

_____

_____

_____

Done ❑

What school needs will be met through the funding and how will this respond to the needs as set forth by the granting agency?

_____

_____

_____

_____

_____

_____

Done ❑

What problems in the technology plan will be solved through receiving the funding?

_____

_____

_____

_____

_____

_____

Done ❑

## 4. GOALS AND OBJECTIVES

Goals and objectives should describe the desired outcome of your project. Objectives must be quantifiable or measurable. They state how you will know when your goals have been met.

*What are the goals of your technology project?*

Goals linked to the original problem:                                            Done ❑

Goals that focus on administrators:                                         Done ❑

Goals that focus on teachers:                                               Done ❑

Goals that focus on students:                                               Done ❑

Goals that focus on parents:                                               Done ❑

*What are the objectives of your technology project? In the objectives, consider target populations and general timelines of completion. Make sure your objectives have a measureable component to them.*

Objectives linked to the original problem:                              Done ❑

Objectives that will benefit administrators:                           Done ❑

Objectives that will benefit teachers:                                Done ❑

Objectives that will benefit students:                                Done ❑

Objectives that will benefit parents:                                 Done ❑

### 5. FUNCTIONAL COMPONENTS OF THE PLAN

It is crucial for grant writers to follow a distinct process when planning or implementing any technology plan. This involves a description of how project objectives will be accomplished, who will be responsible for implementing them, and how each objective will relate to cost.

## Administration and Staffing

It is important to identify administrators and staff that will be working with the project. Many funding agencies base their decision on the quality of leadership associated with the grant. General information collected in Formulating Core Committees, completed in the Project Outline: Phase One: Step Two from Chapter 2, can be extracted to provide this information. Make sure to refer to board trustees, administrators, teacher leaders, and community volunteers.

## Past Success

List other successes with technology grants or technology projects:

Done ❑

## Budget

The budget clearly lists costs to be met by the primary funding source. It states in dollars and cents what the narrative says in words. It provides the financial backbone of the technology project and delineates what the district expects as expenses. The actual budget helps identify and limit project expenditures, and it reinforces the ideas presented in the initial proposal of the plan. Referral to the appropriate sections of Project Outline Activity from Chapter 2 can provide the figures needed for this section.

Staffing

ANTICIPATED COSTS

Salaries

(e.g., program director, technical director)          $_____

Wages

(e.g., secretarial support, etc.)          $_____

Benefits          $_____

Release Time          $_____

Other          $_____

*Totals:*          $_____

Comments:
Professional Development Costs

Anticipated Costs

Site Visits          $_____

Conference Fees          $_____

Training Courses          $_____

Research Resources          $_____

Travel Allowances          $_____

Other          $_____

*Totals:*          $_____

Comments:

Contracted Services

Anticipated Costs

Audit          $_____

Consulting          $_____

Printing          $_____

Maintenance          $_____

*Totals:*          $_____

Comments:
Infrastructure, Technology, and Capital

Anticipated Costs

Hardware and Mobile Devices          $_____

Software and Applications          $_____

| | |
|---|---|
| Remodeling | $_____ |
| Maintenance | $_____ |
| Internet Lines | $_____ |
| Office/School Supplies | $_____ |
| Postage/Shipping | $_____ |
| Moving Charges | $_____ |
| *Totals:* | $_____ |

Comments:

Done ❑

## Future and Other Sources of Funding

This component describes a plan for the continuation of the technology project beyond its initial implementation. This aspect of the plan acknowledges other financial resources and reveals the commitment of the school district to the project.

Anticipated Support:

| | |
|---|---|
| In-School Funding | $_____ |
| District Funding | $_____ |
| Contributions | $_____ |
| Grants | $_____ |
| Donations | $_____ |
| State Initiatives | $_____ |
| Federal Initiatives | $_____ |
| Fundraising | $_____ |
| *Totals:* | $_____ |

Done ❑

## IMPLEMENTATION PLAN

The implementation plan is an essential component. This plan shows that you are very well prepared and have done everything possible to get the technology plan into action. In preparing this component, consider the following questions:

Why have you selected this technology plan?

_____

_____

_____

_____

_____

_____

_____

_____

Done ❑

Why is this approach better than other approaches for your school?

_____

_____

_____

_____

_____

_____

_____

Done ❑

What benchmarks are needed to guide the successful accomplishment of the project objectives?

_____

_____

_____

_____

_____

_____

_____

Done ❑

How will the media and the external community be involved?

_____

_____

_____

_____

_____

_____

_____

Done ❑

| YEAR ONE—Planning Phase | | |
|---|---|---|
| **Month** | **Action** | **Completion** |
| September | Determine initial commitment to project. | Done ❑ |
| | Form technology advisory committee. | Done ❑ |
| | Form project steering committee. | Done ❑ |
| October | Develop project philosophy and mission statement. | Done ❑ |
| | Create calendars for specific committee work. | Done ❑ |
| | Develop project benchmarks and indicators. | Done ❑ |
| November | Finalize goals and targets for project. | Done ❑ |
| | Carry out needs assessment. | Done ❑ |
| December | Review relevant literature. | Done ❑ |
| | Analyze needs assessment data. | Done ❑ |
| January | Disseminate information from literature review. | Done ❑ |
| | Consider possible options available to coordinators. (Look at such things as hardware, software and application programs, bandwidth, implementation strategies, financing, professional development strategies, student needs.) | Done ❑ |
| February | Determine course of action based on available options and needs assessment data. | Done ❑ |
| | List needed materials and resources. | Done ❑ |
| | Confirm and formalize school board commitment. | Done ❑ |

| YEAR ONE—Implementation and Professional Development Phases | | |
|---|---|---|
| **Month** | **Action** | **Completion** |
| February | Establish leadership roles for implementation phase. | Done ❑ |
| | Fix calendar for implementation phase. | Done ❑ |
| March | Plan public relations program. | Done ❑ |
| | Meet with committees to discuss implementation strategies. | Done ❑ |
| | Purchase hardware, software, applications, and supplementary materials. | Done ❑ |
| April | Initiate professional development programs. | Done ❑ |
| | Continue public relations program. | Done ❑ |
| May | Installation begins. | Done ❑ |
| | Complete installation and troubleshooting of system. | Done ❑ |
| Summer | Carry out as much teacher-in-service as possible before classes begin. | Done ❑ |

| YEAR TWO—Implementation Phase | | |
|---|---|---|
| **Month** | **Action** | **Completion** |
| August | Continue with professional development activities. | Done ❑ |
| September | Use of new technology in instructional program begins. | Done ❑ |
| | Administrative monitoring of equipment and programs take place. | Done ❑ |
| | Public relations program continues. | Done ❑ |
| October | Ongoing help to teachers is provided in various forms. | Done ❑ |
| November and December | Continue administrative monitoring of equipment. | Done ❑ |
| **YEAR TWO—Evaluation Phase** | | |
| January | Begin formal project evaluation, which should include: | |
| | Reports from administrative monitoring from September to December | Done ❑ |
| | Continued administrative monitoring | Done ❑ |
| | Feedback from teachers | Done ❑ |
| | Feedback from students | Done ❑ |
| | Feedback from in-house technology experts | Done ❑ |
| February | Continue monitoring and gathering information. | Done ❑ |
| | Complete formal evaluations. | Done ❑ |
| March to May | Make revisions according to information gathered. | Done ❑ |

## Evaluation

Who is conducting the evaluation of the technology project?

_____

_____

_____

_____

_____

_____

Done ❑

## Data Gathering Methods

Administrators, trustees, teachers, parents, and community members' satisfaction:

_____

_____

_____
_____
_____
_____
_____

Done ❏

Success of program objectives:

_____
_____
_____
_____
_____

Done ❏

Degree to which achieved objectives were correlated to the success of the program:

_____
_____
_____
_____
_____

Done ❏

(In)Effectiveness of the program:

_____
_____
_____
_____
_____

Done ❏

Cost-effectiveness of the program:

_____
_____
_____
_____
_____

Done ❏

How will the data be distributed to those involved?

_____

_____

_____

_____

_____

Done ❑

What processes will occur to ensure that alterations in the program will be implemented?

_____

_____

_____

_____

_____

_____

_____

Done ❑

## Attachments

The following depend on specific rules and regulations as required:

Copy of letter (hardcopy or electronic) of support from chair of board of trustees

Needed: Yes ❑ No ❑

Copy of commitment (hardcopy or electronic) from cosponsoring agencies

Needed: Yes ❑ No ❑

Newspaper articles (hardcopy or online) as well as other media samples

Needed: Yes ❑ No ❑

List of awards and recognition for school and staff

Needed: Yes ❑ No ❑

Staff resumes: Directors and coordinators of technology

Needed: Yes ❑ No ❑

IRS letter confirming tax-exempt 501(c)(3) designation

Needed: Yes ❑ No ❑

### Federal Sources

- Block grants
- Discretionary federal funds
- Guide to U.S. Department of Education Programs
- U.S. Printing Office
- The Federal Register
- Office of the Federal Register
- National Archives and Records

### Foundations

- National and International Foundations

The Foundation Center provides informational sources on private philanthropic organizations. The organization's dialogue information services provide an online database on foundation grants (fdncenter.org).

The Foundation Center

New York

79 Fifth Avenue/16th Street

New York, NY 10003–3076

Tel: 212–620–4230

- Community-Based Foundations

Although difficult and complex in nature, creating community-based foundations to help fund innovative school technology programs is becoming more prevalent. This is especially the case at high school levels. These community-based foundations can provide an avenue to collect and dispense large donations of money. According to Dan Green (2012), basic steps to building a local community foundation include

1. Establishing an exploratory team

2. Developing a clear mission statement

3. Creating an inclusive governance structure

4. Negotiating with other groups to avoid competition and duplication

5. Locating available money and raising funds

6. Preparing guidelines for program development and evaluation

7. Inviting teachers to apply for venture capital funding

8. Providing ongoing support

9. Evaluating programs

In summary, grants as well as foundations can be an excellent source of funding for school technology. If not well written, planned, and developed correctly, grants and foundations can also leave school districts open to financial problems in the future. Moreover, administrators and community leaders need to exercise care in relying on grants and foundations as their sole funding source. Keeping with this perspective, school leaders are finding that it is best to establish a successful technology program first, and then find other creative sources of funding to help accentuate programs.

## SUCCESS IN FINANCING TECHNOLOGY

### Setting Priorities

Meeting the needs of school funding clearly requires a rearranging of priorities at all levels. Some believe budgeting changes should involve cutting back or eliminating ineffective programs that will free up money for more promising approaches (Symonds, 2012). Whatever approach is taken by administrators, there needs to be a change in how schools currently plan and fund educational technology. For example, at local school levels, a traditional approach has been for officials to focus on cost first and then to infrastructural needs, ease of implementation, programs and applications, curriculum, and finally, philosophy of teaching. This approach needs to be reversed. For example, school leaders need to *first* establish a philosophy of education and then address the elements of cost and implementation.

The key to setting new priorities for technology is developing a community-driven shared-vision up front. Once a community and school district establish a shared vision, they will be better able to link and support new programs and innovations relating directly to school curriculum and subject areas. For example, in light of shrinking dollars, professional development funds can be shifted

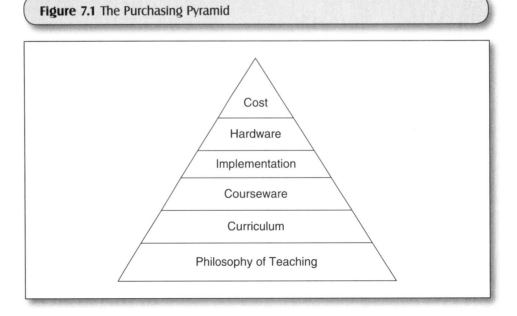

**Figure 7.1** The Purchasing Pyramid

Cost

Hardware

Implementation

Courseware

Curriculum

Philosophy of Teaching

and redirected to support in-house curriculum when needed (Esselman, Lee-Gwin, & Rounds, 2012). The curriculum, in turn, will then determine the scope and sequence of applications and programs used in individual classrooms. Implementation of add-ons will follow. Once all these factors are considered, financing will come into play as support builds within the community. Basically, these types of adjustments are made to meld desired programs with costs at the top of the purchasing pyramid. As can be seen, Figure 7.1 portrayed how this would look (Whitehead, Jensen, & Boschee, 2003).

## Purchasing Policy

Challenges facing purchasers of school technology include compatibility, connectivity, planned obsolescence, maintenance, lease or purchase alternatives, and support of educational objectives. Important questions technology coordinators should ask as they consider investing and purchasing programs and applications are the following:

1. What is the financial capacity of the school district to use, service, and replace items such as mobile devices?

2. What is the processing capacity of the system to efficiently operate current and projected programs and applications?

3. What is the capacity of the system to allow for expansion?

4. What are some possible bandwidth issues?

## E-Rate

The Federal Communications Commission provides virtually every school and public library with a specially discounted "educational rate" (E-Rate) on telecommunications services, internal connections, and Internet access. The E-Rate discount is based on a school's poverty level, which is determined by the federal free and reduced-priced lunch program. Companies providing the discounts are reimbursed through a service fund. Information about E-Rate can be obtained from the U.S. Department of Education.

---

**TECHNOLOGY THOUGHT**

Success with mobile technology is triggering leaders to rethink their budgeting priorities.

---

## Funding Professional Development

One way to fund professional development (involving the use of technology) is through Title II money. School leaders are effectively using block grant money to provide the necessary in-service needed to support their technology programs that relate to science and math. Using federal dollars for professional development is one of the best ways to support and reform education and, at the same time, free up money for infrastructural needs.

## Fundraising Campaign

It is important for school leaders to understand and know the key elements associated with technology fundraising. The following are strategies that vary from district to district and this list is, by no means, an exhaustive formula for passing a levy. The list does provide essential elements for mounting a successful campaign for locally funding technology:

1. *Establish a clear, shared vision of the project.* Before any stakeholders can begin to get onboard financially with your technology program, they need a clear understanding of what you are trying to do. Show stakeholders how your technology project will help students and contribute to the growth and strength of the local community.

2. *Find a point person.* This person's job is to deliver the message about technological change with unflagging enthusiasm.

3. *Devise a public relations message.* Show voters you have a problem, show them how big it is, and then show that you have a solution.

4. *Present to groups who will listen.* You have to communicate ideas to the people who matter most—the taxpayers. School leadership should actively solicit opportunities to meet with local businesses and community leaders, as well as civic organizations.

5. *Involve everyone.* Every person in your community has a potential stake in a technology levy. Don't be shy in asking for support to do the legwork essential for any campaign, such as distributing flyers, raising money, demonstrating technology, e-mailing, texting, and making phone calls. Make it an issue with every person in the community. Try to get as many people as possible excited and committed to the technology-funding project.

6. *Access local media.* Most likely, the media will report the facts and figures of your technology levy or tax to the general public. Their perception of your campaign will be important for convincing the community that spending the money is both prudent and worthwhile.

7. *Community activities.* Once you're certain the crucial part of your funding message has been delivered and people understand what you plan to do with technology, celebrate with a community activity—a barbecue, picnic, or fair. Remember that people are more likely to attend if food is served. This is a great way to reward people for their efforts and support and to help solidify their commitment to the technology project.

8. *Begin process early.* Don't wait until just prior to a vote to explain what your measure is supposed to do. It's not unusual to work two years or longer on developing technology plans and plotting a course to win taxpayer support.

## Finding Local Funds for Technology

Although a majority of technology funds should come from the general fund, some school leaders are finding supplemental funds from alternative sources. The following are ideas on how to find local funds for technology:

- Holding off buying textbooks
- Considering e-textbooks where students access learning materials online
- Purchasing used textbooks rather than expensive new ones and using remainder of money for technology
- Parent-teacher association/organization (PTA/PTO) carnivals
- Technology jog-a-thon
- Technology conferences and fairs
- School business partners and donations

## Strategies for Success

Educational technology is not an option; it must be budgeted and paid for much like any other vital operational need. That said, schools must engage in a strategic budgeting process that targets scarce resources that will help boost performance (Odden, 2012). As a result, school leaders are rethinking and changing budgeting practices that restrict teachers in their quest to innovate and create. Teachers are taking responsibility for success in their classrooms, thus providing success stories to foster technology funding. Costs are coming down, and the quality and speed of technology is rapidly improving. With mobile technology becoming more affordable, school leaders and technology coordinators are now looking for creative strategies to finance new innovations in their schools. The following ideas reflect a number of financial strategies that have been used successfully by school administrators and technology coordinators.

## Effective Finance Strategies

*Technology Line Item.* Successful schools formulate a specific line item in their general fund budget for technology. This not only establishes a priority for technology but also provides a known dollar base for a starting point. Administrators can now plan for technology needs knowing that a specified dollar amount will be available.

*Percentage of General-Fund Budget.* A percentage of the entire general-fund budget should be earmarked as a line item for technology. This allotment provides a stable base of guaranteed dollars for technology planning, purchasing, implementation, maintenance, replacement, professional development, and evaluation.

*Building-Level Technology Budget.* Building-level teachers often want mobile technology or specific applications for their classrooms that may not be determined by the district as a priority. It is important to have a fixed sum of money set aside in building-level budgets to maximize purchasing power.

*Reallocation of Budget.* Schools sometimes find that funds still remain in specific accounts at the end of the budget year. By combining these funds, administrators are often able to apply these reallocated dollars to technology. For example, some educational agencies in northern states encourage school administrators to set aside additional money to pay for heat during the harsh winters. If these states have a mild winter, the school district may have a large amount of money left over at the end of the budget year to reallocate to technology.

*Building Bonds and Reserves.* Setting building levies and reserves at full bonding limits helps finance technology infrastructure. When constructing new buildings, it is best to set the building bond or a building reserve levy at full bonding limits. This provides school leaders with an opportunity to allocate money for technology infrastructure. A number of educational leaders are using this approach to enhance state-of-the-art technology applications for teaching and learning in their schools.

*Emergency Funding.* School leaders experiencing student enrollment increases may be able to use state emergency funds if available. These funds, used in conjunction with the district general fund, can help maximize purchasing power for technology. Some states allow schools to apply for additional money if they have high enrollment increases.

*Fundraising.* Fundraising should be an essential element of your technology project. For example, some parent-teacher associations garner over $20,000 in just 2 two weeks through holiday gift-wrap programs as well as other fundraising projects.

*Corporate Donations.* Schools benefit from donations of hardware and services to schools from local corporate businesses. Telephone and cable companies in many communities continue to donate a plethora of technology related items.

*Low-Interest Loans.* Banks and credit unions can provide special services to schools needing assistance with their technology program. For example, innovative school districts are collaborating with local banks and credit unions as school-business partners to provide low-interest, signature, and payroll deduction loans for teachers and administrators to purchase new technologies.

*Adult Education Funding.* Adult education money in some states can be used to partially fund a technical director's position if the director is an adult education instructor. In addition, adult education classes held in public schools can serve as a source for professional development at a reduced rate or at no cost to the district.

*College and University Partnerships.* Schools are benefiting from collaboration between their school and a local college or university. Some universities provide technology assistance and professional development for local area schools.

*Technology Consortiums and Cooperatives.* Technology consortiums and cooperatives are a cost-effective way to maximize purchasing power, create professional development programs, and provide maintenance service for technology.

The need to formulate financial plans for educational technology is a critical step in improving and reforming schools. Unfortunately, many school purchasing procedures across the country are based on infrequent and unreliable capital outlay that is out of sync with the needs of education today. To increase awareness, numerous local, state, and federal leaders are ratcheting up financial support for school technology. These leaders realize mobile devices, applications, and related technologies need to be reclassified and included as ongoing operating expenses much like salaries, telephone, electricity, and other necessities. It is vitally important, then, that educational leaders continue to work at state, federal, and even international levels to build awareness and an understanding as to the impact of technology on teaching and learning. Even more importantly, it is how communities can best support and finance these new technologies.

## FUTURE CHALLENGES

The future of our schools seems to be largely tied to the future of educational technology, or so it seems. A key is setting priorities and providing strong financial backing and support for technology in schools. Consequently, successful technology programs should be founded on collaborative community efforts as well as sound budgeting practices. This helps generate partnerships and programs relating to school technology that can become economically self-sustaining. All of these forward-looking changes and reforms need to include matching curriculum, funding, objectives, and assessment with appropriate media and transmissions systems. Likewise, collaboration needs to involve P–16 users, libraries, community centers, businesses, homes, consortiums, and museums. It is through this process that we, as a global community, can enhance participation and enrich learning through interactive technologies and multimedia. And in doing so, will give our future leaders, teachers, and students the edge they need to be successful in a highly competitive and rapidly changing interconnected world.

## REFLECTIVE ACTIVITIES

1. Describe the current structure in place at your school for the financial management of your technology program.

2. Analyze the current support you have from both the internal and external community for new technology initiatives.

3. Detail the types of financial support you have for technology in your school. Consider district, state, federal, and private support.

4. Highlight the funding strategies that exist in your state for technology.

5. Evaluate the current administrative structures and procedures you have in place for writing technology grants.

6. Envision your new fundraising program for this technology initiative. Describe its core components, resources, and personnel.

7. Generate a list of creative ways you can locally fund technology in your school.

# 8  Infrastructure: Future-Proofing School Technology Plans

A crucial element of this technology initiative to consider is your school's infrastructure. Infrastructure is composed of equipment, communication lines, networking systems, and software that support education technology in a school or district. Within this are also state and federal regulations for technology. This is a very technically complicated area. Thus, it is essential that administrators consider both internal and external issues so that your technology program is well linked with the systems already in place and with future state and federal technology directives. The more the infrastructure is configured to meet state and federal standards and systems, the more effective the technology plan will be. It is also important to realize that it would be near to impossible for this book to address the specifics of establishing individual school technology infrastructures. This chapter provides a framework for discussion and analysis. The specific details should then be considered with a school's or district's technology expert to see how to best implement it based on the local context. So, in dealing with this issue, it is vitally important that we learn from the mistakes, successes, and barriers that others have experienced. The following list reflects barriers or obstacles that have impeded the effective integration of technology into American schools and classrooms:

- The inability to properly finance a successful technology infrastructure has been a great handicap to bringing technology into the classroom. Local, state, and national efforts will have to be coordinated to eliminate this barrier.
- For rural schools, the inability to provide line service and Internet service continues to be a major problem, because they are at great distances from Internet providers and fiber-optic capability.

- A lack of up-to-date hardware, courseware, support materials, and software quickly frustrates teachers and students. Teachers experience a great deal of anxiety using outdated equipment and materials, which usually means that new software programs lie idle.
- Poor networking capabilities, due to a reliance on stand-alone computers, reduce flexibility in linking technology to the school's curriculum and to the rest of the world.
- The existence of multiple platforms (Apples and PCs) within and among schools makes transferring and coordinating technological efforts complicated.
- There is a problem with a lack of interchangeable parts. For various reasons, many schools have numerous brands of computers and peripherals, and this has made it difficult to upgrade and interchange components. With this as the reality, technology has not been a cost-effective venture.
- Rapidly changing technology has created a backlog of outdated equipment that is not being recirculated.
- Leadership can be a decisive factor in developing a successful technology program. Not having a technology director or coordinator is a major barrier to technology infrastructure development.
- Many schools have suffered because of a lack of maintenance and service capability. Not having access to proper maintenance and service can be a major obstacle to successful implementation.
- The traditional focus for technology in schools has been toward computer labs. Schools using only computer labs are often limiting their teachers' and students' access to technology. Computer labs make it difficult for teachers to easily incorporate technology into daily curricular activities.
- Another barrier to technology has been a lack of staff training and development opportunities. Various technological devices lie idle in schools because few teachers know how to use them effectively.

## CONSIDER LEARNING AND COMMUNICATION

In reflecting on the discussion from Chapter 4, the new reality in 21st century schools is that there is an integrated connection among pedagogy, content, and technology. Understanding this premise, it is essential for school administrators, curriculum leaders, and technology coordinators to have a solid understanding of the learning they want to happen in their schools. With a conscious understanding of the learning, they can then plan for technology infrastructures that align with the needs of student learning rather than just buying technological devices because they are new and create the impression that your school is progressive. If the device doesn't align with what the school is trying to do academically, then it probably won't be fully used. For example,

- Does your school want to focus heavily on e-learning where you develop infrastructures to support increased online learning and classes for your students?

- Do you want to shift to mobile learning where students use a variety of mobile devices connected to the Internet?
- Do you want to have your infrastructure focused on social networking where you use platforms such as ePals or eChalk to coordinate and communicate with students and parents about school activities, assignments, and responsibilities?
- Do you want to develop a technology infrastructure that is derived from the concept of anytime-anywhere learning where students, families, and staff can access school resources and class-level curriculum at any time?

Beyond this, it is also important for school and district administrators to understand how they want to communicate with each other in terms of management of data, alerts, security, and reporting. Considering these two elements, school leaders can begin to make sound decisions about technology infrastructures.

## Concept of Future Proofing

With the reality that local schools operate under a context of regular school reform, change is inherent in the educational process: teachers are changing, students are changing, learning is changing, and technology is changing. In this sense, the schools that can navigate the changing environment are the ones that will see the greatest success in achieving their educational vision. This notion of adaptability is central to a successful school technology plan and infrastructure and one that is future-proof. Future proofing means that a facility anticipates and supports educational change without expensive remodeling. It is inherently a flexible building that can be used as appropriate today, but it also allows future interpretation and reassignment of programs and functions: "A future-proof building is the escort to a probable future" (Locker, 2007, p. 1).

---

**TECHNOLOGY THOUGHT**

Education is fully immersed in a digital age that continues to bring unprecedented and alarmingly fast technological change. To prepare for and take advantage of this, education leaders need to update their infrastructure to support new demands into the future.

---

Thinking about a school that is ready for the future requires school administrators, technology coordinators, and curriculum leaders to work together to see the school in a different way. It is not about seeing the infrastructure as a stable entity, but one that is prepared to evolve and adapt to changing educational contexts and pedagogies (refer to Box 8.1 for some of the dynamics of considering a future-proof school).

| BOX 8.1. BECOMING FUTURE-PROOF |
|---|

**Think mitten not glove.** A good building infrastructure does not operate around a single idea for a school. A future-proof facility can support several ideas of educational delivery.

**Anticipate change.** With budgetary constraints, most teachers operate on educational wishes that are based on getting the things they haven't been able to have for the past 5 years. This traps school technology infrastructures into a design based on current realities and not future practices.

**Engage in succession thinking.** Design your technology plan with the idea that it is not for you, but for those who will inherent it after you leave. What will they want their school to be able to do in 5 years, 10 years, or 20 years?

**Be a multitasker.** Refrain from defining school space and infrastructure under a single lens or function. Visualize your school infrastructure as being able to move around and shift based on the spaces and how they can meet shifting educational and technological realities.

As has been stated throughout this book, designing and conceptualizing a 21st century school are about understanding that the educational processes we engage in today are the ones that are going to prepare students to live, work, and interact in a world they haven't experienced yet. In this sense, today is linked with tomorrow. So when thinking about the technology plan, it is about learning how to connect the future vision of education with past and present school- and district-level assets. Very few schools are in a situation where they can start from scratch with a new building that is linked with a new curriculum that is linked with new technology. Educational leaders need to be considerate of their legacy technology and the continued purpose it can serve within your school and also how that legacy infrastructure can be used to aid in the advancement of a 21st century technology plan. Some of the legacy infrastructures that school administrators will need to be respectful of can include the following:

- Low, medium, or high bandwidth Internet connectivity
- Types of cable or fiber-optic lines bringing connectivity to the school
- Standardized infrastructure systems such as networking equipment, wireless routers, school-level telephones, or projection systems
- Existing WLAN infrastructure
- Schools' current voicemail, e-mail system, types of remote access, or storage databases
- District-level technology safety and protection protocols

**TECHNOLOGY THOUGHT**

Don't get so focused on the new that you forget about what you already have and how it can be adapted. Learn how to balance the desire to have the new with appreciating the applicability of what you already have.

Another component linked with future-proofing schools creates a context where technology is not a tool of learning but is interwoven into the learning and educational experience. Technology coordinators can't base their infrastructure solely on the latest and hottest new technological devices. There is a certain point where the vision of technology is about seeing it as a means where students can connect with the learning experience and the content. You want to design your infrastructure around how technology can be used to solve educational problems, increase student achievement, and help with content understanding. When this is the focus, then your infrastructure will be adaptable to whatever technology device can serve this educational purpose. For example, shifting from wired technology infrastructures to wireless infrastructures has the potential of future-proofing your school to a whole host of educational opportunities and is flexible to changing technological devices. Even though you want your infrastructure to be flexible, there are certain technology decisions that must be addressed and included to help future-proof your school.

1. In your infrastructure, you must make sure you have appropriate wiring in your school. New technologies need certain wiring standards related to copper density, fiber-optic lines, and electricity. Meeting this need today can help your school respond to future adaptations to your technology plan and will limit major infrastructural changes in the future. Consulting with district technology specialists can help you determine your current status.

2. Since the idea behind future-proofing your school infrastructure is about flexibility and adaptability, it is safest to go with industry standards related to wiring, wireless systems, networking, and the like. Going outside of industry standards and working with a variety of technology vendors can limit support, choice, and adaptability of your infrastructure in the future.

3. Don't try to do this on your own. Establish relationships with technology providers, whether it is hardware or software, so that you can really talk about technology and how it can be integrated into your curriculum. They will also be able to help you look closely at how you can advance what you have and blend it into future aspirations or let you know when you need to go new.

4. The direction is for schools to go wireless. Remember that this is somewhat of a misnomer in that all school wireless systems run through a wired network. Don't forget to address your hardwire infrastructure. This means evaluating your network servers, your access points, or your wireless devices.

---

**TECHNOLOGY THOUGHT**

Always keep your budget as the forerunner of your technology infrastructure. Keeping a close eye on the budget will help you clearly picture what technologies are necessary to advancing the curriculum.

## Examples From the Profession on Future Proofing

This first example is not an endorsement of Pearson or Pearson products but is an example of how a school district is working with their selected technology professional to incorporate a 21st century technology infrastructure into their district educational plan.

In response to the changing context of learning and technology, Huntsville City Schools, Huntsville, Alabama, is integrating digital learning into their curriculum through a partnership with a school technology provider—Pearson Products. The plan will switch their 23,000 students into a districtwide one-to-one technology infrastructure. Under the plan, the Huntsville schools will integrate all student achievement data and learning progress into a single environment available remotely anytime and anywhere. That data allow teachers and school district leaders to make instructional adjustments related to learner needs. Students can also review their own progress toward meeting the academic standards of the Huntsville District within the system. In making this switch, the Huntsville City Schools looked closely at their technology infrastructure and had to address their bandwidth, their Wi-Fi, their wireless network, and all the elements that go into a system that supports all students with technology devices including mobile devices, iPads, and laptops. School officials in Huntsville indicated that in the 1st year, it would cost around $3.2 million to switch to digital books. This is in comparison to the roughly $5 million spent on paper books each year. The advantage here is that the digital books don't wear out and can't get damaged. They were also using federal E-Rate reimbursements to help fund the transition to digital. Pearson also uses the Schools Interoperability Framework (SIF), which is a neutral consortium of industry leaders, government agencies, and state departments of education who have developed standards regarding the selection and integration of technology infrastructures into schools. SIF ensures that a school's administrative and instructional software applications can share information seamlessly across multiple technologies and applications. Infrastructural components like Student Information Systems, transportation service software, food service software, library automation systems, learning management systems, assessment management data, and state reporting mechanisms can easily interoperate through SIF. SIF is closely linked to future-proofing your school. Readers can refer to the Huntsville City School District website or the Pearson School System website for further specifics on this effort.

The Durham Public Schools in North Carolina have embarked on a new technology plan and infrastructure responsive to a 21st century learning climate. The strategy of their plan is to infuse technology into classroom learning and school processes. The basic plan comprises three core concepts.

1. A higher concentration of infrastructure within its schools to support the connectivity needed by curriculum-driven collaboration with other classrooms, both nationally and globally.

2. Establishing a long-term plan to ensure a continued ability to provide adequate, agile, and state-of-the-art devices in the classrooms to engage its students to learn more and achieve more.

3. Ensuring high-quality, relevant professional development that gave its teaching professionals the confidence to model, then master, technology with their students who were hungry for learning and energized to excel beyond their dreams.

Durham Public Schools (DPS) technology is a 21st century education strategy that is focused on transforming technology and infusing their classrooms with highly qualified, technology-savvy educators and providing challenging curriculum to propel their students toward achieving knowledge and growth. The key themes of the infrastructure are the following:

- Use minimum baseline technology standards to drive technology decision making; removing aged equipment in our schools and ensure a refresh plan is in place using innovative funding, blended funding, and other means.
- Take advantage of the North Carolina Education Cloud Services wherever possible and with a thorough analysis of DPS requirements and a well-planned migration.
- Create the TLI-IMPACT model in a pilot setting of four schools to prove how the model can work at DPS and use those findings to plan expansion with the vision of modeling in all schools across future years.
- Ensure that after the DPS Technology Plan is in place, each school develops their individual plan to align to the district plan.
- Ensure access to Web resources at all levels possible.
- Create a standing district Media and Technology Advisory Committee.
- Merge the professional development (PD) silos and develop one overall framework for the PD program.
- Expand STEM and one-to-one programs and align Career Technical Education to STEM.
- Ensure sustainable finance options to support technology transformation.
- Create a technology teacher/leader academy.

A Shared Service Model (SSM) is designed to focus on certain services and provide those services in an efficient and effective way, with higher quality and lower costs. When applicable, the shared services should be open and standards based. Clients subscribing to the service model could benefit from leveraging buying power, life cycle replacement, interoperability, and training. DPS is focusing on practices that eliminate redundant activities, improves efficiency, and delivers a higher quality of service. By taking advantage of greater use of SSMs, DPS Information Technology (IT) staff will be able to focus on core technologies and activities that directly support and enhance the classrooms. These services include end-user device support, e-mail, messaging, shared storage, application hosting, filtering, IP (Internet Protocol) phones, network security, backup and recovery, and directory services. Where possible, DPS will increase its SSM strategy in order to reduce the DPS budget and infrastructure requirements. DPS has and is leveraging E-Rate funds, grants, state technology offerings and corporate and public partnerships to meet selective needs. The following are examples of those areas:

### E-Rate

DPS currently leverages E-Rate in the following areas:

- High-speed circuits between district schools
- Local and long distance telephone services
- Cellular services
- Smartphone service
- District Web hosting
- Basic maintenance of network components for schools in need
- Cisco Base maintenance (equipment warranty)
- Basic maintenance of cabling components
- Basic maintenance of video equipment
- High-speed Internet access for the district
- Voice over Internet Protocol (VOIP) services
- Cabling refreshment for schools in need
- Upgrade voice services for schools in need
- Video equipment for schools in need
- Wireless in the neediest schools
- Domain services for schools in need

## Grants

- KidSmart—Young Explorers and Lenovo computers
- Donors Choose
- Other IBM grants such as Translate Now!

### State Technology Offerings

Since July of 2011, DPS has participated in the North Carolina Research and Education Network (NCREN) for all Internet traffic.

### Corporate and Public Partnership

Duke University donates at least 50 computers a month to DPS for use in its classrooms. The Durham Chamber of Commerce also partners with us on our volunteer program and has been instrumental in providing innovative ideas and support. Other partnerships have also been leveraged for bringing in donated computers for the district.

Within the technology infrastructure, DPS is also addressing:

- Internet filtering related to the Child Internet Protection Act
- Voice over Internet Protocol
- Firewall (DPS has currently upgraded its firewall infrastructure and provided training of the product in-house)
- DPS's common data initiative related to sharing relevant student and academic data across the district

A Statewide SSM will enable increased infrastructure and technology efficiency and sustainability by

- Satisfying bandwidth demands
- Providing shared server deployments to support common services across local educational agencies (LEAs)
- Leveraging server virtualization to deploy logical servers
- Automatically scaling server and storage resources to meet demands
- Realizing the efficiency of contemporary IT technologies. By having a standards-based infrastructure, DPS IT will be able to respond more quickly to new technology requirements driven by curriculum. This includes digital textbooks, delivering supplemental curriculum material with textbooks, providing access to remote sites such as the Durham Regional Detention Center and community centers focused on DPS student services. In the future, the same standards-based infrastructure can serve the students who take their devices home.

A Statewide Services Model can provide higher service reliability by

- Categorizing platforms into systems such as learning and instructional, IT enterprise, and business operations to enable the development of an architecture that provides standard learning management, identity, content, and data management interfaces and services in order to simplify connecting provider solutions—shared learning infrastructure transition server hosting and management to cloud providers.
- Providing Service Level Agreements (SLAs) for LEAs rather than best effort Memorandum of Understandings. With limited budget and limited staff, having clear SLAs in place allows all stakeholders to understand the expectations of its partners and be able to make informed decisions when educational changes arise.
- Managing network latency
- Providing hardware and software patches and upgrades

*Source:* Durham Public Schools Technology Plan 2012–2014.

## FUTURE-PROOFING YOUR TECHNOLOGY INFRASTRUCTURE

The following sections describe a variety of components that school administrators, technology coordinators, and curriculum leaders can address or consider in relation to local and district school technology infrastructures.

### National Telecommunications Infrastructure

As research and educational practice continue to show a link between technology and student achievement, national leaders are becoming more interested in funding school technology programs. There appears to be a positive change in Washington, DC, to a belief that technology can drive educational improvement. Government leaders are now coming to the conclusion that technology does impact learning.

The positive attitude on the part of policymakers in Washington, DC, has done much to help pump billions of dollars into school technology initiatives. Federal support for technology infrastructure comes from a multitude of departments, foundations, and competitive grants. The focus has been to decentralize the funding of technological infrastructure through the individual states as much as possible. According to Cheryl Lemke, vice president of education technology for the Milken Exchange Program, "The centralized model is not always the best one. Change happens when local school officials, educators, and parents become part of the program" (as cited in White, 1997).

The Federal Communications Commission (FCC) along with the U.S. Department of Education is intently involved in this national framework and has several key directions for helping schools across the United States increase their connectivity, digital learning, and infrastructure.

## Online Learning

- The U.S. Department of Education, with support from the National Institute of Standards and Technology (NIST) and the FCC, should establish standards to be adopted by the federal government for locating, sharing, and licensing digital educational content.
- The federal government should increase the supply of digital educational content available online that is compatible with standards established by the U.S. Department of Education.
- The U.S. Department of Education should periodically reexamine the digital data and interoperability standards it adopts to ensure that they are consistent with the needs and practices of the educational community, including local, state, and nonprofit educational agencies and the private sector.
- Congress should consider taking legislative action to encourage copyright holders to grant educational digital rights of use, without prejudicing their other rights.
- State accreditation organizations should change kindergarten through twelfth grade (K–12) and postsecondary course accreditation and teacher certification requirements to allow students to take more courses for credit online and to permit more online instruction across state lines.
- The U.S. Department of Education and other federal agencies should provide support and funding for research and development of online learning systems.
- The U.S. Department of Education should consider investment in open-licensed and public domain software alongside traditionally licensed solutions for online learning solutions, while taking into account the long-term effects on the marketplace.
- The U.S. Department of Education should establish a program to fund the development of innovative broadband-enabled online learning solutions.

- State education systems should include digital literacy standards, curricula, and assessments in their English Language Arts and other programs, as well as adopt online digital literacy and programs targeting STEM (Science, Technology, Engineering, and Mathematics).
- The U.S. Department of Education should provide additional grant funding to help schools train teachers in digital literacy and programs targeting STEM. States should expand digital literacy requirements and training programs for teachers.

Unlock the Value of Data and Improve Transparency

- The U.S. Department of Education should encourage the adoption of standards for electronic educational records.
- The U.S. Department of Education should develop digital financial data transparency standards for education. It should collaborate with state and local education agencies to encourage adoption and develop incentives for the use of these standards.
- The U.S. Department of Education should provide a simple Request for Proposal (RFP) online "broadcast" service where vendors can register to receive RFP notifications from local or state educational agencies within various product categories.

Modernizing Educational Broadband Infrastructure

- The FCC should adopt its pending Notice of Proposed Rulemaking (NPRM) to remove barriers to off-hours community use of E-Rate funded resources.
- The FCC should initiate a rulemaking to set goals for minimum broadband connectivity for schools and libraries and prioritize funds accordingly.
- The FCC should provide E-Rate support for internal connections to more schools and libraries.
- The FCC should give schools and libraries more flexibility to purchase the lowest-cost broadband solutions.
- The FCC should initiate a rulemaking to raise the cap on funding for E-rate each year to account for inflation.
- The FCC should initiate a rulemaking to streamline the E-rate application process.
- The FCC should collect and publish more specific, quantifiable, and standardized data about applicants' use of E-rate funds.
- The FCC should work to make overall broadband-related expenses more cost-efficient within the E-rate program.
- Congress should consider amending the Communications Act to help tribal libraries overcome barriers to E-rate eligibility arising from state laws.
- The FCC should initiate a rulemaking to fund wireless connectivity to portable learning devices. Students and educators should be allowed to take these devices off campus so they can continue learning outside school hours.

- The FCC should award some E-rate funds competitively to programs that best incorporate broadband connectivity into the educational experience.
- Congress should consider providing additional public funds to connect all public community colleges with high-speed broadband and maintain that connectivity.

Readers can refer to www.broadband.gov/plan/11-education for more specific details on this information and how it could be a resource to your school or district technology plan/infrastructure. Readers may also want to review Infrastructure: Access and Enable on the Ed.gov website. The national level project is about creating a national level educational infrastructure where all students and educators will have access to a comprehensive infrastructure for learning when and where they need it. Some of the elements addressed in this effort include: broadband everywhere, access devices for every student and educator, addressing E-Rate provisions, cell phones as a means to support learning, student safety on the Internet, Open Educational Resources, interoperability standards, cloud computing, and using students as technological resources.

## State Telecommunications Infrastructure

State leaders are becoming more interested in the impact technology is having on teaching and learning in the classroom. Understanding infrastructure design and how it relates to integrating technology in classrooms is becoming the foundation for the change process. Many states are now establishing financial funding that promotes and protects the integrity of technology use in classrooms and across networks. Making sure that schools are able to purchase proper wire, wireless servers, high-speed network servers, and high-speed computers with large amounts of memory continues to be of critical interest to state lawmakers.

Several states are looking at what they can do to speed up the implementation of technology in school classrooms. Of primary importance are those communications that support IP-based data and multimedia delivery. Many state and federal agencies, university systems, and private businesses now work collaboratively to deliver stable and sustainable multimedia-based applications. Networking current infrastructure systems within each state has facilitated this effort by establishing models for connectivity, training, and curricula for P–16 education. Requests for large blocks of IP addresses are being made using an IP addressing scheme to support efficient routing and IP-based connectivity to schools and libraries throughout each state.

Multimedia delivery for individual states is often supported through partnerships with other online services, compressed video networks, satellite uplinks available from the university systems, tribal and technical colleges, or private industry—as well as from community access television stations and television cable infrastructures. Many states now have multiple telecommunications corporations, resource centers, and other commercial entities that are coming forward to invest in developing statewide, infrastructural telecommunications systems that can be accessed by schools.

## State Telecommunications Networks

Community and school leaders want statewide computer networks that provide dedicated access for voice, video, and data transmissions. Communities and schools are now linked through fiber channels. Linking independent school networks together with state fiber channels remains the primary economic challenge for many states. Telephone companies are now discussing how to offer price breaks on usage fees to allow sustained use of these fiber networks by schools. While compressed video is less expensive than fiber-optic, interactive TV, it suffers from similar scheduling problems. As the use of site networks grows, conflicts in scheduling when all sites are free can be expected to become increasingly problematic. Compressed video sites often have two screens, one that shows the home site and a central "speaking" or point-of-origin site. Interactive sites typically have several TVs that allow viewers and speakers to see participants at all or some sites simultaneously or alternately. Frame relay is one method of providing high-bandwidth data communications statewide, such as Internet access.

A few states have been funding their telecommunications programs by requiring companies that are seeking deregulation to contribute to school technology. Companies must provide discounted telecommunications services to schools and contribute an agreed dollar amount per year over a period of 10 years. This money is used to fund and upgrade technology infrastructure.

The use of satellite networks will help to reduce technology barriers and equity issues in schools across the country. The Texas satellite network, known as T-STAR, links districts, regional educational service centers, and the Texas Education Agency together (Woodard, 1997). Each district in Texas has a satellite dish that allows it to participate in the system. As costs come down, more schools in the future will depend on satellite technology to enhance their contact with the external community. There are thousands of school-based satellite dishes throughout the country, and more schools will be turning to satellite to increase desktop Internet access. The problem is the logistics of organizing enough sites to receive the same broadcast and to justify the expense of transmission and use.

South Dakota provides a cost-effective, innovative model for creating infrastructure. Former governor William J. Janklow provided fiber-optic cable and training for inmates in the state penitentiary. Schools hired the prison inmates at penitentiary salary to wire every school from kindergarten through higher education in the state of South Dakota to create the Dakota Digital Network, a two-way audio, two-way video telecommunications network.

## State Regulations and Guidelines

One direction being taken is to tie the funding of technology infrastructure to specific standards and guidelines. The following sections are areas of concern in relation to state and federal regulations and guidelines.

## Equity Issues

Technology equity is a major concern for state lawmakers and leaders. States continue to work to eliminate a wide disparity among individual districts as to how they use technology. In order to address equity concerns, some state leaders now allocate federal funds to districts according to the number of low-income children in a district. Free and reduced-cost student lunch counts are used as a measure for identifying the number of low-income families in districts. State officials also use low property values as a way of determining which schools should receive financial support for technology. Another direction is that districts consider the development of technology consortia to help decrease the gap between the haves and the have-nots.

*what is the # of low income students?*

## Technology Plans

Before money is approved for technology, many state agencies are requiring schools to develop a comprehensive network technology plan. These state leaders are requiring that districts take certain steps in developing their technology infrastructure before receiving competitive grants in technology.

## Evaluation

Program evaluation and a school's ability to assess student performance are now critical elements that must be included in the formation of most states' technology plans if schools are to receive funding.

## Staff Development

Teacher training is being recognized as one of the main reasons that schools have difficulty implementing technology. Therefore, state leaders are now requiring that all technology plans include a provision that addresses how staff development will be funded. Some states are requiring teachers to have advanced skills in technology before a school district can receive state technology funds.

## Maintenance and Service

Maintaining and servicing networked equipment continues to be a challenge for schools' effective use of technology. More states are now requiring that districts and schools have a technology specialist or coordinator who supports teachers in integrating instruction and technology before that district can receive state funding.

## Infrastructure

Integrating technology into classrooms has been a major priority of many states. Numerous state competitive grants are based on how school districts will develop a higher level of connectivity in classrooms.

## REGIONAL CENTERS AND TECHNOLOGY HUBS

Regional technology service centers, sometimes called technology hubs, have the capability of serving as informational resource centers, information management systems, professional-development centers, procurement centers, and research and evaluation centers, as well as grant-writing centers. Technology service centers can often make the transfer of student records easier, and they can also enhance the opportunity for state agencies and schools to share reports on student achievement, attendance, enrollment, demographics, and budgets.

## Distance Learning Programs

Most learning centers should have the capacity to train teachers in how to integrate technology into their classrooms as well as how to evaluate instructional resources. School leaders now agree that training and content knowledge will become more important as faculty and students have regular access to technology. Regional centers will thus act as staff development centers or learning academies that offer courses for teachers on how to have a closer link between technology and the curriculum. Teachers and other educators will be provided with workshops and conferences at the regional center with the expectation that they will return to their districts and share what they have learned with their peers. The National Science Foundation uses regional technology centers as a base of operations for electronic learning.

Regional centers also provide distance inservice learning. Technology hubs have the capability of housing sophisticated distance learning classrooms that can serve all schools within a state. Participants using these interactive classrooms will be able to see, hear, and interact with other educators, classes, and presenters within their state as well as around the world. Centers can thus provide a way for high school dropout students to graduate by allowing them to take courses over the Internet.

College classes can also be offered electronically to students and teachers. A full menu of classes, such as foreign language, art, anatomy, and advanced math, can be offered through an interactive television network based at the regional technology center. Using Internet and telecommunications strategies, technology hubs can go a long way to "filling in the holes of school curriculum" when necessary.

## Procurement

 Districts can apply for state funds, which may include matching grants, to provide school districts with electronic connections for voice, video, and data transmissions. The service centers can also work with state education departments to buy technology equipment for school districts through special lease-purchase agreements. School districts can also use regional technology centers as sites to try out hardware and software products before deciding what to buy. Using regional technology hubs as procurement centers helps eliminate unnecessary duplication and increases buying power for schools.

## Research and Evaluation

Regional technology service centers can also act as a hub for educational research and evaluation of technology programs. Many states have a variety of agencies that can provide research and evaluation services, but currently, there is often no coordinated statewide approach. Regional technology hubs, on the other hand, provide a central processing location for the coordination of research and evaluation activities. This is often what is needed to help generate data that are essential to best restructure education throughout the country.

In addition, technology centers have specialists who assist local school leaders in formulating strategies for the planning, implementation, and evaluation of technology. Data from research projects is used to inform administrators and technology coordinators of what works and what doesn't work. This provides a mechanism through which research results can now be shared with educators on a faster time frame because of the Internet. According to Donald Leu Jr. (2002), professor at Syracuse University:

> Increasingly, classroom teachers, not researchers, may define the most effective instructional strategies for literacy and learning. Teachers can evaluate instructional effectiveness and quickly spread the word on the Internet faster than researchers who require substantial time before results are published. (p. 315)

## Financial Advice on Technology Implementation

Regional centers also prove to be effective in providing financial advice on the implementation of technology into schools. Staff specialists work with state government and school leaders on the best ways to disperse money for technology. They know and understand the best ways to integrate technology into classrooms and work with schools to ensure that grant dollars are being well used. Centers also have the capability of providing training to administrators and technology coordinators on how to successfully write and receive competitive technology grants.

## Technology Cooperatives

One of the best ways to purchase, service, and upgrade school technological infrastructure is through technology cooperatives. School leaders are now realizing the benefits of technology cooperatives. Cooperatives are making schools more efficient in how to buy, what to buy, and where to buy the latest technology.

National organizational leaders are now assisting school leaders in developing technology cooperatives. Such organizations include the American Association of School Administrators (AASA) (www.aasa.org), the National Association of Elementary School Principals (NAESP) (www.naesp.org), the National Association of Secondary School Principals (NASSP) (www.nassp.org), the National Education Association (NEA) (www.nea.org), and the National School Boards Association (NSBA) (www.nsba.org). These organizations also work with state legislators and members of congress to encourage the development of technology cooperatives.

# MANAGEMENT, SERVICE, AND MAINTENANCE

## Technical Coordinator or Director

One of the most important steps to developing a successful technology program is hiring a technical director or coordinator. Technology is becoming too complex and too expensive to leave to untrained teachers and administrators. Networking computers and multimedia tools today is presenting a series of difficult challenges to schools. School leaders need to know what type of equipment to purchase, where to obtain the best buys, how to train teachers to use it, and when it should be upgraded. It is, therefore, important that administrators have access to personnel who have a technology background and understand how to address these problems.

There continues to be a nationwide shortage of information-technology specialists. Large and better-funded districts are often able to lure the best-trained technologists to their schools first. Small and rural districts are, however, finding it essential to share the services of a technical coordinator. More schools are banding together to create technology cooperatives that have greater buying power and can attract top-notch people.

Optimally, it is best if technical coordinators have experience in the classroom, but it is not a necessity. Under the proper administrative guidance, technical directors will learn how to best consider technical matters in direct relation to the needs of teachers, students, and the curriculum. For example, Box 8.2 highlights the general job description of a typical school technology coordinator.

---

### BOX 8.2. GENERAL JOB QUALIFICATIONS OF A SCHOOL TECHNOLOGY COORDINATOR

- A broad general education and dedication to lifelong learning; overall intelligence and perseverance; a strong work ethic; high ethical standards; self-confidence; good time-management skills; budgeting and other fiscal skills.
- Knowledge of and support for the district's educational system; appropriate skills in teaching school children as well as educators and other adults; knowledge of curriculum, curriculum development, and school reform; knowledge of testing and assessment.
- Interpersonal relations skills, especially in being a good listener; skills in written and oral communications; administrative skills; good telephone and electronic mail communication skills.
- Technical knowledge in the fields of computer science, computer education, and the broad range of technologies used in hypermedia environments; knowledge of the theory and practice of instructional technology; substantial experience in working with students and educators in the instructional technology field; knowledge of teaching and learning theory as they relate to the roles of technology in content and pedagogy.

## Teacher Technology Coordinators

One of the most common ways that small and rural schools have addressed the problem of maintaining and servicing their computer infrastructure has been to train their own experts. Training a technology coordinator on-site has had mixed results but continues to be a common practice in many small and rural schools. Librarians and teachers are sometimes asked to become half-time technologists. Half-time technologists need to lead technology planning, purchase and assemble equipment, load software, train teachers, and troubleshoot the system as well as doing their jobs as librarians or teachers.

The part-time technology coordinator often becomes the lightning rod of political struggles over technology funding, training, and service. Although some staff members make it through this gauntlet and become full-time technology coordinators, most do not.

Whether the technology coordinator is a part-time teacher/librarian or an outside expert, Craig Nanson from the Minot School District provides practical advice (see Box 8.3) on how technology coordinators should cope with their diverse responsibilities.

---

### BOX 8.3. COLLECTIVELY DEFINED JOB DESCRIPTION

PART I: Things you want to DO:

(You need to be the one doing these things)

- Develop technology team (visionaries, people on-site, troubleshooters, people you can delegate pieces to)
- Define a technology plan
- Communicate your priorities to others
- Delegate pieces to your technology team
- Act as liaison for implementing technology plan
- Finding champions ("special friends," visionaries, parents, community)
- Staff development (could also be delegated)
- Presentations to staff, PTA, district council, board, etc. (can also give input or delegate)
- Community/Parent/Staff/District/Board Liaison
- Attend conferences & workshops
- Research & development (could also be delegated)

PART II: Things you want INPUT on:

(You don't have the ultimate responsibility, but you want to be consulted and involved)

- Define technology plan
- Define technology goals
- Prepare budgets
- Develop Acceptable-Use Policies

*(Continued)*

(Continued)

- Develop Scope and Sequence
- Write grants
- Preview equipment & software (could also be delegated)
- Order, install and maintain equipment & software (could also be delegated)

PART III: Things you want to DELEGATE or COORDINATE:

(You are responsible for these things, but other people can do them. This is why you built a team of supporters & champions!)

- Troubleshoot problems
- Take inventory
- Manage network
- Develop and maintain website
- Provide parent and community classes
- Run a student group

*Source:* Nansen, C. (2002).

## Student Technology Assistants

Small and rural schools continue to turn to students for technical support. Schools are having success in organizing their middle and high school students into teams to maintain networks and run the school's Internet services. As part of their student career services, districts are also sending teams of students into the elementary schools to help make wiring connections, load software, train teachers and students, manage Internet accounts, and perform routine maintenance and repair functions. Students obtain course credit, and their skills lead to well-paying summer jobs or permanent employment.

Some school leaders, however, are cautious about relying too heavily on students to help maintain the district's technology program. Their concern is valid in that there may be litigation concerns. Whatever the outcome, educators need to make sure that the students helping to maintain technology programs are being supervised and are working under designated guidelines.

## Work-Tracking System

To best manage and attend to problems on network servers and hubs, schools are using work-tracking systems. Without leaving their offices, technicians can use these types of management systems to address network problems quickly and efficiently. School technical directors and teachers can now receive technical assistance by contacting a company's troubleshooting division 24 hours daily. Company software can analyze the school's network and individual machines electronically and provide solutions on how to correct problems. Troubleshooting a network electronically has vastly improved how schools maintain and service their equipment even though the parent company may be thousands of miles away.

## Strategies for Success

The following strategies are effective for implementing a technological infrastructure in schools.

1. **Rule of Three.** The rule of three is one of the most important tips provided in this book: *"Ask three and then me."* Teachers and staff members are required to ask three other staff members before requesting help from the technical director or coordinator. The purpose of the rule is to reduce the burden on the technology staff so that they are not troubleshooting minor problems such as a computer that is not plugged in, a print cartridge that needs changing, or a loose wire. The rule of three reduces time restraints on the technical staff and allows them to be much more productive and helpful to the staff.

2. **Teacher Application of the Rule of Three.** This same rule, *"Ask three and then me,"* also helps teachers save time in the classroom. Teachers simply require students to ask three other classmates to help solve a computer problem before going to the teacher. Students know which students are more proficient on the computer and will usually go to them first. Students knowledgeable about the computer eventually become great troubleshooters for the class.

3. **Teacher System Operators.** Successful school technology leaders train selected staff members to become system operators. At least two grade level teachers (or two teachers in adjacent grade levels within rural schools) are provided with inservice to become technology troubleshooters. It is crucial that at least two system operators be trained so that if one becomes tired or changes jobs, the other team member can continue providing technical support to the staff.

- A system operator's role is to mentor other teachers having difficulty in implementing the technology initiative. Teachers like to talk to teachers, especially teachers they know and respect. Teachers trained as troubleshooters are often more credible and more accepted into classrooms than technology directors or coordinators. System operators or teacher troubleshooters help provide on-site technology instruction during recesses and breaks, after school, or on weekends. It is easy for them to develop collegial relationships with other teachers in their grade level or at other primary, intermediate, middle, or high school levels.

- Besides developing a collegial relationship and mentoring other staff members in technology, system operators also help save technical directors and coordinators enormous amounts of time. System operators are trained to look for obvious technology problems. Minor problems can occupy much of a technology coordinator's time. With the help of teacher system operators, technical directors and coordinators can address larger and more pressing issues as well as have more time to plan. System operators are generally not paid but are rewarded with the latest upgrades in equipment or are sent to local, state, and national technology conferences. This gives them a sense of pride and accomplishment in that they are improving themselves as well as helping others in their respective school districts.

4. **Internet, Scanner, and Multimedia Applications**. School technology leaders are finding that a triad of Internet, scanner, and multimedia presentation applications provides a strong base for teacher and student use of

technology. This combination allows teachers and students to more efficiently gather data from local, state, national, and international sources as well as providing them with a way to present their material in a multimedia format. Teachers at intermediate levels are finding that the combination helps teach students how to sequence and outline material for electronic presentations.

5. **Intranet.** The Intranet is a communication link similar to the Internet but is developed within the district. Networked computers can access current academic standards and tips on teaching strategies and can recommended technologies. School districts are developing Intranets to act as multimedia libraries and repositories. Intranets are now connecting classrooms and media centers as well as offices electronically so that students, staff, and administration can find and locate previously stored information and communicate with each other. Such connections can include everything from telephones and e-mail that allows staff to exchange ideas more conveniently to centralized databases.

Some teachers and students are using Intranets to store media presentations and electronic research papers as well as lesson plans. For example, a high-quality student report on pyramids could be linked to a set of lesson plans on the Middle East developed by a teacher within the district. Other teachers could use the district Intranet to electronically obtain the Middle East lesson plans as well as the student report on pyramids (for information on any relevant intellectual property laws, contact your district office). If used in this manner, the Intranet can become a locally developed, districtwide, electronic resource file for teachers and even for students.

When all is said and done, there are three main components to a school technology infrastructure. The following section is derived from information contained on the computer strategies, LLC, and website that is used with permission.

## Three Main Parts

Generally, a network is a communications system used to connect two or more users. A computer network connects users of devices such as computers, printers, or application programs so they can share information. The largest of these networks is, of course, the World Wide Web—the network of networks. In the simplest sense, every computer network consists of three parts:

**Clients:** The user workstations and peripherals

**Infrastructure:** The wires, fiber-optics, or transmission media that the data moves through

**Networking electronics:** Devices that move, route, and store data for users

A network with 5,000 users might have thousands of components, but each would be one of the types described above. The simplest networks are called *peer-to-peer* networks. In these networks, each client has its own storage area, which might be shared with other clients. There is no central storage in this type of network. Peer-to-peer networks are often used in small classroom computer labs.

The most common are *client-server* networks. These networks have storage devices on the network that may hold data for users to share. The term *file server* is used in reference to these storage devices. A client may use the network to connect to one of these storage devices and get some documents to view or edit.

Computer networks come in all sizes. They are usually referred to by their size and scope. LAN has become almost synonymous with the word network. A LAN is a network in which all clients share a common infrastructure (wires) and are usually in the same building or group of buildings. In contrast, a WAN is one that spans a larger geographic area. For instance, a network that links two or more LANs that are separated by some distance might be called a WAN (see Figure 8.1).

A really big network made up of several diverse LANs and WANs is often called an *Internet.* The largest group of interconnected networks in the world is

**Figure 8.1** Daviess County (Kentucky) Public School Network

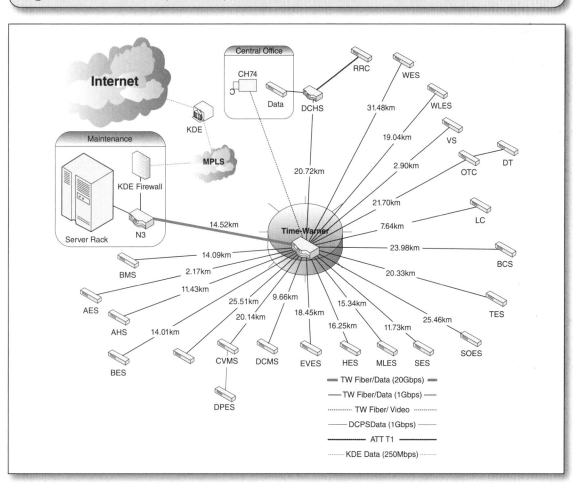

*Source:* Daviess County Public Schools DCPS Network Layout, designed by Steve Burton, manager of computer operations for the Daviess County Public Schools district. Retrieved from http://www.daviesskyschools.org/content_page2.aspx?cid=826

the global network known as the Internet. Increasingly, large groups of networks are interconnected within an organization. As explained above, this type of network has come to be called an *Intranet.*

Intranets have become enormously popular because they often rely on the same standard software packages that most of us use for the Internet. For example, using a standard World Wide Web browser, teachers in a large district might navigate their own district's Intranet to find class schedule information or a message board for sharing curriculum ideas. Such Intranets may look and feel just like the Internet, but access to them is often limited to users within an organization.

Based on this information, a technology coordinator could call up a networking vendor and say, "We are looking to build a district WAN made up of 14 LANs. We estimate about 1,200 clients eventually, and of course, we want to link our WAN into the Internet." That should get their attention!

## Networking Costs

Building and operating a network costs money. Generally, costs are determined by a number of factors. Among them are

Everyone should have the same type of computer to be more cost effective.

- How many users will there be?
- Over what distance will the users be spread?
- At what speed of communication will the network run?
- How complex or simple will the network be?
- What type of client service is needed?
- How well designed is the network?

It is logical that a network connecting 20 students in a single classroom computer lab will be cheaper than a network that connects 300 teachers across large districts. But some of the other cost factors are not as obvious. For instance, a network in which every user has the same type of computer will be cheaper to build and operate than one in which there are several different types of computers.

The type of services needed is another good example. A network where everyone needs only e-mail will be much cheaper than one where everyone needs live video conferencing. Accordingly, in the planning process, it is really important to separate the need-to-have services from the nice-to-have services. Remember that you will be networked for a long time; there will be plenty of time to add those bells and whistles.

1 support person for every 50 to 75 users.

Networking cost analysis should also take into account ongoing support costs. Many network coordinators use the rule that one full-time support person will be required for every 50 to 75 users. In schools, students and teachers are often involved in the network support. Using certified staff for day-to-day technical support may not be appropriate or practical in many situations. Remember, managing a school network can be a full-time job. What happens when the network goes down and the teacher-network manager is teaching a chemistry class? If the choice is to use student or teacher time, it is important to be realistic about the time demands that will be created by your network-support needs.

Other ongoing costs are related to maintenance and upgrades for the network. In a successful situation, demands for network services will increase steadily, and so will monitoring and maintenance costs. The phenomenal rate of change in the world requires technology coordinator to plan for costs due to growth, improvements, and upgrades. As well with each major change or improvement, there will be costs related to training, both for network users and the network support staff.

*Futureproof your plan.*

## Infrastructure Costs

It is surprising to many school administrators when they come to realize where the typical costs for network components are spent. In reality, only a small percentage of the costs are spent on infrastructure (see Table 8.1).

Notice, too, that while infrastructure accounts for very little of the overall network cost, it also tends to last longer than the other networking components.

### Component Typical Life Span

- Client stations (PC, Apple): 18–36 months
- Network electronics (hubs, routers): 3–5 years
- Infrastructure (wires, racks, wiring closets): 10–20 years

Since infrastructure is relatively inexpensive and long-lasting, the obvious conclusion is to build the best infrastructure that is possible. Unfortunately, in practice, many networks are built on poor infrastructure, usually because the network was not planned for growth or costs were cut in the wrong places. For example, when a less-expensive and lower-rated wire is selected, it may not accommodate higher transmission speeds when you want to upgrade. Another common infrastructure mistake is to reduce costs by limiting the number of data ports (or drops) per classroom below the recommended four to six. Most network professionals say that the bulk of the problems a network could encounter come from a poor infrastructure. Think of network infrastructure as you would the foundation of a house. If you were to build a poor foundation under a house, wouldn't that house have problems? It does not matter how well built the house is above ground if the foundation is not solid.

*Build the best infrastructure possible!*

| Table 8.1 Relative Costs for Network Components | |
| --- | --- |
| Software | 53% |
| Hardware | 35% |
| Networking electronics | 7% |

*Source:* Computer Strategies, LLC. (2002). Oakland, California. Used with permission.

A final note concerns the use of volunteers and students to install network infrastructure. The schools that have done this successfully have used the services of experts to train, oversee, or test the installations. In other words, make expert advice available to get the job done properly.

Building a good, well-planned infrastructure is just one of the many tasks ahead, but it illustrates something that is true of the whole network infrastructure implementation process: planning pays off! A well-planned network will be

1. **More reliable:** Less downtime

2. **Lower in cost:** Less expensive to support, expand, and use

3. **More flexible:** Based on standards, easy to expand, uses parts from many vendors

4. **Simple to support and use**

The alternative to good planning is building a network ad hoc. Some people mistakenly assume that eliminating a planning process can save money. They prefer to spend their budgets right away on new hardware and software. The next time there is money in the budget, they run to buy more equipment. This strategy may work for the smallest of systems, but on larger networks, ad hoc networking ends up being expensive, hard to support, and very complex for users.

## TECHNOLOGY INFRASTRUCTURE ELEMENTS IN 21ST CENTURY SCHOOLS

### Cyberinfrastructure (CI)

This infrastructure brings together data, technology, and human resources as a means of generating knowledge and sharing expertise. Cyberinfrastructure is a technological reality based in the sciences, economics, social sciences, and the humanities. In essence, it is a virtual research community. The construction brings together high-speed networks with high performance computational resources. Management systems control the usage, performance, and availability of computing systems, with security systems protecting the activity. The National Science Foundation has indicated that CI provides an opportunity for a new kind of scholarly inquiry and education, empowering communities of researchers and learners to innovate and revolutionize what they do (www.nsf .gov/pubs/2007/nsf0728/nsf0728.pdf). The advantage is that it gives schools access and the opportunity to be involved with cutting edge research, data, and facilities that they could never afford. The following is a case of CI in a high school classroom:

*Sherry is a tenth-grade science teacher. In preparing an earth sciences class, she downloads recent seismological data and incorporates them into a game-like, inquiry-based classroom activity. She feels a bit unsure about how to best structure the student groups and how to design her class activity, so she logs into her online professional development environment where her mentors provide advice and assistance. Her refined activity then becomes available to other teachers for use and adaptation. Along the way, Sherry learns more about the physics of shock wave propagation. Indeed, she learns to use a software tool that models this phenomenon.*

*In class, Sherry walks about the room, offering help and advice as students work through the activities. Because of the extended nature of the activity, students continue working collaboratively on the project at home. The environment includes a simulated scientist agent who can offer advice. As part of the activity, they use sensors connected to handheld devices to explore and collect vibration data in different physical environments. One student continues working on the problem during his after-school technology club. Other students in the club become engaged and suggest other resources for solving the problem.*

*Sherry, meanwhile, can assess students' progress and learning activity by accessing tools that visually display real-time analyses of their performance, attitudes, and the nature of their collaborative activity. She can consult her online assessment mentor to help her interpret these dynamically generated analyses and offer tailored and developmentally appropriate feedback. Report generation software helps her prepare reports for parents and district administrators. These analyses can also help Sherry reflect on the quality of the instructional activity, student learning, and ways to implement improvements.*

*Source:* Computing Research Association. (2012). *Cyberinfrastructure for Education and Learning for the Future.* Retrieved from http://archive.cra.org/reports/cyberinfrastructure.pdf

## Cybersecurity

Generally speaking, cybersecurity are the hardware and software devices designed to protect sensitive and private data. School systems hold a great deal of sensitive data related to particular students and families. Since the bulk of these data is now stored in computer and server databases, it is essential that this information is protected from outside access. School leaders should consult with district and system-level specialists to ensure confidential school data are protected from outside access.

## Wireless Infrastructure

With the ease of using and accessing wireless technologies in the classroom, the direction for school technology infrastructures is centered on setting up a strong wireless network (Wi-Fi) across the school. The benefit of a sound Wi-Fi network is that it inherently supports technology growth and change because the network can accommodate a variety of digital learning devices. It also supports one-to-one technology learning strategies and anytime-anywhere learning. Within your wireless network, it is essential to address safety. Service Set Identifiers (SSIDs), WPA2 Encryption, and restricted IP ranges in your wireless infrastructures can help you address security matters in your network.

*Considerations in your wireless infrastructure:*

1. Depending on the degree to which you are going to go digital through programs like Bring Your Own Device (BYOD), you may want to have an access point (AP) in every classroom to ensure sufficient connectivity for 30 students operating mobile devices at one time in one classroom. Some schools are also bringing wireless connectivity out to school parking lots, fields, and lunchrooms.

2. There is a lot of high bandwidth demanding programs and websites that students will need access to on your WLAN. The latest information suggests that you should be upgrading to an 802.11n wireless network. The advantage with this system is that it can transmit multiple data streams through multiple antennas.

3. Know what applications will work on the network you have or are setting up. You want to make sure that your technologies and applications can run smoothly without delay or interruption.

4. Plan for Guest Access and BYOD. Make sure your system can support students and teachers connecting to your school network.

---

*Source:* Aruba Networks (2013).

## Interactive Whiteboards/Smart Boards

For many schools across the nation, Smart Boards are a common technology in the classroom. The challenge for many schools and school districts is that regular smart boards are quite expensive. One of the authors of this book, Devon Jensen, used to serve as the president of the parent council for his local school. The parent council had a source of funds that could be used to support the academic programs happening at the school. The council would then work with the principal and the school to determine how those funds could best be used to support the actual needs of teachers and learning at the school. In one year, the entire allocation went to purchasing five Smart Boards for the school. They could have never been able to do this with their regular technology budget allocated to them by the district. So it is a huge investment as part of a school's technology infrastructure although worth it because of how it can impact the creativity of student instruction. Schools with a more focused budget could consider other technologies that do the same thing but at a lower cost.

As shown following, eBeam or Mimio Interactive Displays—uses existing technologies that a school will have—laptop and LCD projector—to turn any surface into interactive digital content. The small receiver unit attaches to the wall and activates and image area up to 9 feet by 5 feet. Students an teachers can then use a Stylus pen to interact with the data being projected. This can all be accomplished on an existing whiteboard or on the wall.

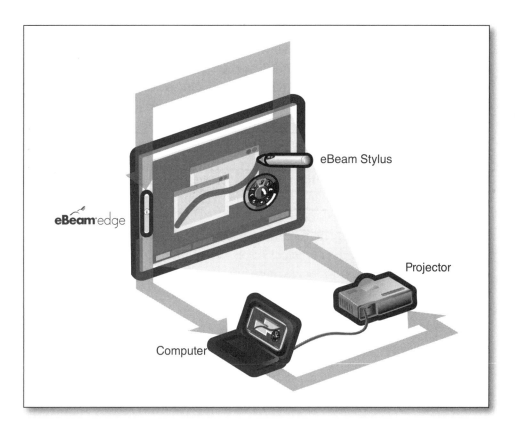

## Cloud Computing

Districts can consider moving to cloud computing, which involves shifting from the procurement and maintenance of servers in local datacenters to purchasing software as a service (SaaS) and Web applications from datacenters running in the cloud. In this realm, there are both private and public cloud applications. Cloud computing derives from the concept of utility computing. Utility computing is the packaging of computing resources as a metered service similar to how public utilities package and sell electricity through our nation's power grid.

Cloud computing can support both the academic and administrative services required for learning and education. It can enable students and educators to access the same learning resources using different Internet devices anytime and anywhere, both in and out of school. This will not happen automatically, however. School systems and other youth-serving organizations—public libraries, public broadcasting, after-school clubs, and so on—will need to engage each other and seek common platforms or at least technical interoperability.

Cloud computing is still in a nascent stage with obstacles to overcome to fully realize its potential. Still, now is the time to move forward with investments that contribute to the shift to cloud computing, with the primary benefits being cost savings and an ability for educational institutions to refocus on their core mission, educating students (Ed.gov, Access and Enable).

## E-Rate

E-Rate is a federal program that supports connectivity in elementary and secondary schools and libraries by providing discounts on Internet access, *discounts from 20-90% based on poverty level.*

telecommunications services, internal network connections, and basic maintenance. Schools, school districts, and consortia can receive discounts on these services ranging from 20% to 90% depending on their level of poverty and geographic location. Schools' eligibility for E-Rate money is contingent on compliance with several federal laws designed to ensure student privacy and safety on the Internet. The Children's Internet Protection Act (CIPA) requires any school that funds Internet access or internal network connections with E-Rate money to implement filters that block students' access to content that may be harmful to minors, including obscenity and pornography. CIPA also requires schools receiving E-Rate discounts to teach online safety to students and to monitor their online activities.

Ensuring student safety on the Internet is a critical concern, but many filters designed to protect students also block access to legitimate learning content and such tools as blogs, wikis, and social networks that have the potential to support student learning and engagement. More flexible, intelligent filtering systems can give teachers (to whom CIPA restrictions do not apply) access to educationally valuable content. On the other end of the spectrum, some schools and districts filter students' online activities with proxy servers that meet CIPA requirements but are easy to get around, minimizing their utility for managing and monitoring students' online activity. CIPA also has posed challenges to accessing school networks through students' own cell phones, laptop computers, and other Internet access devices to support learning activities when schools cannot afford to purchase devices for each student (Ed.gov, Access and Enable).

## FUTURE CHALLENGES

Schools and libraries of the future will continue to encourage teachers and students to best use local, state, national, and global informational resources. Schools of the future will not only be considered processors of knowledge, they will also become connectors of knowledge. School leaders will be providing students and teachers with portable technology that will allow them to travel electronically around the world faster than ever before. Wireless portable technology will provide a very high level of connectivity for everyone. New innovations will provide resources, arrangements, and lifelong learning experiences for the full development of all individuals and their communities. New creative designs will provide self-directed, other-directed, individually supported group learning, team building, and societal connections for our world and its people. In sum, educational technology will unfold in a way that nurtures learning and fosters communication among all members of the global community.

## REFLECTIVE ACTIVITIES

1. List the infrastructure barriers that you have experienced in your school as you have tried to implement a technology program.

2. State your opinions regarding networked classroom technology centers.

3. Outline the administrative structure for technology that exists in your school, district, and state. Consider wiring and hardware structure.

4. Explore the things you are doing to ensure that your technology plan incorporates the concept of future-proofing.

5. Based on the information about connectivity in this chapter, evaluate where your technology program would rate. Explain your school's perceived need to change this level.

6. Detail what your school is doing to maximize the interchangeability, adaptation, and use of its technology resources. Identify the infrastructure that exists for the management, maintenance, and service of the computer technology in your school.

# 9 Technology Plan Evaluation

## THE FINAL PIECE OF THE PUZZLE

Innovative schools are using technology to make assessment and evaluation an integral part of the instructional design and development process. Built into this technology initiative are procedures for school leaders to monitor and evaluate the direction and implementation of the plan. When appropriate technology is used to facilitate teaching and learning, it becomes an established part of your school. The development of a statewide electronic communication network infrastructure will help assist school leaders in best using and sharing information gained through meaningful program evaluation.

## Challenges to Program Evaluation

The single biggest barrier to widespread school technology implementation continues to be basic awareness of the measurable benefits. Unprecedented support for school technology is spurring an investment of billions of dollars, but the lack of research and quality measurement has led to unclear results. The key issue is establishing more effective and accurate ways in which we can measure the real benefits of educational technology and measure the true associated costs in money and time spent learning to use these technologies. Sociological acceptance and adoption of the use of these new communication technologies continues to represent a challenge as well.

Another concern is the lack of quality leadership in establishing strong evaluation and assessment agendas and programs and supporting teachers. Authors Williams and Engel (2012) noted that if one understands the teaching process, then building a nation's capital calls for hiring teachers with potentially good teaching traits and providing support to teach well. As part of that support, administrators need to assist teachers with technology integration. Thus, there is a special need for leadership and more understanding as to the process of evaluation and how it relates to technology development in schools. Quality leadership is a key component to the success of any educational technology implementation process. One of the most important aspects of that leadership role is that educational planners understand the process of evaluation and how it should be administered.

The rapid changes occurring in technology also pose a challenge to establishing effective evaluation programs. Technology capabilities have continued to change faster than educational researchers can keep up. For example, initial evidence on the use of technology applications in the classroom showed that drill and practice activities were successful in reinforcing skills. Now, with continued advances in mobile devices and applications being used extensively in classrooms, teachers are becoming even more creative in their approach to integrating technology. Subsequently, it has been difficult for researchers to complete large-scale, controlled studies that lead to solid conclusions because by the time their research is published, new technologies are providing new opportunities for teachers and students.

Of concern is the need to better align technology standards and guidelines with current teaching and curriculum evaluation frameworks. Fortunately, the move toward Common Core State Standards and the work of numerous states in developing new multimeasure frameworks for teaching and evaluation is helping to fill this gap (Depascale, 2012). As part of this evaluative process, there appears to be increased interest in determining possible links between technology integration and characteristics of high-performing schools. To be sure, administrators, teachers, and parents want to know and understand the impact that technology has made on district goals relating to student learning, professional development, and curricular content.

## Focusing on Student Performance

According to Robert Marzano (2012), an evaluation system that fosters teacher (and student) learning will differ from one whose aim is to measure teacher competence. With this in mind, it is essential for administrators to focus the direction of any technology initiative on student performance. The key, then, is to create a more symbiotic relationship between teacher and students as well as a connection between technology and the curriculum. In doing so, correlations between student performance and the use of technology in the classrooms will become more evident. This means that appropriate mechanisms and administrative structures will need to be made so that student performance can be measured and assessed in relevant ways. The key here is that we want teachers, students, administrators, and the external community to see that technology is having a positive impact on student achievement and that students are performing better because of the technological changes enacted within the school.

## Data Collection

Data collection is a major key to finding out how technology is being used to impact teaching and learning. A number of national marketing companies are collecting data on technology use. These commercial marketing firms collect information on school technology and sell that information to technology manufacturers. They conduct mail and telephone surveys of schools throughout the nation, determining what type of high-tech equipment is being used and how it is being used. Results are supplemented by information from departments of education and other surveys. State and school leaders, upon request, may obtain this information after a certain amount of time.

State and school leaders do have to be careful in placing too much emphasis on data collected by marketing companies. One of the weaknesses of these data is that they are usually based on small-sample populations. This can generate misleading statistics that tend to favor the direction of the company sponsoring the survey. Another problem is that district administrators do not always take surveys seriously or rush through them without real consideration. As a result, some states are collecting their own data because they feel that schools take government surveys more seriously and the results will be more accurate. In addition, these surveys have an educational and student achievement focus on technology and are less likely to have a hidden technological agenda like that found in market research. These data are also public property and can be shared more easily among districts and states for comparison studies.

There continues to be a move nationally to gather technology data for research. Federal and state officials are, at times, having schools submit a list of inventory of technology as a requirement for grant applications.

## LEADERSHIP

Quality leadership is a key component in the success of any educational evaluation process. One of the most important aspects of that leadership role is for educational planners to understand the process of evaluation and how it should be administered. Educational planners can contribute to the process by understanding the evaluation process and how it relates to program development. Understanding the evaluation process means leaders will have to convey knowledge of technology as well as instructional strategies. They will also have to convey their expectations of how technology can be used throughout the curriculum.

### Technology Plan Assessment

An assessment of the technology plan should reveal the quality of change that occurred during the actual implementation process. Assessment indicators need to reveal the quality of change rather than just a snapshot of current conditions. The evaluation process should help determine if the school's vision of technology truly reflects a focus on student learning. School leaders must examine and review the technology plan to make sure that it encourages teachers to use current research and academic development practices in their classrooms. The following questions can provide direction during a review of a technology plan:

- Does the technology plan address the meaningful involvement of community members, parents, and other stakeholders who have shown an interest in developing and promoting informational technology?

- Should the technology plan be changed to increase community involvement?
- Does the technology plan facilitate instruction?
- Do action steps in the plan reflect the alignment of up-to-date technological practices with student-learning patterns?
- How effective is the technology plan in accounting for student performance?
- Are objectives for student performance responsive to the learning needs of students?
- Are student achievement goals being met?

In sum, an evaluation of the technology plan should reveal a dynamic perspective of growth in the area of technology use.

## Professional Development and Evaluation

Often a strong association exists between effective leadership and the evaluation of professional development programs. Effective professional development programs can be evaluated as well as analyzed by using indicators of success developed early in the project.

Objectives of any quality professional development program involving the use of technology should be consistent with the school district's shared vision. Indicators of staff development success can be measured through the staff's ability to

- Understand and follow school vision and goals as shown by surveys and documents
- Be involved in a variety of technology workshops and conferences
- Access district operating and informational systems
- Understand the use of data collection and multimedia
- Demonstrate an ability to access cloud and use of mobile technology
- Identify technology resources involving support and service
- Use emerging technology to support instruction
- Understand equity and legal issues involving the use of technology
- Evaluate and assess student performance and outcomes

## Assessing Teaching and Learning

Determining how technology enhances the integration of curriculum as well as curriculum content is a way to measure the effectiveness of technology. Development of an integrated curriculum is based on expectations for student learning achievement. The formulation of learning objectives is an important component in assessing student growth via the use of technology. The design of the curriculum should provide students with the essential knowledge and skills in information technology that can be applied across the curriculum. Students can use their school's technology resources to access the cloud and/or access a library online (with supervision), as a way of finding information that relates to different curricular areas.

## Classroom Technology Environment

The importance of organizational climate for school success is well known. The classroom must be designed technologically to foster active involvement of students in the learning process. Lessons should be based on high expectations and an application of higher-order thinking skills whenever applicable. The pace of learning should take into account learning styles of children and stages of growth and development. Application of instruction should be based on individual needs of the students and allow them to explore and investigate new forms of informational technology.

The amount of student writing, as well as the completion rate of projects, can be used to measure positive changes. Pointedly, there appears to be a trend of student attendance rates going up in classrooms using technology. Students participating in interactive technology seem to want to come to school. Attendance rates can easily be cross-correlated with classrooms using interactive technology to give administrators a feel as to whether technology may be having an effect on attendance.

Another indicator of technology success in the classroom is teacher and parent support. Teacher and parent support of technology can be monitored via questionnaires or surveys as well as by the collection of positive correspondence. In addition, minutes from board of trustee meetings can provide documentation of positive feelings toward technology and thus reflect possible organizational climate changes.

## Student Outcomes

Documenting the effectiveness of improvements made in electronic applications is a way of assessing the impact of technology in schools. Student learning outcomes can include measures of how well students learn, think, reason, and solve complex problems through the use of computers in the classroom. Program attendance, graduation rates, standardized testing, teacher-made pre- and post-tests, observation, portfolios, grades, and the degree of student participation can provide indications of program success.

Teacher and student use of technology can be documented easily by logging the number of times an individual uses some type of online source. A log of all Internet queries and messages sent and received can be noted. These data can be graphed and shared with the community to show how technology is being used in classrooms.

## Equity Issues

Monitoring equity issues as they relate to technology planning and implementation is a key to reforming education. On the other hand, an equity problem can arise due to a lack of technology. Wealthier school districts almost certainly have an advantage over economically deprived urban and rural schools when it comes to accessing technology. This has a tendency to create a situation referred to as "pockets of excellence." That said, thousands of rural and economically disadvantaged schools need to upgrade equipment and programs if they are to keep up with emerging technologies. Hopefully, with more research and support, better access, and additional funding, all of these rural and disadvantaged schools will be able to address this problem.

## MEASURING CONNECTIVITY

Measuring student access and maintaining equity is of paramount importance to school leaders. Many states are concerned that many school technology applications and programs are not being used—or used wisely. Thus, some technology planners are measuring student use as per a connectivity rate. A school's connectivity rate can be formulated by calculating the number of minutes students are actually using their technology applications divided by the number of applications provided. This can be tracked daily and averaged at the end of the month. A school's connectivity rate can become an important factor when administrators are allocating technology funding or competitive grants.

### Accreditation Standards

States are attempting to link technology funding with standards for student performance. To avoid developing paste-in technology approaches, schools are realigning their curricula and technology around student performance standards. Program evaluation for schools using technology is becoming centered on meeting student performance benchmarks. In an attempt to avoid prepackaged technology approaches, schools are realigning their curricula and technology around student performance standards. Program evaluation for schools using technology is becoming centered on meeting student performance benchmarks.

#### Student Performance Assessment

Technology grant applications in some states are now requiring schools to include student performance objectives and assessments in proposals. As a result, school leaders are continuing to search for the best ways to incorporate assessment packages in grant applications.

#### Integrated System Assessments

A popular way to access student achievement and performance is through the use of integrated data-based systems. These programs allow individual students to learn and work at their independent challenge levels but, at the same time, are able to digitally track student performance. These data-based approaches also have a teacher management component that provides diagnosis, adjustment, and evaluation features. Information collected from these databases can then be used as part of a larger program evaluation process.

### Program Guidelines

Technology is ever-changing and so the best of technology plans must change as well. Due to the scope of most technology plans, it is critical that the evaluation process be viewed as ongoing. Statewide educational agencies should review and evaluate technology in their states at a minimum of every three years. Such evaluations should be coordinated with appropriate resource centers, schools, and other agencies. This type of review process helps to identify standards and interconnection issues that should be evaluated and addressed. It will also identify the success stories and research that is needed to validate the cost and implementation of technology.

Guidelines for program evaluation are listed below:

- Indicators of success for the technology program should be developed at the onset of the project.
- Indicators of success should relate to the original vision of the project as well as to the mission statement.
- An evaluation component for staff development should be a major component of the technology plan.
- A feedback process for information should be incorporated in the evaluation plan.
- Clear indicators of success expressed in terms of student outcomes should drive improvement efforts.
- Assessment should derive from multiple sources of data, both quantitative and qualitative.

## Evaluation Checklist

Evaluation checklists are helpful to educational planners trying to gauge the success of their classroom technology program. The checklist below is easy to administer and provides a quick assessment of program components:

Does the program provide evidence of administrative and school board support?

Does the plan incorporate a technology mission statement?

Does the plan establish a technology task force or advisory committee?

Does the technology plan facilitate community school-business partnerships?

Does the technology program provide for a public relations plan?

Does the technology program allow for research development?

Does the technology plan use student learner outcomes as a measure?

Does the plan have an evaluation tool that provides for the collection of qualitative data?

Evaluation tools such as the checklist are often digitally based and do not have to be complicated. They are also helpful as to ensuring that key components are present in any classroom technology program.

## STRATEGIES FOR SUCCESS

Successful school administrators use the following strategies in developing assessment and evaluation programs relating to school technology:

## Setting Goals and Indicators

The evaluation and assessment process must be linked to the original mission statement and objectives of the district. Indicators of successful technology integration for the purposes of evaluation should be established during the early planning stages of the program.

## Identifying Target Populations

Successful evaluation and assessment procedures should focus on targeting specific external and internal population groups. Parents and community-related organizations and businesses represent external groups. Trustees, administrators, teachers, and students represent internal target groups. Data collection needs to specifically focus on these target areas and how they relate to technology integration.

## Evaluation Centers

The National Study of School Evaluation located in Schaumburg, Illinois, provides a wealth of information on technology evaluation and assessment (see www.ecs.org/html/Document.asp?chouseid=3654).

## Regional Technology Training Centers

Educational Northwest (see educationnorthwest.org) and other regional technology centers across the United States provide a plethora of information on best practices involving assessment and evaluation. They also provide conferences and workshops on evaluation strategies.

Regardless of the process used to evaluate a program, planners need to be willing to use data and to make changes and adjustments where necessary. They must understand that curriculum improvement and instructional improvement are interconnected and that a change in one area will probably elicit a change in another area. Problems and concerns can cloud issues at hand, making evaluation an important tool. With higher quality and more detailed information at our disposal, school leaders will be able to focus more on how technology can help teachers with student achievement in the future.

## Technology Plan Evaluation Activity

1. Locate two technology plans for schools or districts similar to where you currently work. Carefully read through these documents.

   a. How do these plans compare to each other?

   b. How do these plans differ from each other?

2. Analysis of your technology plan.

   a. Review the Technology Maturity Benchmarks Rubric using either your school or district as the focus.

Technology Maturity Benchmarks Rubric

| Category | Type | | Administrative Filter | | |
| --- | --- | --- | --- | --- | --- |
| | | Emergent | Islands | Integrated | Intelligent |
| Policy | Behavioral | Appropriate technology use is considered, but it is informal and inconsistent. | Appropriate technology use is formalized, but it is mostly ignored by many in the school. | Appropriate technology use is formalized and embraced in many parts of the school. | Appropriate technology use policy is formalized and fully supported at all levels of the organization. |
| | Resource/ Infrastructure | No technology policy exists. | Some policy exists, loosely articulated and mostly informal, with no formal approval. | Formal policy exists, but it is not comprehensive in nature or has not been approved by the governing body. | Comprehensive policy exists and has been approved by the organization's governing body. |
| Planning | Behavioral | Informal planning process is isolated to projects and is budget driven. | Formal planning takes place but is isolated to specific projects with some connection to other planning efforts. | Schoolwide comprehensive planning receives informal review and is connected to other planning efforts. | Schoolwide comprehensive planning exists with formal evaluation and connection to other planning within the school and district. |
| | Resource/ Infrastructure | There is an informal plan. | There is a formal plan with isolated implementation and little or no connection to other planning efforts. | There is a comprehensive technology plan that receives informal review and some connection to planning efforts. | There is a comprehensive technology plan with formal evaluation and connection to planning in the school and district. |
| Budget | Behavioral | Some policy exists, loosely articulated and mostly informal with no formal approval. | Formal technology budgeting process exists, but with relatively simple resourcing. | Technology budgeting process with high priority; multiple budgets considered, but long-term budgeting is not. | There is a comprehensive long-term budgeting for the institution; multiple budgets including upgrades, etc. |
| | Resource/ Infrastructure | Little budget allocated for technology. | Specific technology budget is provided, but other budgets are not considered for technology. | Specific technology budget is provided in addition to line items in other budgets. | Specific budget is provided in addition to line items in other budgets for long-term budget needs. |

**Administrative Filter**

| Category | Type | Emergent | Islands | Integrated | Intelligent |
|---|---|---|---|---|---|
| Administrative Information | Behavioral | Administrative systems are utilized by a few of the staff members, primarily to benefit administration. | Administrative systems are utilized by many staff members but are not integrated into regular practice. | Administrative systems are utilized by most of the staff members; some paperless systems are in place. | The daily use of electronic systems is required for support activities; paper systems are replaced. |
| | Resource/ Infrastructure | Administrative systems are available to administration and/or a few staff only. | Administrative systems are available to many administrators and staff. | Administrative systems are available to most administrators and staff. | Administrative systems are available to all administrators and staff. |

**Curricular Filter**

| Category | Type | Emergent | Islands | Integrated | Intelligent |
|---|---|---|---|---|---|
| Electronic Information | Behavioral | Staff and students rarely depend upon electronic resources and use them sporadically. | Students and staff are somewhat dependent upon information resources and utilize them often. | Students and staff are very dependent upon information resources and utilize them regularly. | Students and staff are heavily dependent upon information resources and use them daily. |
| | Resource/ Infrastructure | Resources are scarce, limited to materials like electronic encyclopedias. Few students have access. | Resources are beyond basic, but they lack depth and are not available to all areas of the school. | Resources are fairly comprehensive providing depth or diversity, but not both. Access is available to most. | Resources are comprehensive providing depth and diversity. All students have regular access. |
| Assessment | Behavioral | Few staff and no students use technology for evaluation of student work. | Used by many of the staff and some of the students for the evaluation of work and self-assessment | Used by most of the staff and many students for the evaluation of work and self-assessment | Technology is an essential part of the assessment process for students, teachers, and parents. |

*(Continued)*

(Continued)

| Category | Type | Curricular Filter | | | |
|---|---|---|---|---|---|
| | | Emergent | Islands | Integrated | Intelligent |
| | **Resource/ Infrastructure** | Electronic tools are rarely used for assessment and are not readily available. | Some reporting and assessment tools are available, with a focus on traditional assessment measures. | Many reporting and assessment tools are available, with instruments limited in scope and availability. | Fully integrated reporting and assessment tools are available for student and staff use. |
| **Curriculum Integration** | **Behavioral** | Some of the technology is used in the curriculum on a limited basis. | Curriculum is somewhat dependent on technology and used in multiple ways. | Curriculum is very technology dependent and used comprehensively throughout. | Technology and related resources are available for all curricular areas. |
| | **Resource/ Infrastructure** | Technology is limited to only a few curricular areas. | Technology related resources are available for some curricular areas. | Technology and related resources are available for most curricular areas. | Technology and related resources are available for all curricular areas. |
| **Teacher Use** | **Behavioral** | Occasional use by teachers for curriculum enrichment and material generation | Regular use by teachers, but not integrated into daily work | Daily use by teachers for administration and curriculum | Teacher's work not possible without technology |
| | **Resource/ Infrastructure** | Few teachers have access to appropriate technology in their work area. | Some teachers have access to appropriate technology in their work area. | Most teachers have access to appropriate technology in their work area. | All teachers have access to appropriate technology in their work area. |
| **Student Use** | **Behavioral** | Student use of technology is sporadic, primarily for remediation and enrichment. | Students use technology often, but in limited ways. | Students use technology frequently and comprehensively, but outcomes are not dependent on its use. | Students use technology frequently and comprehensively, and they cannot meet outcomes without it. |
| | **Resource/ Infrastructure** | Few students have consistent and regular access to appropriate technologies. | Some students have consistent and regular access to appropriate technologies. | Most students have consistent and regular access to appropriate technologies. | All students have consistent and regular access to appropriate technologies. |

| Category | Type | Support Filter | | | |
|---|---|---|---|---|---|
| | | Emergent | Islands | Integrated | Intelligent |
| **Stakeholder Involvement** | **Behavioral** | Some of the groups are aware of the planning and implementation procedure, but few are engaged in the process. | Many of the groups are aware of the planning and implementation procedure, but few are engaged in the process. | Most of the groups are aware of the planning and implementation procedure, and many are engaged in the process. | All of the groups are aware of the planning and implementation procedure and are engaged in the process. |
| | **Resource/ Infrastructure** | Few groups are represented in the planning and implementation process. | Many of the groups are represented in the planning and implementation process. | Most of the groups are represented in the planning and implementation process. | All of the groups are represented in the planning and implementation process. |
| **Administrative Support** | **Behavioral** | Support is limited to peripheral discussion, but no involvement. | There is peripheral involvement by the administration in planning, practice, and implementation. | There is an ongoing discussion with the administration. | There is an extensive administration involvement in the planning, practice, and implementation. |
| | **Resource/ Infrastructure** | No formal administration, time, and support allocated to the planning and implementation process | Little formal administration, time, and support allocated to the planning and implementation process | Some formal administration, time, and support allocated to the planning and implementation process | Significant formal administration, time, and support allocated to the planning and implementation process |
| **Training** | **Behavioral** | Few staff members participate in technology training activities. | Many staff members participate in technology training activities. | Most staff members participate in technology training activities. | All staff members participate in technology training activities and seek additional training. |
| | **Resource/ Infrastructure** | Limited formal training | Ongoing formal training provided by limited personnel | Ongoing teacher training provided by site and district resources | Training at all levels of the organization, with area experts in each building |

*(Continued)*

(Continued)

| Category | Type | Support Filter | | |
| | | Emergent | Islands | Integrated | Intelligent |
|---|---|---|---|---|---|
| Technical & Infrastructure Support | Behavioral | Few staff utilize formal and informal support. | Many staff utilize formal and informal support. | Most staff utilize formal and informal support. | All staff utilize formal and informal support to find help efficiently. |
| | Resource/ Infrastructure | No formal technical assistance. Users are on their own to find help. | Limited formal technical assistance, usually a mentor, teacher, consultant, etc. | Formal technical assistance provided through staff release time, hired help, and/or formal district support. | Full-time personnel to address all technical support needs. |

| Category | Type | Connectivity Filter | | |
| | | Emergent | Islands | Integrated | Intelligent |
|---|---|---|---|---|---|
| Local Area Networking (LAN) | Behavioral | Staff and students use available network sporadically, usually only for print sharing and limited data. | Staff and students use available networks often, but use is unsophisticated and limited. | Staff use is limited to data but is extensive and sophisticated. | Staff use available WAN services for video, voice, and sophisticated data needs. |
| | Resource/ Infrastructure | No networking installed, or limited, slow speed networking for print sharing | High-speed networking, limited to isolated areas | High-speed networking with access to all working environments | Networking comprehensive and expandable for data, voice, and video |

| | | Connectivity Filter | | | |
|---|---|---|---|---|---|
| Category | Type | Emergent | Islands | Integrated | Intelligent |
| **District Area Networking (WAN)** | **Behavioral** | Little or no use of area services exists. | Staff use district services often, but in very traditional and basic manners. | Staff use is limited to data but is extensive and sophisticated. | Staff use available WAN services for video, voice, and sophisticated data needs. |
| | **Resource/ Infrastructure** | Little or no district-area networking infrastructure, with little or no applications or available data | Limited district-area networking through dial-up services or dedicated lines; applications and data are limited. | District area networking infrastructure with dedicated, high-speed lines; several data services are available. | Comprehensive network services with high-speed lines, voice, video, and data capacity; data services are available. |
| **Internet Access** | **Behavioral** | Few staff and students use the Internet frequently, and curriculum integration is not apparent. | Many staff and students use the Internet frequently, and curriculum integration is limited. | Most staff and students use the Internet frequently. Use is integrated into the curriculum. | All staff and students use the Internet extensively for video, voice, and sophisticated data needs. |
| | **Resource/ Infrastructure** | There is no Internet access. | There is a limited Internet access via dial-up lines. | There is a direct LAN Internet access in some locations. | There is a direct Internet access to all locations. |
| **Communication Systems** | **Behavioral** | E-mail is used sporadically with little or no impact on communication. | E-mail is used often but has no significant impact on the communication process. | E-mail is used frequently to form administrative and learning activities. | E-mail is an integral part of the school learning and support communications. |
| | **Resource/ Infrastructure** | E-mail is available to some staff and few or no students. | E-mail is available to most staff and some students. | E-mail is available to all staff and many students. | E-mail is available to all staff and students. |

| Category | Type | Innovation Filter | | | |
| --- | --- | --- | --- | --- | --- |
| | | Emergent | Islands | Integrated | Intelligent |
| **New Technologies** | **Behavioral** | New technologies are readily rejected by staff members, with few opportunities for experimentation. | New technologies are accepted by many staff members, although opportunities for experimentation are limited. | New technologies are readily accepted by most staff members. | There is a systematic adaptation of new technologies throughout the school. |
| | **Resource/ Infrastructure** | New technologies are readily rejected with implementation limited to a few areas and staff. | New technologies are readily accepted by many staff with little implementation. | New technologies are readily accepted by the staff with moderate implementation. | Systematic adaptation of new technologies throughout the school |
| **Comprehensive Technologies** | **Behavioral** | Technology is limited to computers, VCRs, overheads, etc. | Technology is becoming more comprehensive including A/V, digitizing, and scanning. | Technology is fairly comprehensive, but it lacks more advanced techniques. | Readily available comprehensive technology, including video conferencing, voice recognition, etc. |
| | **Resource/ Infrastructure** | Available technology is limited and underutilized. | Available technology utilization is limited to one or two types of technology for most staff and students. | Available technology is used including voice, etc., but equipment has not reached full potential. | Available technology is used very comprehensively, incorporating video, etc. into regular practice. |

*Source:* Adapted from the Technology Use Plan Primer by Sibley & Kimball (1998).

b. Complete the Technology Maturity Benchmarks Survey Sheet.

## Technology Benchmarks Survey Sheet

Name: _____ Date: _____
District: _____
School: _____

Clearly mark the box that best represents the level of technology use achieved at your school site. Please refer to the attached Maturity Model Benchmarks Rubric for detailed descriptions of the categories. Return this sheet to your district technology coordinator.

| | | | Emergent | Islands | Integrated | Intelligent |
|---|---|---|---|---|---|---|
| **ADMINISTRATIVE** | Policy | behavioral | | | | |
| | | resource/infrastructure | | | | |
| | Planning | behavioral | | | | |
| | | resource/infrastructure | | | | |
| | Budget | behavioral | | | | |
| | | resource/infrastructure | | | | |
| | Administrative Information | behavioral | | | | |
| | | resource/infrastructure | | | | |
| **CURRICULAR** | Electronic Information | behavioral | | | | |
| | | resource/infrastructure | | | | |
| | Assessment | behavioral | | | | |
| | | resource/infrastructure | | | | |
| | Curricular Integration | behavioral | | | | |
| | | resource/infrastructure | | | | |
| | Teacher Use | behavioral | | | | |
| | | resource/infrastructure | | | | |
| | Student Use | behavioral | | | | |
| | | resource/infrastructure | | | | |
| **SUPPORT** | Stakeholder Involvement | behavioral | | | | |
| | | resource/infrastructure | | | | |
| | Administrative Support | behavioral | | | | |
| | | resource/infrastructure | | | | |
| | Training | behavioral | | | | |
| | | resource/infrastructure | | | | |
| | Technical/Infrastructure Support | behavioral | | | | |
| | | resource/infrastructure | | | | |

*(Continued)*

(Continued)

| Clearly mark the box that best represents the level of technology use achieved at your school site. Please refer to the attached Maturity Model Benchmarks Rubric for detailed descriptions of the categories. Return this sheet to your district technology coordinator. | | | Emergent | Islands | Integrated | Intelligent |
|---|---|---|---|---|---|---|
| CONNECTIVITY | Local Area Networking (LAN) | behavioral | | | | |
| | | resource/infrastructure | | | | |
| | District Area Networking (WAN) | behavioral | | | | |
| | | resource/infrastructure | | | | |
| | Internet Access | behavioral | | | | |
| | | resource/infrastructure | | | | |
| | Communication Systems | behavioral | | | | |
| | | resource/infrastructure | | | | |
| INNOVATION | New Technologies | behavioral | | | | |
| | | resource/infrastructure | | | | |
| | Comprehensive Technologies | behavioral | | | | |
| | | resource/infrastructure | | | | |

    c. After reviewing this material, write up a summary of where you would portray your school or district in the Technology Maturity Model.

3. Review the following two Technology Planning Analysis Rubrics. Select one of them and analyze your school or district's technology plan in relation to the rubric you select. Write a short brief that explains how your technology plan is related to the rubric. What are you doing well? Where is the room for growth and change?

**Technology Planning Analysis Rubric From the Technology Use Plan Primer by Peter H. R. Sibley and Chip Kimball (1998)**

| Criteria | Level of comprehensiveness | | | |
| | 1 | 2 | 3 | 4 |
| --- | --- | --- | --- | --- |
| **Broad Based Support Contributions (Administration, Teachers, Students, Community, and Staff)** | A list of contributors is not provided. | A list of contributors is provided, but it does not describe the constituencies they represent. Equitable representation is not apparent due to the lack of detail. | A comprehensive list of contributors is provided with the constituencies they represent. Representation is provided by at least three of the five areas of the objective. The principal is included. | A comprehensive list of contributors is provided with the constituencies they represent. Representation is across all five areas of the objective. The principal is included. |
| **Broad Based Support Process** | No process for equitable representation is described. | | The process to ensure equitable representation is briefly mentioned, but not emphasized. | The process to ensure equitable representation is emphasized and mentioned in detail. |
| **Needs Assessment Breadth** | A needs assessment is not provided. | A needs assessment is referenced, but it only covers one element of the school environment (equipment or staff development, but not both). | A needs assessment is referenced with more than one element analyzed, but completely assessing staff, student, and community needs. | The needs assessment is comprehensive in breadth, consisting of detailed information about staff development needs and competencies, attitudinal surveys, equipment inventories, and school and district context. |

*(Continued)*

(Continued)

| Technology Planning Analysis Rubric From the Technology Use Plan Primer by Peter H. R. Sibley and Chip Kimball (1998) | | | | |
|---|---|---|---|---|
| | **Level of comprehensiveness** | | | |
| **Criteria** | **1** | **2** | **3** | **4** |
| **Needs Assessment Depth** | Broad generalizations are made about what the school needs with no reference to an assessment. | A needs assessment is referenced, but the instrument is informal, brief and generally not very specific. For example, a computer count is provided with no specificity as to where or how they are used. | A needs assessment is referenced with what appears to be some level of detail. However, the instrument and data are not provided, and there may be room for additional detail in the collection and analysis. | The assessment in any given area is detailed and thorough. The instrument is provided with generalizations about the data. Raw data may be provided in an appendix. |
| **Needs Assessment Equipment** | No equipment inventory was provided. | An inventory exists but is limited to computers only and does not represent vintage. | The inventory moves beyond computers only (phone, TV) but does not address infrastructure or vintage of equipment. | A comprehensive equipment inventory was provided, including computers, infrastructure, access, ITV, telephone, and other equipment. |

From: TPAR ver 2.5mm 2/6/981 copyright © 1998 EDmin Open Systems

**Technology Planning Analysis Rubric From the Technology Use Plan Primer by Peter H. R. Sibley and Chip Kimball (1998)**

| Criteria | Level of comprehensiveness | | | |
|---|---|---|---|---|
| | 1 | 2 | 3 | 4 |
| Mission and/or Vision | No clear mission and/or vision is articulated. | Vision is skill based only and does not address the larger outcomes by the school or district. | Vision focuses on the technology outcomes and skirts around the learning outcome issue. | Vision is comprehensive, which deals with large learning outcomes of students, not technology outcomes. The statement identifies the learning process skills and values. |
| Goals and Objectives | General learning goals are not clear or are absent. | Goals are equipment based instead of based upon learning outcomes. Objectives are not linked to goals or are absent. Objectives and/or goals do not appear to be measurable or obtainable. | Goals are broad and comprehensive but are not completely clear. They are linked to objectives, but are not readily obtainable or measurable. Goals are loosely tied to the state or district documents. | Goals are broad and comprehensive, addressing teaching and learning needs. The goals are clear, attainable, and measurable. Objectives are delineated from goals, further defining how they will be met. |
| Action Plans With Timelines, Responsibilities and Budget | An action plan exists, but timelines and responsibilities are nonexistent or limited. Assessment is not mentioned. The action plan is not curriculum based. | The action plan is specifically tied to the goals and objectives. The identified task, timeline, responsibility, funding, and assessment are incomplete and several elements are missing. | The action plan is specifically tied to the goals and objectives. The identified task, timeline, responsibility, funding, and assessment components are thorough, but one or more elements are missing. | The action plan is specifically tied to the goals and objectives. Each task identifies a task, timeline, and responsibility, funding, and assessment. |

*(Continued)*

## Technology Planning Analysis Rubric From the Technology Use Plan Primer by Peter H. R. Sibley and Chip Kimball (1998)

| Criteria | Level of comprehensiveness | | | |
|---|---|---|---|---|
| | 1 | 2 | 3 | 4 |
| Program Integration | Connection to other efforts is not mentioned throughout the document. | The TUP mentions other efforts but is not explicit in connection with the other efforts. | The TUP is loosely coupled to the other documents with needs and program changes integrated much of the time. | The TUP is tightly coupled to the other reform, curriculum, or accountability documents with the approach fully integrated. |
| Curriculum Integration | The plan focuses upon technology outcomes and skill based goals and does not address how it can enhance the curriculum. | The plan mentions curriculum integration and enhancement, but it lacks detail. | The plan specifically identifies how the curriculum can be enhanced by the use of technology with detail. A technology-rich environment is described, but strategies for enhanced teaching are not explored thoroughly. | The plan specifically identifies how technology enhances the curriculum, and what a student using the technology may do in such an environment. The plan addresses strategies of teaching and learning that can be enhanced as a result of technology integration. |

From: TPAR ver 2.5mm 2/6/982 copyright © 1998 EDmin Open Systems

**Technology Planning Analysis Rubric From the Technology Use Plan Primer by Peter H. R. Sibley and Chip Kimball (1998)**

| Criteria | Level of comprehensiveness | | | |
|---|---|---|---|---|
| | **1** | **2** | **3** | **4** |
| **Evaluation** | No formal evaluation is described. | An evaluation process is described, but it lacks detail and comprehensiveness. It does not refer to learning outcomes. | An evaluation process and instrument is described in detail, but it lacks complete comprehensiveness. The link to goals and objectives is not apparent. | An evaluation process and instrument are described in detail, and they are comprehensive in nature. Assessment is timely, and tied to the objectives. |
| **Multiyear Planning** | A timeline is not mentioned | The plan only covers 1 academic year or project. | The plan covers more than 1 year but is short term in nature with no reference to ongoing planning and support. | The plan is multiyear and references multiyear funding, support, and planning activities. |
| **Standards** | No equipment and/or software standards are mentioned in the document beyond brand names. | Equipment standards are mentioned, but they are limited in their specificity. | Equipment standards are specific but limited to a narrow scope. | Equipment standards are specific, comprehensive, and a process is mentioned as to how they will be employed. |
| **Funding** | Funding resources are not mentioned. | Funding is mentioned, but it primarily focuses upon budgeting or specific site funding and does not address other incoming funding required to implement the plan. | Specific funding sources are described but are limited to traditional sources without specific budget figures. | Specific funding sources are described including current and future funding sources. Including the reallocation and employment of resources and attached budget figures. |

*(Continued)*

(Continued)

| Technology Planning Analysis Rubric From the Technology Use Plan Primer by Peter H. R. Sibley and Chip Kimball (1998) | | | | |
|---|---|---|---|---|
| | **Level of comprehensiveness** | | | |
| **Criteria** | **1** | **2** | **3** | **4** |
| **School Pilot Projects Research and Development** | No R&D projects are mentioned or planned as part of the project. | R&D efforts are mentioned, but they lack detail. No timeline, assessment, or scalability is mentioned. | Specific R&D efforts are described, but scalability is not articulated; timelines and measurements are mentioned, but are not specific. | Specific R&D efforts are described, with implications for future work (scalability) articulated. The R&D efforts have a timeline and measurable instruments in place. |
| **Educational Research** | No educational research is mentioned as part of the project. | Educational research is mentioned, but only in the broadest sense. | Specific educational research is mentioned, but no connections are made to the efforts in the school. | Specific educational research is mentioned, and connections are made to the efforts in schools. |

From: TPAR ver 2.5mm 2/6/983 copyright © 1998 EDmin Open Systems

**Technology Planning Analysis Rubric From the Technology Use Plan Primer by Peter H. R. Sibley and Chip Kimball (1998)**

| Criteria | Level of comprehensiveness | | | |
|---|---|---|---|---|
| | 1 | 2 | 3 | 4 |
| **Model Classroom Configurations** | No classroom or school configurations are described. | Classroom configurations are mentioned, but lack detail (i.e., there will be three computers and a printer in each room). | Classroom configurations are described in detail, but they may be restrictive in nature as the "only" right way. Usually only one type of configuration is described. | Classroom and school configurations are specifically described, with links to teaching and learning outcomes. They are provided as possible solutions to particular problems but are not prescriptive in nature. |
| **Facilities (Electricity, Security, etc.)** | Facilities issues are not mentioned. | Facilities issues are mentioned, but they lack the detail to build into an action plan. | Facilities issues are identified and articulated, but solutions and suggestions lack detail or clarity. | Specific facility issues are identified and addressed, with recommended solutions, budgets, and responsibilities. |
| **Maintenance and Support** | No maintenance and support are provided. | Support plans are mentioned, but they do not have the detail or clarity to implement. | Support plans are mentioned with clarity and detail, but they do not take into consideration long-term issues. | Specific support plans are articulated. This included the process for specific support issues and ongoing equipment replacement, staff development, and repair. |
| **Software Agreements (Site Licensing, etc.)** | No software agreements or policy are mentioned. | Software agreements and policy are mentioned, but the specific policies are not articulated in the plan. | Specific software policy is articulated, but it is not tied to the needs of the site. | Specific software policy is articulated with plans to accommodate software needs at the site. |

*(Continued)*

(Continued)

**Technology Planning Analysis Rubric From the Technology Use Plan Primer by Peter H. R. Sibley and Chip Kimball (1998)**

| Criteria | Level of comprehensiveness | | | |
|---|---|---|---|---|
| | 1 | 2 | 3 | 4 |
| **Copyright and Acceptable Use Policy** | No copyright or acceptable use policy is described. | Copyright and acceptable use are mentioned, but specific policies are not articulated in the plan. | | Copyright and acceptable use are mentioned, but specific policies are not articulated in the plan. |
| **Gifts and Disposal** | No policy is provided for the disposal and receiving of gifts of equipment and service. | Policy is provided, but it is not clear or articulated. | Specific policy is articulated regarding disposal and gifts, but it is not tied to the standards. | Specific policy is articulated regarding moving and disposal of equipment. Gift acceptance is tied directly to standards. |
| **Staff Development** | Staff development is not mentioned in the document. | Staff development is mentioned, but it is not clearly articulated as to how it will be accomplished, or evaluated. | Staff development is articulated, but it is limited to single modalities and is not clearly provided for with resources. | Staff development is addressed either in the action plan or in a separate section. It included multiple strategies, incentives, and resources. |

From: TPAR ver 2.5mm 2/6/98 4 copyright © 1998 EDmin Open Systems

| Technology Planning Analysis Rubric | | | |
|---|---|---|---|
| **Components** | **3** | **2** | **1** |
| **Executive Summary** | It identifies clearly and concisely for the reader the vision, mission, goals and objectives, background, findings, issues, conclusions, and recommendations of the technology plan. Submitted on time. | It provides adequate and accurate information in Executive Summary. Submitted on time. | Executive summary is absent or incomplete. It has missing two or more components of information or is submitted late. |
| **Identifies Contributors and Stakeholder Groups** | Membership list has complete description of constituencies/ stakeholder groups. All areas are equitably represented. Submitted on time. | Membership list is provided and describes constituencies represented. Submitted on time. | Membership is not listed or is inadequate to determine representation of stakeholder groups or is submitted late. |
| **Vision Statement** | Vision is comprehensive and deals with learning outcomes, not just technology outcomes. Clearly and concisely states your team's vision for using technology to improve learning; identifies who will be the users of technology and how it will be used to enhance learning; indicates the benefits that you envision will result from the use of technology by students, teachers, administrators, or others. Submitted on time. | Vision statement provides adequate description of how technology will improve learning, but instructional outcomes are not fully addressed. Submitted on time. | Vision statement is not included or does not address learning outcomes; it is difficult to understand or is submitted late. |
| **Mission Statement** | Mission statement is focused on instructional outcomes and indicates clearly what the school or district will do to make its technology | Mission statement addresses learning outcomes but provides limited information about what, why, and for | Mission statement is missing or does not address instructional outcomes. Provides |

*(Continued)*

(Continued)

| Technology Planning Analysis Rubric | | | |
|---|---|---|---|
| **Components** | **3** | **2** | **1** |
| | vision a reality; why the school or district wants to do this; and for whom the school or district is doing this. Submitted on time. | whom the school or district is doing the plan. Submitted on time. | incomplete and/or is difficult to understand, or is submitted late. |
| **Goals** | Goals are broad, comprehensive, and realistic in addressing teaching and learning needs. Goals clearly answer the following questions: Who? What? By when? By how much? According to which instrument? Submitted on time. | Goals are mostly equipment based and loosely linked to improvement plans. Submitted on time. | Goals are absent or seem to be only equipment based; are not measurable; are incomplete, difficult to understand; or are submitted late. |
| **Objectives** | Objectives are measurable and delineated from goals; they clearly define steps to be taken to achieve goals and are clear and realistic. Submitted on time. | Provides most of the objectives. Some objectives may not be readily attainable or measurable. Submitted on time. | Objectives are absent or incomplete; are difficult to understand, unrealistic; appear immeasurable; or are submitted late. |
| **Needs Assessment** | Assessment is comprehensive and contains detailed information from hardware resources, technology needs assessment, and Maturity Model Benchmark surveys; it identifies use by students and staff, and training received and desired. Submitted on time. | Technology has been assessed and analyzed, but it may not include summaries of information from all elements in the technology surveys. Submitted on time. | Needs Assessment is absent, incomplete, or is submitted late. |
| **General Issues** | Clearly addresses issues of staff development, technical support, technology standards; | Adequately addresses most, but not all, of the most significant issues | |

| Technology Planning Analysis Rubric | | | |
|---|---|---|---|
| **Components** | **3** | **2** | **1** |
| | student access to computers; integrating new with old technologies; capacity of present facilities to accommodate new technologies; how technology resources and budget will be distributed among schools for equitable access; how needs of students with disabilities or limited English proficiency will be addressed; student access to computers; integrating new with old technologies; capacity of present facilities to accept new technologies, etc.<br><br>Submitted on time. | specified in Excellent column.<br><br>Submitted on time. | General issues missing or very incomplete, difficult to understand, or submitted late. |
| **Conclusions and Recommendations** | Clearly identifies the most important needs and challenges confronting the school or district and recommends the projects and steps to be taken to achieve the vision. Conclusions are strong and relevant.<br><br>Submitted on time. | Conclusions and recommendations are adequately justified although the basis of some conclusions are not entirely clear.<br><br>Submitted on time. | Conclusions and recommendations are missing or are not adequately justified based on the information gathered in planning process or are submitted late. |
| **Acceptable Use Policy** | It describes policies that are needed to ensure proper use of the technology resources (e.g., guidelines, software and facilities use policies, parental consent for Internet use, etc.). | It provides an adequate description of the most relevant policy issues. It includes an adequate draft of Acceptable Use Policy. | Policy issues are absent, incomplete, or difficult to understand; lack of Acceptable Use Policy draft or submitted late. |

*(Continued)*

(Continued)

| Technology Planning Analysis Rubric | | | |
|---|---|---|---|
| **Components** | **3** | **2** | **1** |
| | It includes well-written draft of Acceptable Use Policy. Submitted on time. | Submitted on time. | |
| **Technology and Learning Statement** | It provides clear and strong description of how technology is currently used in learning environment and ways it will be used to achieve instructional outcomes; describes how technology will enhance curriculum and teaching and learning strategies; is tightly coupled to other reform efforts; indicates what students will do in the learning environment. Submitted on time. | It provides overview of the current and future use of technology in enhancing the teaching-learning process for students. There is little detail on how technology will be integrated into learning and curriculum. Submitted on time. | Technology and Learning Statement is absent or provides incomplete information on the current use or future role of technology in the school or district and how it will enhance learning, or is submitted late. |
| **Technology Standards, Requirements, and Models for Technology and Learning** | It provides clear and comprehensive description of the capabilities of hardware and learning environments. It identifies minimum standards and requirements for computer hardware, software, and connectivity; describes the types of learning environments that currently exist and those to be created by the plan. Submitted on time. | It provides general description of hardware, software and connectivity standards, and requirements. Although clear, it may miss some information elements. Submitted on time. | Technology standards, requirements, and models are missing, incomplete, vague, or submitted late. |
| **Staff Development** | It clearly describes current and needed technology competencies; describes how plan will take teachers and other staff from present level of | It provides a general overview (not detailed) of current and needed technology competencies; describes | Staff Development is absent or provides only minimal information on |

| Technology Planning Analysis Rubric | | | |
|---|---|---|---|
| **Components** | **3** | **2** | **1** |
| | technology competency and knowledge to the level of skill required in the plan; describes staff development strategies and recommendations for incentives and professional development resources. Submitted on time. | a few strategies and recommendations for incentives and resources. Submitted on time. | current and needed technology competencies or how the plan will help staff achieve the needed competencies, or is submitted late. |
| **Technical Support** | Provides clear and comprehensive requirements and plans for services available and needed to support technology use (network, computer, and software support). Submitted on time. | Provides adequate but not comprehensive description of technical support requirements and services. Submitted on time. | Technology support is absent or provides vague or little information on technical support requirements for plan, or is submitted late. |
| **Projects, Budgets, and Timelines** | Provides a prioritized list of major tech plan projects, tasks, and timelines; provides budget summary estimate of capital expenses (hardware, software, facilities, infrastructure, staff development, tech support, etc.); identifies possible alternative funding resources; projects, timelines, and budgets are realistic and consistent with plan goals and objectives. Submitted on time. | Provides most, but not all, of the project, timelines, and budget estimate information. Appears to be generally consistent with plan goals. Submitted on time. | Projects, budgets, or timelines missing; provides vague or little information on project, budgets, or timelines; projects appear not relevant to plan goals; budget estimates appear incongruent with plan or unrealistic; or not submitted on time. |
| **Clarity of Writing** | Writing is concise and clear; uses active voice when appropriate. No misspelling, grammar, or punctuation mistakes evident. | Writing is clear but unnecessary words are used. Meaning is not clear in some instances. Few errors in spelling/grammar. | Writing is difficult to understand. There is evidence of spelling, grammar, and punctuation errors. |

Created by Dr. Paul Allen at the University of Texas

## FUTURE CHALLENGES

Once people know firsthand and are able to measure the benefits of advanced technology applications, public support for funding will become viable. Indicators of success used to measure the impact of technology in schools are noted in Chapter 1. It is hoped that future research will be based on these indicators to give educational planners a more complete picture as to the impact of technology on teaching and learning in our nation's classrooms. A key to the success of any technology program in the future is the ability of school leaders to develop awareness and understanding through the implementation of an effective evaluation program. Throughout the entire evaluation process, the focus for administrators should be on combining appropriate technology with measurable results indicating positive correlations between teaching and learning.

## REFLECTIVE ACTIVITIES

1. List the current practices and procedures your school has for evaluating technology. Consider elements such as administrative structures, staff, and lines of communication.

2. Describe the current methods that your school uses for collecting data about technology and student achievement. List the internal and external sources.

3. Evaluate your current technology assessment procedures and then consider alternative approaches for your school.

# References

Abilock, A. (2012). How can students know whether the information online is true or not. *Educational Leadership, 69*(6), 70–74.

Alliance for Excellent Education. (2012). *The digital learning imperative: How technology and teaching meet today's education challenges.* Retrieved from http://www.all4ed .org/files/DigitalLearningImperative.pdf

Allison, E. (2012). The resilient leader. *Educational Leadership, 69*(4), 79–82.

Ananiadou, K., & Claro, M. (2009). 21st century skills and competences for new millennium learners in OECD countries. *OECD Education Working Papers, No. 41,* OECD Publishing. doi: 10.1787/218525261154

Aruba Networks. (2013). *Best practices for Wi-Fi in K–12 schools.* Retrieved from http:// www.arubanetworks.com/pdf/technology/TG_K-12BestPractices.pdf

Attewell, J. (2005). *From research and development to mobile learning: Tools for education and training providers and their learners.* Retrieved from http://www.mlearn.org.za/ CD/papers/Attewell.pdf

Banchero, S., & Simon, S. (2011, November 12). My teacher is an app. *The Wall Street Journal.* Retrieved from http://online.wsj.com/article/SB1000142405297020435800457703060006625014 4.html

Bandura, A. (1977). *Social learning theory.* Englewood Cliffs, NJ: Prentice Hall.

Blair, N. (2012). Technology integration for the new 21st century learner. *Principal, 91*(3), 8–11.

Bridgstock, R. (2009). The graduate attributes we've overlooked: Enhancing graduate employability through career management skills. *Higher Education Research & Development, 28*(1), 31–44.

Bruner, J. (1973). *Going beyond the information given.* New York, NY: Norton.

C21 Canada. (2012). *A 21st century vision of public education for Canada.* Retrieved from www.c21canada.org/ . . . /C21-Canada-Shifting-Version-2.0.pdf

Carr, N. (2011). The juggler's brain. *Phi Delta Kappan, 92*(4), 8–14.

Caudill, J. G. (2007). The growth of m-learning and the growth of mobile computing: Parallel developments. The International Review of Research in Open and Distance Learning. Retrieved from http://www.irrodl.org/index.php/irrodl/article/ view/348/873

Characteristics of virtual learning communities. (n.d.). Retrieved from http://www .usask.ca/education/coursework/802papers/communities/characteristics.HTM

Chesley, G. M., & Jordan, J. (2012). What's missing from teacher prep? *Educational Leadership, 69*(8), 41–45.

Cobcroft, R., Towers, S., Smith, J., & Bruns, A. (2006). Mobile learning in review: Opportunities and challenges for learners, teachers, and institutions. In Proceedings Online Learning and Teaching (OLT) Conference 2006, pp. 21–30, Queensland University of Technology, Brisbane.

Coffield, F., Steer, R., Hodgson, A., Spours, K., Edward, S., & Finlay, I. (2005). A new learning and skills landscape: The central role of the Learning and Skills Council. *Journal of Education Policy, 20*(5), 631–655.

Computer Strategies, LLC. (2002). Oakland, CA.

Computing Research Association. (2012). *Cyberinfrastructure for education and learning for the future.* Retrieved from http://archive.cra.org/reports/cyberinfrastructure.pdf

Covey, S. R. M. (2006). *The speed of trust.* New York, NY: Simon & Schuster.

Cushman, K. (2012). Backtalk: How kids get to be "tech experts." *Phi Delta Kappan, 92*(4), 80.

Cyberbullying Research Center. (2013). Retrieved from http://cyberbullying.us/research

Damani, B. (December 2011/January 2012). Tell me about: How you are doing more with less: Going to the cloud. *Educational Leadership, 69*(4), 94–95.

Daviess County Public Schools. (2013). DCPS network layout. Retrieved from http://www.daviesskyschools.org/content_page2.aspx?cid=826

Dede, C. (2010). Comparing frameworks for "21st century skills." In J. Bellanca & R. Brandt (Eds.), *21st century skills: Rethinking how students learn* (pp. 51–74). Bloomington, IN: Solution Tree. Retrieved from www.watertown.k12.ma.us/dept/ed_tech/research/pdf/ChrisDede.pdf

Demski, J. (2012, June 7). 7 habits of highly effective tech-leading principals. *The Journal: Transforming Education through Technology.* Retrieved from http://thejournal.com/articles/2012/06/07/7-habits-of-highly-effective-tech-leading-principals.aspx

Depascale, C. A. (2012). Managing multiple measures. *Principal, 91*(5), 6–12.

Devine, P. A. (2012). A technology enabled journey. *Principal, 91*(5), 4.

Dewey, J. (1916). *Democracy and education: An introduction to the philosophy of education.* New York, NY: The Macmillan Company.

Dobler, E. (2012). Flattening classroom walls: Edmodo takes teaching and learning across the globe. *International Reading Association, 29*(4), 12–13.

Dron, J. (2005). Digital students and their use of e-learning environments. *IADIS Conference on WWW/Internet 2055,* p. 306. Retrieved from http://www.academia.edu/2656264/Digital_Students_and_their_Use_of_eLearning_Environments

Dufresne, A., Martial, O., Ramstein, C., & Mabilleau, P. (1996). Sound, space, and metaphor: Multimodal access to windows for blind users. Proceeding of ICAD 96. Retrieved from http://www.icad.org/Proceedings/1996/DufresneMartial1996.pdf

Durham Public Schools. (2012). Technology plan 2012–2014. Retrieved from http://www.dpsnc.net/about-dps/departments/technology-services/e-rate-requirements/dps-320-technology-plan-2012–14

Education Week. (2012). Education week teacher: Teacher leader network. Retrieved from http://www.edweek.org/tm/collections/teacher-leaders-network/

Ellis, K. (2003). Moving into m-learning. *Training, 40*(10), 12–15.

Engeström, Y. (1987). *Learning by expanding: An activity-theoretical approach to developmental research.* Helsinki, Finland: Orienta-Konsultit.

Espinoza, R. (2012). Finding pivotal moments. *Educational Leadership, 69*(7), 56–59.

Esselman, M., Lee-Gwin, R., & Rounds, M. (2012). Rightsizing a school district. *Phi Delta Kappan, 93*(6), 56–61.

Fiscal Year 2012 budget summary and background information. (n.d.). Retrieved from http://www.all4ed.org/federal_policy/budget_FY2012

Georgieva, T. (2004). M-learning: A new stage of e-learning. Presentation to International Conference on Computer Systems and Technology. Retrieved from http://ecet.ecs.ru.acad.bg/cst04/docs/siv/428.pdf

Gliksman, S. (2012). Making the case for student controlled devices. Retrieved from http://ipadeducators.ning.com/profiles/blogs/device-control

Goslin, K. G. (2012). Is modeling enough? *Phi Delta Kappan, 93*(7), 42–45.

Goudvis, A., & Harvey, S. (2012). Teaching for historical literacy. *Educational Leadership, 69*(6), 52–57.

Green, D. (2012). Investing in high school. *Phi Delta Kappan, 93*(8), 28–33.

Green, K. C. (1999). The 1999 National Survey of Information Technology in U.S. Higher Education—The Continuing Challenge of Instructional Integration and User Support. The Campus Computing Project, Center for Educational Studies, The Claremont Graduate University, Claremont, CA 91711.

Green, K. C. (2000). Technology and instruction: Compelling, competing, and complementary visions for the instructional role of technology in higher education. Retrieved from http://www.campuscomputing.net

Gross, R., & Acquisti, A. (2005). Information revelation and privacy in online social networks. ACM Workshop on Privacy in the Electronic Society. Retrieved from http://portal.acm.org/citation.cfm?id=1102214

Guess, K. (2011, November 20). Schools paying closer attention to cyber-bullying. *The WCF Courier,* pp. A1, A6. Retrieved from http://wcfcourier.com/news/local/schools-paying-closer-attention-to-cyber-bullying/article_29497291-c2c7-5fc2-8fda-6d8fb6f5907a.html

Hemmen, S. (2012). Principal's bookshelf: Review of customized schooling: Beyond whole school reform. *Principal, 91*(5), 48–49.

Hew, K. F., & Brush, T. (2007). Integrating technology into K–12 teaching and learning: Current knowledge gaps and recommendations for future research. *Educational Technology Research and Development, 55*(3), 223–252.

Hodge, M. J. (2006). The Fourth Amendment and privacy issues on the "new" Internet: Facebook.com and MySpace.com. *Southern Illinois University Law Journal, 31,* 95–122.

Hoerr, T. R. (2012). Principal Connection: Talking to the reverend. *Educational Leadership, 69*(7), 90–91.

Huffman, J., & Hipp, K. (2003). *Reculturing schools as professional learning communities.* Lanham, MD: Rowman & Littlefield.

Institute for Global Ethics. (2006). *The schools of integrity project.* Retrieved from http://www.globalethics.org/soi.php

International Society for Technology in Education. (2011). Retrieved from http://www.iste.org/standards

International Society for Technology in Education. (2011a). Iste.nets: The standards for leading, and teaching in the digital age. Retrieved from http://www.iste.org/standards/nets-for-teachers

International Society for Technology in Education. (2011b). NETS-T teacher standards. Retrieved from http://www.iste.org/docs/pdfs/nets-t-standards.pdf?sfvrsn=2

Internet Keep Safe Coalition. (2009). C3 Matrix: Digital citizenship. http://www.curriki.org/xwiki/bin/download/Coll_iKeepSafe/iKeepSafeC3Matrix/C3%20Matrix.pdf

Jetter, R. (2012). Creative communication strategies. *Principal, 91*(3), 42–43.

Jones, S. (2002). *The Internet goes to college: How students are living in the future with today's technology.* Pew Internet and American Life Project. Retrieved from http://www.pewinternet.org/~/media/Files/Reports/2002/PIP_College_Report.pdf.

Kalamazoo Public Schools. (2012). Kalamazoo public schools technology plan 2012–2015. Retrieved from http://www.kalamazoopublicschools.com/files/Technology%20Plan%202012–15%20.pdf

Keane, M. (2010). The uncertain journey. In *The QUT creative industries experience* (pp. 61–65). Retrieved from http://eprints.qut.edu.au/39735/1/16684_QUT_CI_Experience_Lres.pdf

Kelly, J. (2011, October 10). Hall passages: Hellgate Elementary students make leap in learning. *Missoulian*, pp. A1, A8.

Kember, D. (1997). A reconceptualisation of the research into university academics' conceptions of teaching. *Learning and Instruction, 7*(3), 255–275.

Kennedy, A., Deuel, A., Nelson, T. H., & Slavit, D. (2011). Requiring collaboration or distributing leadership? *Phi Delta Kappan, 92*(8), 20–24.

Key components in state anti-bullying laws. (2013). *Stopbullying.gov.* Retrieved from http://www.stopbullying.gov/laws/key-components/index.html

Kielsmeier, J. C. (2010). Build a bridge between service and learning. *Phi Delta Kappan, 91*(5), 8–15.

Koehler, M. J., & Mishra, P. (2009). What is technological pedagogical content knowledge? *Contemporary issues in technology and teacher education, 9*(1), 60–70.

Kowalski, T. J. (2011). *Public relations in schools* (5th ed.). Upper Saddle River, NJ: Pearson Education, Inc.

Leh, A. S. C., Kouba, B., & Davis, D. (2005). Twenty-first century learning: Communities, interaction and ubiquitous computing. *Educational Media International, 42*(3), 237–250.

Lenhart, A. (2009). Teens and social media: An overview. Pew Internet and American Life Project. Presentation to New York Department of Health and Mental Hygiene. Retrieved from http://www.pewinternet.org/Presentations/2009/17-Teens-and-Social-Media-An-Overview.aspx

Lenhart, A., Madden, M., Purcell, K., & Zickuhr, K. (2011). *Teens, kindness and cruelty on social network sites: How American teens navigate the new world of digital citizenship.* Washington, DC: Pew Research Center. Retrieved from http://www.pewinternet.org/Reports/2011/Teens-and-social-media.aspx

Leu, D., Jr. (2002). The new literacies: Research on reading instruction with the Internet. In A. Farstrup & S. Samuels (Eds.), *What research has to say about reading instruction* (pp. 310–336). International Reading Association.

Levin, B. (2012). Failing students is a (financial) loser. *Phi Delta Kappan, 93*(5), 72–73.

Linebarger, D. L. (2011). Teaching with television: New evidence supports an old medium. *Phi Delta Kappan, 93*(3), 62–65.

Locker, F. (2007). Future-proofing schools. Retrieved from http://www.schoolfacilities.com/cd_2898.aspx

Lytle, J. H. (2012). Where is leadership heading? *Phi Delta Kappan, 93*(8), 54–57.

Marzano, J. R. (2012). The two purposes of teacher evaluation. *Educational Leadership, 70*(3), 14–19.

Masie, E., & Chan, J. (2011). Refreshing the classroom survey. The MASIE Center. Retrieved from http://masie.com/classroom2011

Massachusetts Educational Technology Advisory Council. (2010). *Responsible technology use in public schools: Internet safety task force.* Retrieved from http://www.doe.mass.edu/boe/sac/edtech/safety.pdf

McGovern, J., & Gray, K. (2005). Directions for organisation and management of university learning: Implications from a qualitative survey of student e-learning. Proceedings of ASCILITE 2005. Retrieved from http://www.ascilite.org.au/conferences/brisbane05/blogs/proceedings/46_McGovern.pdf

McMahon, M., & Pospisil, R. (2005). Laptops for a digital lifestyle: Millennial students and wireless mobile technologies. Proceedings of ASCILITE 2005. Retrieved from http://www.ascilite.org.au/conferences/brisbane05/blogs/proceedings/49_McMahon%20&%20Pospisil.pdf

Mid-Continent Research for Education and Learning. (2012). Technology audit. Retrieved from http://www.mcrel.org/products-and-services/services/service-listing/service-51

Mirk, P. (2009). Ethics by example. *Principal Leadership, 10*(2), 18–23.

Motiwalla, L. (2007). *Computers and education, 49,* 581–596.

Mulholland, J. (2011). iPads in the classroom. *Government Technology.* Retrieved from http://www.govtech.com/education/iPads-In-The-Classroom.html

Nansen, C. (2002). District technology coordinator for Minot, ND, public schools. Retrieved from http://pages.minot.k12.nd.us/nansen/content/print/job_description.html

National Council of Professors of Educational Administration. (n.d.). Ethical administrators: Tools for the trade. Retrieved from http://cnx.org/content/m14495/latest/

National Research Council. (2000). How people learn: Brain, mind, experience, and school. National Academy of Sciences. Retrieved from http://www.nap.edu/catalog.php?record_id=9853#toc

Nichols, R., & Allen-Brown, V. (1996). Critical theory and educational technology. In D. Jonassen (Ed.), *Handbook of research for educational communications and technology* (pp. 226–252). New York, NY: Simon and Shuster Macmillan.

Nidus, G., & Saddler, M. (2011). The principal as formative coach. *Educational Leadership, 69*(2), 30–35.

North Dakota Education Association. (2012). *Public relations: Building relationships handbook.* Retrieved from http://ndea.org/teachers/?public_relations_building_relationships_handbook

Northwest Regional Educational Laboratory. (1990). Modified and adapted by Whitehead, B. M., Jensen, D. F. N., & Boschee, F. (2003), *Planning for technology: A guide for school administrators, technology coordinators, and curriculum leaders.* Thousand Oaks, CA: Corwin.

Oblinger, D. G. (2003). Boomers & gen-Xers, millennials: Understanding the "new students." *EDUCAUSE Review, 38*(4), 37–47.

Odden, A. (2012). Schools can still improve, as part of four takes on tough times. *Educational Leadership, 69*(4), 14–15.

Oldfield, A. (2012). iTEC teacher's survey and students' Power League activity: Findings and recommendations. Retrieved from http://itec.eun.org/c/document_library/get_file?uuid=8f765dcf-3e88-444b-a684-d2958b3ed106&groupId=10136

O'Malley, C., Vavoula, G., Glew, J., Taylor, J., Sharples, M., & Lefrere, P. (2003). *Guidelines for learning/teaching/tutoring in a mobile environment. Mobilearn project deliverable.* Retrieved from http://www.mobilearn.org/download/results/ guidelines.pdf

Organisation for Economic Co-operation and Development. (2012). *Transferable skills training for researchers: Supporting career development and research,* OECD Publishing. Retrieved from http://www.keepeek.com/Digital-Asset-Management/oecd/education/21st-century-skills-and-competences-for-new-millennium-learners-in-oecd-countries_218525261154

Organization for Economic Co-operation and Development. (2011). *Education at a glance 2011: OECD indicators,* OECD Publishing. Retrieved from http://www.oecd.org/edu/skills-beyond-school/48631582.pdf

Overbay, A., Mollette, M., & Vasu, E. S. (2011). A technology plan that works. *Principal, 68*(5), 56–59.

Partnership for 21st Century Skills. (2013). Framework for 21st century learning. Retrieved from http://www.p21.org/overview/skills-framework

Peterson, T. (2011). Innovation in action: Leading by example. *EDTECH, 9*(3), 49–51.

Piaget, J. (1973). *Memory and intelligence.* New York, NY: Basic Books.

Pianfetti, E. S. 2001. Teachers and technology: Digital literacy through professional development. *Language Arts, 78*(3), 255–262.

Portin, B. S. (2010). Shared leadership at its best. *Principal, 89*(5), 22.

Prensky, M. (2013). Our brains extended. *Technology Rich Learning, 70*(6), 22–27.

Rau, P., Gao, Q., & Wu, L. (2006). Using mobile communication technology in high school: Education motivation, pressure, and learning performance. *Computers and Education, 50*(1), 1–22.

Ravenaugh, M. (2013). 10 tips for school technology planning. Retrieved from http://www.scholastic.com/browse/article.jsp?id=52]

Richardson, J. (2009, December/2010, January). Playing "catch-up" with developing nations makes no sense for US: An interview with Yong Zhao. *Phi Delta Kappan, 91*(4), 15.

Richardson, J. (2011). Tune in to what the new generation of teachers can do. *Phi Delta Kappan, 92*(8), 14–19.

Rosen, L. D. (2011). Teaching the iGeneration. *Educational Leadership, 68*(5), 10–15.

Rothman, R. (2012). A common core of readiness. *Educational Leadership, 69*(7), 10–15.

Routman, R. (2012). Mapping a pathway to schoolwide highly effective teaching. *Phi Delta Kappan, 93*(5), 56–61.

Ruebel, K. (2011). *Research summary: Professional learning communities.* Retrieved from http://www.amle.org/Research/ResearchSummaries/PLCs/tabid/2535/Default.aspx

Salpeter, J. (2012). 21st century skills: Will our students be prepared? *Tech & Learning,* Retrieved from http://www.techlearning.com/assessment-&-testing/0034/21st-century-skills-will-our-students-be-prepared/45157

Saltman, D. (2012). Flipping for beginners: Inside the new classroom craze. *Harvard Educational Letter, 27*(6), 1, 2. Retrieved from http://www.hepg.org/hel/article/517

Scholastic Administrator. (2012). BYOD to school? Retrieved from http://www.scholastic.com/browse/article.jsp?id=3756757

School Improvement Network. (2012). PD 360. Retrieved from http://www.schoolimprovement.com/products/pd360/

Sharples, M. (2002). Disruptive devices: Mobile technology for conversational learning. *International Journal of Continuing Engineering Education and Life Long Learning, 12*(5/6), 504–520.

Shulman, L. (1986). Those who understand: Knowledge growth in teaching. *Educational Researcher, 15*(2), 4–14.

Sibley, P. H. R., & Kimball, C. (1998). Technology use plan primer. Retrieved from http://brandonworkentin.files.wordpress.com/2012/07/technology-use-maturity-benchmarks.pdf

Speak Up 2012. (2012). Mapping a personalized Learning Journey: K–12 students and parents connect the dots with digital learning. Retrieved from http://www.tomorrow.org/speakup/pdfs/SU11_PersonalizedLearning_Students.pdf

Stein, L. (2012). The art of saving a failing school. *Phi Delta Kappan, 93*(5), 51–55.

Sterling, D. R., & Frazier, W. M. (2011). Setting up uncertified teachers to succeed. *Phi Delta Kappan, 92*(7), 40–45.

Symonds, W. C. (2012). Pathways to prosperity. *Educational Leadership, 69*(7), 35–39.

Technology Standards for School Administrators Collaborative. (2001). Retrieved from http://www.kyepsb.net/documents/EduPrep/tssa.pdf

Thinking hard while running on empty. (n.d.). Retrieved from http://www.21stcenturycollaborative.com/2011/07/thinking-hard-while-running-on-empty/

Thornton, P., & Houser, C. (2004). Using mobile phones in education. In J. Roschelle, T. Chan, T.-W. Kinshuk, & S. Tang (Eds.), *Proceedings of the 2nd IEEE International WMTE Workshop* (pp. 3–10).

Toch, T. (2012). A dream deferred. *Phi Delta Kappan, 93*(6), 66–67.

Tondeur, J., van Braak, J., Sang, G., Voogt, J., Fisser, P., & Ottenbreit-Leftwich, A. (2012, August). Preparing pre-service teachers to integrate technology in education: A synthesis of qualitative evidence. *Computers & Education, 59*(1), 134–144.

Toy, C. (2008). Leadership and effectively integrating educational technology: Ten lessons for principals and other educational leaders. *NASSP.* Retrieved from http://www.nassp.org/Content.aspx?topic=58730

Traxler, J. (2009). Learning in a mobile age. *International Journal of Mobile and Blended Learning, 1*(1), 1–12.

Tynan, D. (2011). From STEM to star. *ED TECH, 9*(3), 42–44.

Uden, L. (2007). Activity theory for designing mobile learning. *International Journal of Mobile Learning and Organization, 1*(1), 81–102.

U.S. Department of Education. (2010). Transforming American education: Learning powered by technology. Retrieved from http://www.ed.gov/sites/default/files/netp2010.pdf

Victoria Department of Education and Early Childhood Development. (2013). Student acceptable use agreement. Retrieved from http://www.education.vic.gov.au/school/teachers/health/Pages/lolaua.aspx

Vollmer, J. (2011). Welcome to the great conversation. *Educational Leadership, 68*(8), 69–73.

Vygotsky, L. S. (1978). *Mind and society.* Cambridge, MA: Harvard University Press.

Wagner, E. (2005). Enabling mobile learning. *EDUCAUSE, 40*(3), 40–53.

Wagner, T. (2008). *The global achievement gap.* New York, NY: Basic Books.

Wang, Y., Wu, M., & Wang, H. (2009). Investigating the determinants and age and gender differences in the acceptance of mobile learning. *British Journal of Educational Technology, 40*(1), 92–118. DOI: doi:10.1111/j.1467–8535.2007.00809.x

Wherry, J. H. (2009). Using the right communication tool. *Principal, 88*(3), 6.

White, K. (1997). A matter of policy. *Education Week's Technology Counts, 17*(11), 40–42.

Whitehead, B. M., Boschee, F., & Decker, R. (2013). *The principal: Leadership for a global society.* Thousand Oaks, CA: Sage

Whitehead, B. M., Jensen, D. F. N., & Boschee, F. (2003). *Planning for technology: A guide for school administrators, technology coordinators, and curriculum leaders.* Thousand Oaks, CA: Corwin.

Williams, J. H., & Engel, L. C. (2012, December/2013, January). How do other countries evaluate teachers? *Phi Delta Kappan, 94*(4), 53–57.

Woodard, L. (1997). State by state profiles. *Education Week's Technology Counts, 17*(11), 88.

# Index

**CORWIN**

A SAGE Company

The Corwin logo—a raven striding across an open book—represents the union of courage and learning. Corwin is committed to improving education for all learners by publishing books and other professional development resources for those serving the field of PreK–12 education. By providing practical, hands-on materials, Corwin continues to carry out the promise of its motto: **"Helping Educators Do Their Work Better."**